'FUNNY... YOU DON'T LOOK JEWISH'

Sidney Brichto is a well-known rabbi, preacher and controversial theologian. Born in America, he came to London in the 1960s, and soon rose to the post of Executive Vice-President of the Union of Liberal and Progressive Synagogues. After 25 years in this role, he moved on to direct the Joseph Levy Charitable Foundation, to act as consultant to various Jewish communal organizations, and to lecture at the Oxford Centre for Hebrew and Jewish Studies. He also enjoys a hectic schedule of writing, and media appearances.

'FUNNY… YOU DON'T LOOK JEWISH'

A Guide to Jews and Jewish Life

SIDNEY BRICHTO

With illustrations by
DAVID MYERS

PILKINGTON PRESS

To my wife Cathryn
who thinks I am too Jewish
and
in memory of my father
for whom
I was not Jewish enough.

First Published 1994
Reprinted 1996
By Pilkington Press Ltd
Yelvertoft Manor
Northampton NN6 7 LF

ISBN 1 899044 00 0

Produced, Designed and Typesetting by
A.H. Jolly (Editorial) Ltd
Yelvertoft Manor
Northamptonshire NN6 7LF

Printed in Great Britain
By Balding + Mansell

Contents

Preface

'I could tell you were Jewish,' said the Portobello Road shopkeeper. 'It's in the eyes, I can always tell from the eyes.' Others can tell from the nose, the manner of speaking or some other characteristic. But whether or not there is a universal means of recognition, why should people care if they can recognize a Jew? What difference does it make?

If non-Jews are speaking of someone and one of the group says, ' I think he's Jewish,' it often leads to a long debate on that person's identity without anyone indicating why it should be of any concern. What seems to be implied is that being Jewish covers an array of sins or talents, possibilities and dangers, and that it is important to be aware of these.

Many people still believe that Jews have 'influence' in high quarters, but the source of this influence is a mystery to them. Jews are also credited with a pool of knowledge to which they alone have access. Strangely enough, respect for Jews also feeds prejudice. When non-Jews pat themselves on the back for engaging an astute lawyer, a clever accountant or a brilliant surgeon, if these happen to be Jewish their success may be ascribed to racial characteristics, based on genes or environmental conditioning, rather than to individual intelligence and skill.

What it is like to be Jewish is the subject I seek to unravel in this book, for the benefit of those non-Jews who may not understand their own curiosity about 'those Jews' who seem to be everywhere, living next door, working in the shopping parade, or in the solicitor's or accountant's office, appearing on television or splashed across newspapers for some financial scandal or an attack on Palestinians.

Who are the Jews, where do they come from, why are they always in trouble or causing trouble, what makes them tick and in what do they believe? These are some of the questions I will try to answer, in addition to others which have been asked of me by interested non-Jews.

There are many books written about Jews, Jewish history, faith and practice, but none seem to meet the needs of non-Jews looking for simple information and eager for an understanding of what the Jews are all about. An additional failure of most books now available on Jewish subjects is that they do not deal with the common prejudices held even by the friendliest of non-Jews. Rather, they seek to show the enormous contribution of Jews and Jewish intellectual and artistic genius to the world. In the process, they may unintentionally feed the belief that Jews are both arrogant and genetically superior.

This book is intended not to defend the Jews or the Jewish way of life. While I would welcome the removal of prejudice against Jews, this is not my main intention. What I do is to answer from my own personal perspective the questions which non-Jews wish to have answered but do not feel comfortable about asking their Jewish friends or associates, because they could be misunderstood or cause offence. Tentative enquiries often produce responses of embarrassment. I can assure the reader that this was due to the ignorance of the people to whom they were talking and not to any desire to withhold information. My determination to write this book was reinforced by the discovery that many non-Jews married to Jews complained that their spouses were unable to answer the simplest of questions about the Jews, their history, religion or ideals. This book is for all of them, Jews and non-Jews alike.

Sidney Brichto
1994

ACKNOWLEDGEMENTS

Christian Tyler's interview of me in the *Financial Times* and subsequent conversations inspired me to write the book. He read the first tentative draft and made important suggestions. Brian Pilkington's enthusiasm spurred me on to complete the manuscript, as I knew that it would see the light of day. Peter Levy's friendship is a source of continuous encouragement. Critical and generous readings from The Revd Barrie Hibbert and Professor Erich Segal were also reassuring. Jeremy Schonfield put his literary abilities at my disposal and I took full advantage of them. Cathryn, Anne, Daniel, Adam and Jonathan suffered patiently as I explored the concepts of the book with them in their embryonic state. My son Daniel was the last to go through the manuscript with his pencil before proof stage and I endorsed the alterations with my own pen. Beverley Taylor saw the manuscript through from the first word to its final submission to the printer with love and patience. To all these individuals, and also to Alec Jolly for making it such a beautiful book, my deepest gratitude.

Note on the name of God, the Rabbis and the Christian Era

Wherever the name of God appears in the Hebrew Bible, it is read by Jews as 'Lord'. As the actual name of God was according to tradition pronounced only once a year – by the High Priests in the inner sanctum of the Temple on the Day of Atonement – and as Hebrew has no written vowels, we can only guess its correct pronunciation. But in order to give the reader a sense of personal relationship between God and the Hebrew Patriarchs and their descendants, I have employed the name 'Yahweh', which many biblical scholars believe is the closest approximation to how it was once spoken. My intention is not to offend Orthodox Jews, who believe that no mention of God's name or any approximation of His name should be articulated, but only to make the Bible as alive for the modern reader as it was for our ancestors thousands of years ago.

I refer to the rabbis who were responsible for the composition of rabbinic literature – the Talmud and Midrash – as 'Rabbinic Masters' to distinguish them from modern rabbis. The rabbis of ancient days enjoyed civil as well as religious authority and in many instances had the aura of Gurus, so without disrespect to contemporary rabbis, I thought it right to make this distinction clear.

In the non-Jewish world, the calendar years are reckoned as BC (Before Christ) and AD (Anno Domini). As Jews do not recognize Jesus as their lord, I have employed BCE (Before the Common Era) and CE (Common Era) to indicate these periods.

When quoting from the Bible, I used the Revised Standard Version (1952) but allowed myself the freedom to make slight changes without altering the meaning of the text.

1 Jewish Persecution

*'There must be a reason people
always pick on the Jews'*

Two poor Jews in America looking for a meal passed an evangelical church which advertised, 'Convert to Christianity and we will give you $100'. They look at the sign, at each other and agree that they must try this. Moshe agrees to go in first. An hour later, he emerges. Impatiently, his friend asks him, 'Well Moshe, what happened?' 'I converted.' 'Yes, I know, but did they give you the $100?' Moshe replied, 'All you damn Jews ever think about is money!'

This joke told by Jews is full of irony. It assumes of course that Jews tend to see anti-Semitism as integral to Christianity, but it also implies that even in every Jew are the seeds of anti-Semitism. Why is this so? Jews, as well as friendly non-Jews, find it hard to understand why Jews should have suffered so much, especially as there is no clear reason for it. But surely, it is thought, no nation on earth is picked on without any reason.

Yet women who are raped or children who are sexually abused, psychologists tell us, often suffer guilt, though they have done nothing to deserve their fate. In the same way, a people subjected to constant verbal or physical abuse may end up feeling that there is something wrong with them. So the very fact that Jews are victims has the effect of intensifying anti-Semitism and promoting forms of self-hate among Jews.

Imagine a child who is brought up to have a poor opinion of Jews, and finds this confirmed by parents, grandparents and neighbours. Does the child think the whole world is wrong because he has a nice Jewish classmate? One day I came home from work and my wife told me that our son Jonathan, then aged 5, had a friend over for tea. When in the course of conversation it came out that we were Jewish, his friend insisted, 'But you can't be Jewish.' Jonathan repeated that he was, but the little boy did not want to believe it. One can only guess what he had heard about Jews at home, or how the name had been used.

Christian attitudes towards Jews have been formed by the supposed Jewish involvement in the death of Jesus. Today it may be a mark of civilization not to condemn children for their fathers' sins, but however liberal we are, consider the impact of the following verses from Matthew, in which Pontius Pilate offers the Jewish mob to free either Barabbas or Jesus:

'Which of the two do you want me to release for you?'
'Barabbas.'
'Then what shall I do with Jesus who is called Christ?'
'Let him be crucified.'
'Why? What evil has he done?'
But they shouted all the more, 'Let him be crucified.'

So when Pilate saw he gained nothing, but rather that a riot was beginning,
he took water and washed his hands before the crowd, saying,
'I am innocent of this man's blood, see to it yourselves.'
And all the people answered, 'His blood be on us and on our children.'

This has been read and preached to almost 200 generations of Christian faithful: and to an unsophisticated reader it can only mean that the wicked Roman Procurator declared his innocence and that the Jews accepted the guilt for themselves and their children.

These verses from Matthew must have instilled a hatred for the Jews beyond imagining. Family vendettas were common in most countries of the world until very recently, and revenge was considered a matter of honour, even after generations. In the minds of simple Christians living in the Middle Ages, when power was supreme and irresponsible, when Popes and bishops made political pacts and went to war, when torture was used, and burning people alive for heresy was a common practice, there could be no more convenient scapegoat than a Jew for all one's misfortunes, especially if, as Matthew says, they are guilty anyway.

When there was a plague, it was believed that the Jews had poisoned the wells. When a child was killed by some sexual pervert, it was said that the Jews had done so to drink its blood at Passover. The Crusaders could provide for their needs, on their way to free the Holy Land from the infidels, by plundering and killing Jews; and why not, if it was believed that they had killed their Lord?

Anti-semitism of the Christian variety seems almost inevitable. The Bible – which was believed literally, as millions still do to this day – said, or implied, that Jews were to be despised. They were referred to as 'Perfidious Jews' in Christian prayer. But to the impartial eye they had no more faults than any other people – unless, of course, they *were* responsible for killing Christ. If you believed that, you would also have good reason to think that the sin for killing him was passed on to Jews for ever, just as Christians believe that Adam's original sin was inherited by all mankind.

The 'scapegoat' is a biblical concept. On the holiest day of the Jewish year, when the Temple stood in Jerusalem and the High Priest prayed for forgiveness for himself, his household and all the people of Israel, the sins of everyone were placed on a goat, which was then taken to a place called Azazel, where it would be thrown from a cliff and killed. This was the symbolic ritual by which Jews sought to rid themselves of their sins. To this very day, some Orthodox Jews, during the season of repentance, place their sins on a chicken, which they lift over their head before it is slaughtered. Many Jews on the Jewish New Year, following the synagogue service, walk to the closest river or brook, and cast bread on the water, the bread representing their sins which they wish to be washed away.

To Christians, in some sense, Jesus seen as the Suffering Servant is also the symbolic bearer of the sins of humanity. He is sacrificed, he lays down his life because of the sins of all God's children. But the modern concept of a scapegoat is different – not the bearer of sins, but the innocent victim on whom the more powerful can lay the blame for all that goes wrong. It is an unfortunate but natural psychological tendency of ordinary people to seek scapegoats. Who does not kick the cat, bellow at the children at breakfast when suffering from a hangover, or turn on one's spouse after a horrid day at the office or at home? It must happen at least sometimes to everyone.

The Bible makes this very point with its usual wry economy of means. Adam's second sin, after he is found out for the first one, is to blame Eve and even God, and to make them his scapegoats. 'The woman *you* gave me, she did give me of the tree, and I ate.' Eve in turn blames the sly serpent. Neither are prepared to take responsibility, and this, one might say, is the 'fall of man' as far as Jewish history is concerned.

Jews have been ideal scapegoats. Perceived as killers of God, they also had the good grace not to disappear, but to remain available to bear further blame. And as ideal scapegoats, they could be used for all the dirty work. They were forbidden in medieval Europe to own land or enter the guilds of craftsmen and were permitted only to be middlemen, peddlers, pawnbrokers, money-lenders and rent-collectors. People still bear a resentment to middlemen: how much cheaper to buy directly from a craftsman; and how tempting it is to resent someone who earns a livelihood by doing nothing but lending money, usually other people's money. And who thanks the rent-collector? What a convenience to have the Jew serving in all those capacities. When things got tough, a pogrom was organized and debts would be cancelled if the lender was killed. The peasants' anger at exploitative rents could be ventilated on the Jewish bailiff rather than the Christian landowners, and so on.

What was even luckier was the fact that the Jews of medieval Europe were totally defenceless. They had no army to protect them and nowhere to go if they were expelled. After all, most countries within travelling distance were Christian, where their treatment would be little better or even worse. There was no escape. The world was the Jews' prison! Even in Muslim countries, they were only tolerated so long as they acknowledged their dhimmi (second-class) status. By maintaining their religious identity, Jews were a living refutation of Islam as well as Christianity.

In spite of this, the Jews had good periods, when the governments of the countries or city states in which they lived realized that their presence was of benefit: it was known that they stimulated trade and provided finance, as merchants always do. Under the rule of good despots, who appreciated that 'their' Jews lubricated prosperity, Jews were allowed to get on with life. During these peaceful times they gathered strength, and acquired a sense of security which made the next pogrom seem very distant. When troubles loom, it is natural to hope that they will simply pass away. Was this the basis of Jewish optimism? And was there an alternative?

But in addition to scapegoating, is there a Jewish contribution to anti-Semitism, which adds fuel to the flames of prejudice against them? The answer must be, yes. It is difficult for people to escape an image which history has imposed on them. Their faults as well as their virtues become intensified by persecution. Consider the accusation that Jews are devious and suspicious. These two traits seem ideally designed for self protection against an assumed enemy. With so much anti-Semitism about, both unexpressed and virulent, one should not be surprised that many Jews would act in this way. What is more remarkable is that so many Jews optimistically go about their business as though they had no enemies. Many thousands, perhaps millions of Jews might have escaped the Holocaust had they believed the stories of what the Nazis were doing. Bruno Bettelheim, the distinguished psychoanalyst, maintained in *The Informed Heart* that Jews unwittingly co-operated in their destruction by believing in the humaneness of their murderers.

Exclusivity is another trait of which Jews are accused. The sense of being under constant threat will make any group of people prefer the company of those they can trust. But consider the Jews who luxuriate in their association with a wide variety of non-Jewish friends and acquaintances. Consider also that such behaviour has been known to provoke the opposite accusation, that Jews are pushing themselves into circles where they do not belong.

Jews may also be told that they are over-sensitive to criticism, see an anti-Semite round every corner, and interpret opposition as prejudice. Some Jews admit this about themselves, and castigate each other over it. But this does not mean that they have no right to these feelings. I heard one leading rabbi declare to a mixed group of church representatives, 'We are not paranoid. We are being persecuted.'

And what of assertions of Jewish arrogance and aggressive behaviour? This too seems natural if one feels victimized or under threat of victimization. One can either 'stand proud' and take the offensive, in which case one appears aggressive, or become submissive and servile, and be equally despised as insecure and cowardly.

Are Jews more ostentatious than others? Arguably, but what society on the move does not pass through a *nouveau-riche* stage? Their grandchildren, if not their children, will be different. With a history of transiency they may have inherited the feeling of 'here today, gone tomorrow', and be inclined to enjoy their wealth by spending it. Equally, for the very same reason many Jews will live modestly in order to set aside a nest-egg for a rainy day.

Jews are as confused about the motives for anti-Semitism, and their reaction to it, as non-Jews. When they explore its motives, they may find what in some sense appears a justification for it. But this is not so! Anti-Semitism, like all prejudice, is a disease of moral weakness. It is symptomatic of those who cannot accept personal or collective responsibility for their actions.

Prejudice, and the fear of those who are different, will continue until humans grow up. Blacks, Catholics, Protestants, Arabs, Pakistanis or any group, as well as Jews, can be made to bear the blame for economic recession or political tyranny. The same cowardly tendency can be witnessed today as homosexuals become the convenient scapegoat for AIDS, as though they had created the disease rather than been its first victims.

But for the reasons I have given, historically Jews have been the scapegoat par excellence. They have been attacked for being, paradoxically, both the leaders of communism and of capitalism, the socialist reformers as well as the exploiting landlords, the leaders of the Trades Unions and the owners of the capitalist press that seeks to suppress them. The zenith of blaming the Jew for everything appeared in the famous forgery called the 'Protocols of the Elders of Zion', written in the last century and debunked long ago, but still published and read today. It claims that there is a world-wide Jewish conspiracy to control the world, and it is nowadays used to prove Hitler was right to attempt to destroy the Jews.

Suffice it to say that racial prejudice in general, and anti-Semitism in particular, are the result of human immaturity and weakness. Only when people judge others not on their history or collective identity, but on their own merits and achievements, will the world be rid of the gratuitous hatred which always divides and sometimes destroys the very fabric of human society.

Now there arose a new King over Egypt, who did not know Joseph. And he said to his people, 'Behold, the people of Israel are too many and mighty for us. Come, let us deal shrewdly with them, lest they multiply, and, if war befall us, they join our enemies and fight against us and escape from the land.' Therefore they set taskmasters over them to afflict them with heavy burdens; and they built for Pharaoh store cities, Pithom and Ra-am'ses.

Bible, Exodus I

And all the King's servants who were at the King's gate bowed down and did obeisance to Haman; for the king had so commanded concerning him. But Mordecai did not. And when Haman saw that Mordecai did not bow down he was filled with fury. But he disdained to lay hands on Mordecai alone. So, as they had made known to him the people of Mordecai, Haman sought to destroy all the Jews, the people of Mordecai, throughout the whole Kingdom of Ahasu-e-rus. Then Haman said to King Ahasu-e-rus, 'There is a certain people scattered abroad and dispersed among the peoples in all the provinces of your Kingdoms; their laws are different from those of every other people, and they do not keep the King's laws, so it is not for the King's profit to tolerate them. If it please the King, let it be decreed that they be destroyed, and I will pay ten thousand talents of silver ... into the King's treasuries.'

Bible, Book of Esther 3

JEWS ARE NEWS...

2 Jews are News

'You can't pick up a newspaper without
reading something about Jews'

Anyone who lives in the West can be excused for thinking that the world is more interested in Jews than their numbers warrant. This interest is more than contemporary. Jews have been around since almost the beginning of recorded history. Even before the advent of Christianity or Islam, Jews were admired or despised but never ignored.

In the days when Judaea was a vassal state of Rome, Jews left their land, either because they were exiled or to follow commercial opportunities, and established communities throughout the Roman Empire. The historian, Salo Baron, estimated that 10 per cent of the Empire's population was Jewish. Their influence was felt, and it is unlikely that Christianity would have succeeded in harvesting the Roman Empire had not Judaism sown the seed.

The fact is that the ancestors of modern Jews made an impression. The example of the biblical Joseph saving Egypt from famine, and on behalf of Pharaoh buying up the entire country from Egyptian landowners in return for grain and seed, can be seen being repeated in varying degrees throughout history. Jews have been agents of kings, princes, lords, barons, viziers, and bailiffs; and they have also been doctors and scribes.

As a group they have tended to act as an irritant because they were so different. After Alexander's conquests, the world rushed to be Hellenized, to become citizens of art-loving Hellas. Many Jews did the same, but most retained a fierce loyalty to a God who was never depicted in form. This led to revolt and civil war. Jews insisted on being different, and these differences made their neighbours uneasy. Their tenacity, their refusal to worship the conquering gods, as most other defeated nations were prepared to do, appeared most peculiar. Gentiles must have been in constant puzzlement: 'What makes the Jews behave the way they do? Is it something good and to be admired, or is it due to some mysterious power and thus to be feared?' The Jewish general and historian, Josephus, who, after taking part in the unsuccessful Jewish rebellion against Rome in 67–70 CE, became a courtier at the palaces of Vespasian and Titus, felt compelled to write *Contra Apionem*, in which he put up a defence against the anti-Jewish attacks made by Apion, a popular writer of his day.

Jumping ahead to the present century, the fact that Hitler was able to convince an entire nation that the Jews were the source of the world's ills is proof of the vast store of mistrust and dislike that had built up over the generations.

Jews living as strangers in foreign lands always offered a special problem to their neighbours. As individuals they were like other people, some good and kind, some malicious. To what extent their personal behaviour reflected their

Jewishness was a question constantly being asked by those who had regular contact with them. It is part of human nature to categorize individuals who stand out from the mainstream. Members of any group may treat other members of the group as individuals, but they will tend to feel more comfortable if they can find a generalization to encompass outsiders, and it is usual to compartmentalize other religious or national groupings. Jews, Christians and Muslims do the same, and so do Americans about the English and the French, and vice versa.

But the Jews, as has been said, are 'just like everybody else but more so'. The truth of this aphorism lies in the prominence of Jews throughout Western history. Not only do Jews have their own collective consciousness, but non-Jews have a collective memory about them; they have inherited the judgement and prejudices of their ancestors towards them.

So while other nations and religions differ from each other, Jewish differences are often more visible and evident because they lived scattered as minorities in foreign lands. Furthermore, Jews, because of their religion, were in constant confrontation first with pagans and then with Christians and Muslims in the modern world. Jews were perceived as different even at the beginning of their history. The pagan prophet Balaam says in the book of Numbers, that Israel was 'a people who dwell alone'. Balaam had been paid by the king of Moab to curse and weaken the invading Israelites. But, according to the biblical tale, God compelled Balaam to bless the Israelites instead. The very aloneness of the Jewish people, once intended as a blessing, later became their curse.

When Christianity dominated the Western world, the uniqueness of the Jews became a challenge, even a threat to Christians. The Jewish people had given them a Saviour, had rejected him, and according to Christian Scriptures, had crucified him. It is painful but necessary to understand the consequences of such a historical perception.

Put yourself into the mind of Christian believers living among Jews, and you may be able to appreciate the psychological impact of such beliefs. Such Christian believers could have lived in any historical period – in Constantinople after the Emperor Constantine converted to Christianity, in London during the Crusades, in Toledo after Ferdinand and Isabella had taken Spain from the Muslims, in Budapest during the Black Death, or in Berlin when the Reichstag was burnt down. Let us summarize these Christians' process of thinking.

Their lives are circumscribed by faith in Jesus Christ, the son of a Jewish carpenter and a virgin mother, but also the Son of God, who died for their sins so that they, on death, would enjoy eternal bliss and salvation. They live good lives according to Christian doctrine, and hope to achieve salvation. And because they were born in sin, they require God's grace which can only be found through the Church of Christ. They must confess all their sins, and because they are mortal and sinners, are in constant need of the Church to help them atone and to escape the fires of damnation. This they do by sharing in the death and resurrection of their Lord and by partaking in the sacrifice of his flesh at the Mass.

What do they think about the Jews who live in their village or city? The Saviour came from their people, but their ancestors rejected Him and are believed to have been implicated in his murder. But in spite of this, Jews seem happy. They prosper. They live in big houses. They enjoy a warm family life. They worship their God with many rituals, and celebrate their Sabbaths and Festivals. They do not appear to be living under threat of eternal damnation. They are civil to Christians and indeed most respectful. 'How is all this possible?' a Christian might ask. 'Can there be more than one way to God? Can there be more than one truth? Yet, I am taught that there is only one way to salvation and that is through my Lord, the living Christ.'

Consider the spiritual turmoil of Christians living among Jews. Some will be thinkers, some will be peasants living as tenants on baronial estates run by the landlords' Jewish agents, some will be merchants who cannot meet their debts to Jewish money-lenders. Some will be ill, and depend on the skills of a Jewish doctor. Several may even be gentlemen who have been captivated by the beauty and wit of a Jewish banker's daughter. Some will be ignorant priests who cannot understand why Jews continue to walk past their churches on their twice-daily journey to pray in their synagogues.

What would be the attitude of Christians towards Jews? Would they admire or hate them? Would they become their enemies or seek a way of living with these strange people who reject their Lord with impunity? When Christians turned to the Church for an understanding of the Jews, they might be told that these people were spiritually blind but had been forgiven by Jesus because 'they know not what they do'. More likely the clergy would condemn them as 'perfidious', the word used to describe Jews in the Catholic liturgy. Looking to their parents for an explanation, the views they would hear would have been passed down through the generations, whether from relationships with Jews, the hearsay of others, or the sermons of the clergy.

Jewish survival and endurance would pose another problem for the Christian. How, it would be asked, could the Jews have survived so long in a hostile world? Is it God's work or the devil's? If the former, what does it suggest about the validity of the Jewish or the Christian faith? If the latter, why should they be tolerated?

However one considered them, the Jews must have seemed not merely outsiders, but constant moral and intellectual thorns in the religious Christians' side. In Muslim countries Jews were treated no worse or better than Christians. Both had rejected Allah and His Prophet. Both were regarded as subordinate communities, to be tolerated so long as they accepted their inferior status until Islam's domination of the world would be achieved.

Even today, can the Jews be anything but an anomaly? It must be of special interest to the present world to witness, among other revolutions in human affairs, the radical change in the Jewish situation. After centuries of pogroms and persecutions, culminating in the Holocaust, Jews have re-emerged like a phoenix from the ashes; they have thrown off their victims' mantle, put on armour, conquered their homeland and have become a fiercely independent and sover–eign military power.

Yet even with the triumphant return to Zion and the opening of its doors to all Jews, they cling to their homes in 'foreign' lands, expressing their full potential as citizens while maintaining a discreet loyalty to their community and to the

State of Israel. Wherever they enjoy democracy, many of them rise to the top. Numerous are the Jews in business, the professions, the arts, media, sciences and academia. Thirty per cent of all Nobel Prize winners are Jews, although Jews number less than three-tenths of one per cent of the world population. The three individuals who have most radically shaped the modern world in science, psychology and politics were either Jewish or of Jewish parentage – Albert Einstein, Sigmund Freud and Karl Marx.

In comparison to their small numbers (less than 1 per cent in Great Britain, and 2.5 per cent in the USA) it is incredible that many readers of this book will have contact in their daily lives with Jewish doctors and dentists, lawyers, accountants, professors and teachers, businessmen and shopkeepers. They will read about, and see on their TV screens, Jews in every public aspect of life – in government, the arts and entertainment. In the days when Margaret Thatcher had four Jews in her cabinet, I recall with amusement a neighbour refusing to believe that the UK had only 350,000 Jews. He insisted that there had to be at the very least three million!

In the light of all this, is it a wonder that Jews should be of such interest? Proportionally they are more successful than others and therefore tend to be in the limelight. And conversely, because they have been of such interest throughout their history until the present, the non-Jewish world continues to focus its attention on them; more, indeed, than they wish or even deserve. A Jew such as Ivan Boesky, accused of fraud, tends to receive more attention than a non-Jew. Israel is sometimes perceived as the centre of the Middle East; her conflict with the Arabs gives the Palestinians the status of being the foremost example of oppressed and persecuted national minorities, while the 25 million oppressed Kurds, who for centuries have been frustrated in their attempts for national self-determination, have few sympathizers, even when attacked by gas-laden rockets by Saddam Hussein at the end of the Iraq–Iran war. Only when Saddam decided to confront the world did the Kurds begin to win limited support. However, had Kurds formed a non-Jewish minority in Israel (instead of in Iraq, Turkey, Iran and the Commonwealth of Independent States) in place of the Palestinians, they would, one suspects, have received far more publicity.

The Christian world is interested in Jews because they, their faith and history are one of the mysteries of the world. Just as Jews seek to understand the reasons for their own identity, so non-Jews seek to comprehend the meaning of this peculiar people, who gave birth to their own faith but rejected it, who as outsiders remain somewhat aloof, but who as integrated citizens make a disproportionate impact on the lives of everyone.

I don't like 'Ebrews. They work harder; they're more sober; they're honest; and they're everywhere.
Loyalties, John Galsworthy

3 Jewish Standards

'Jews should behave like Christians'

The double standards of Christians towards Jews were illustrated during the Israeli invasion of the Lebanon in 1982. During the early days of the war, I had a meeting with an Independent Television producer who criticized Israel's siege of Beirut. Only medicine and water were allowed into the city. She felt that it was terrible for Israel to behave in this manner. When I asked her if she did not agree that the purpose of sieges was to force cities to surrender without risking lives through bombardment, she confessed that while this was true she expected 'Jews to behave like Christians'. My reaction to this was, 'When Christians don't behave like Christians, why should Jews?'

She, like many non-Jews, demanded that Jews be better; but why? If you wish to cause a traditional Zionist a paroxysm of anger, tell him that Israelis behave immorally towards the Palestinians. He will tell you of the Holocaust, the refusal of the Allied forces to bomb the train lines to Auschwitz, which cost ten thousand Jewish lives for every day they were not bombed. He will rant about the bombing of Dresden, the Japanese treatment of Australians, the atomic bombing of Hiroshima and Nagasaki, the American massacre at My Lai in Vietnam. There will be no abatement to his fury, and he will finish his diatribe by advising you not to teach Israel morality.

But Jews also expect better from themselves. The Torah provides a moral code for creating a stable and harmonious society. The pursuit of righteousness, and the care of widows, orphans, the crippled, poor and strangers, are the very core of its civil laws. Today there are countless internal debates between those Jews who demand that their co-religionists behave better than others, and those who see this as a form of self-hatred. What is the point of a Jewish State, the idealists demand to know, unless it is different from others? 'Have we given up being oppressed in order to become an oppressor?' The reply from the realists is, 'Yes, better *that* than becoming victims again.' Nevertheless, 400,000 Israelis, 10 per cent of the population, demonstrated in Tel Aviv against the Israeli invasion of the Lebanon.

Jews also have pragmatic reasons for wishing to be better. The evil action of one Jew reflects on the others and feeds anti-Semitism. A misbehaving Jew lets the side down and promotes the caricature of the Jew as mean, avaricious, a hater of non-Jews, or some other pernicious image.

It is not surprising that Jews demand more from themselves than from others. What is ironic is that Gentiles, who for centuries have been taught that Jews were responsible for the death of Christ drank Christian blood at Passover, poisoned the wells of medieval Europe, took a pound of flesh in redemption of an unpaid loan, and were motivated purely by the desire for self-advancement and greed, should be disappointed when Jewish morality is not superior to their own.

Are these double standards simply a devious form of anti-Semitism, just one more excuse for attacking Jews, and the way to put them into a no win situation? When Jews *do* attain higher moral standards and boast of it, they are told that they are self-righteous and have the arrogance of a people claiming chosenness or even racial superiority. It seems a matter of 'heads the anti-Semites win and tails the Jews lose'.

Yet anti-Semitism is not the whole story. It seems to me that buried deep in the psyche of Christians (and it is significant that Muslims do not expect Jews to have higher moral standards) may be the identification of the Jewish people with the suffering of Christ. Christians know, at least those who are intellectually aware, that Jews have suffered enormously with small justification; that none the less they have courageously remained loyal to their faith and people; that they, like most people, are decent and honest with their neighbours and associates. So why should they suffer so much? Is it possible that the Jew has become a Christ figure? As Christ suffered for the sins of the world, so must the Jews! And as Christ forgave and remained pure, so must the Jews! Yet, when Jews react differently, they betray those Christians who for some reason believed they would do what Jesus told everyone to do – but what most people with power have never done – and that is to turn the other cheek and to love their enemies.

Moses said to the Israelites, 'Love the stranger because you were strangers in the land of Egypt.' Christian men and women in the West, or people whose origins are Christian, seem really to be saying, 'you know what it is to be the victims of history, therefore never make others into victims.' While others may be excused for seeking vengeance for their affliction, or for rising up against society and committing crimes, Jews, collectively and individually, are expected to be purified by their suffering.

The explanation would be insufficient if it were offered as the only one, but taken as an element in the warp and woof of attitudes towards Jews – particularly the view that they should behave better (although, according to Christian theology, having been responsible for killing Christ, no one has behaved worse) – it recommends itself for consideration.

It is too small a task for you to be my servant,
only to preserve the tribes of Jacob,
and to restore the survivors of Israel: [but]
I will make you a light to the nations,
that my salvation may reach to the ends of the earth.

Bible, Isaiah 59

4 Jewish Survival

'The Jews just won't give up'

Jews are no different in their make-up from any other national or religious group-ing. Among them you will find patriots and fanatics, but also people who are apathetic and in the process of assimilation. In between are the largest numbers, who remain loyal out of filial piety, folk memory, peer pressure, inertia, or – last but not least – sincere belief.

It was not so at the beginning of history. The ancestors of today's Jews were a tribal nation, and like all nations, their members and citizens took pride in their country and their spiritual inheritance. They felt secure within their own bor-ders; and some were even warriors crossing boundaries to conquer and exact tribute from other cities and nations. As children feel special to their parents, the Jews, like other nations, felt special to their land, their God and their traditions.

The Jews began as a group of Semitic tribes that united to conquer and settle Canaan. The determination to achieve this objective derived from the conviction that God had promised their ancestors the land on condition that they would enter into an agreement with Him to worship Him and obey his ethical and ritual laws. The God of the Covenant was described metaphorically as a 'Man of War', for He redeemed his people from Egyptian bondage and, after a period of forty years in the wilderness under the leadership of the great prophet and law-giver Moses, they had the courage to invade the promised 'land of milk and honey', to subdue its inhabitants and to establish themselves as its inheritors and rulers.

It is natural to love the land of one's birth and childhood; and the land of Israel, with its varied topography and climatic conditions, was particularly love-able. It had, however, the misfortune of being at the cross-roads of rival empires to the north and south and was drawn into their conflicts. This was the case before Alexander's conquest of the Middle East, and even after, when his empire was split up between the Ptolemies of Egypt and the Seleucids of Syria.

Before then, however, two events provide clues to the secret of Jewish sur-vival. The first of these was the conquest by the Assyrians of the northern part of the kingdom in 722 BCE. King Sennacherib exiled the Ten Tribes of Israel which had declared their independence of the Davidic dynasty in the south after the death of Solomon. The Israelites of the north were never to return home, for their defeat was utter and complete. They are now known as the Ten Lost Tribes, because they assimilated and disappeared in a foreign land. Those who were left behind became known as the Samaritans, and it was they who provoked the sympathy of Jesus.

In 586 BCE, a similar fate befell the southern tribes of Judah and Benjamin, and

25

the tribe of Levi which ministered to God at his Temple in Jerusalem. They too were forced into exile soon after the Babylonian King Nebuchadnezzar destroyed Solomon's Temple. But these exiles 'wept by the rivers of Babylon' and swore to return. And this many of them did fifty years later, when Cyrus, King of Persia, conquered Babylon. He gave them a royal dispensation and even encouraged them to return and to become a tributary state with their capital in Jerusalem. Judaea was reborn.

But the questions are, why did the Judaeans maintain their loyalty in a strange land for over two generations, and why, unlike other peoples whose gods had suffered defeat and who had been forced into submission and exile, did the Judaeans have the will to return to the land of their ancestors? The answer lies in the genius of their prophets. These people posited a moral God, and predicted the punishment of Judaean society and even the destruction of God's House for the sins of their kings, princes and plutocrats.

Other peoples blamed their military defeats on the weakness of their gods and worshipped instead the gods of the conquering armies. The Judaean prophets, however, saw the defeats as the deliberate acts of their own God, and saw Him as using others to punish his recalcitrant children. The prophetic message sank in and took root. The prophet Jeremiah, for instance, warned that God would allow his own house to be destroyed, and then joined his people in exile and promised that repentance would lead to their return and to the restoration of God's glory on his holy mountain. Because the Judaeans accepted that their defeat was at the hands of God, faith in Him remained alive and vibrant.

A people with a living God in their midst and a dream of national restoration does not die. And having survived exile to return to rebuild their Temple, the Jews established a precedent which would loom large in their view of themselves – having survived exile once they could do it again. Rome destroyed Jewish independence and ended its autonomy, when it conquered Jerusalem in 63 BCE. Titus destroyed the Temple in 70 CE and the Romans crushed the Bar Kochba rebellion in 135 CE. But the Judaeans' faith was not shaken, and for over two thousand years they prayed for a return to their homeland. Some of the pious did indeed return to the land, and for centuries some Jews – descendants of the exiled Judaeans – lived in the land under foreign rule. Finally it became fully theirs in 1948, reborn as 'Israel', and bearing the name of its first incarnation in ancient times.

The second historical fact that helps account for the Jews' survival is that Jewish *national* feelings and yearnings blend with Judaism. Even when there was no nation-state, the religion ensured survival by creating internal motivation and external pressure. Internally, there was a concrete objective: the return to the land under a quasi-political religious leadership, a spiritual Messiah who would be the descendant of the earthly King David. This return was not, however, dependent solely on the advent of a Messiah. The land of Israel was holy, and those Jews who went to live there achieved a dimension of holiness. Some made the journey in order to end their days on holy soil. But psychologically the existence of a material goal – a land to which all Jews aspired – had greater power even than the belief in God. The land was reality – it could be reached – while God was elusive. One could kiss the dust of Judaea; but the existence of a protecting God seemed very distant.

It is clear from the growth of the modern political movement of return to the Holy Land that the pull of the land of Israel could be more powerful than the faith in God. In the course of centuries in exile pious Jews would visit Palestine, or financially support those who sanctified their lives by ascending to the Holy Land. In fact the Jewish State has been the creation of secular and not religious Jews.

Beyond these historical factors, however, there are external reasons for the survival of the Jews. The most important is the refusal of Gentiles to allow Jews civil rights. The freedom of integration leads to assimilation, but Jews were encouraged by persecution to mistrust the countries in which they lived. The fact that the Holy Land was their ultimate goal merely confirmed that Jews were 'foreigners'. So why, Gentiles argued, should they be allowed to vote or be given the privileges of citizens?

In the end, therefore, Jews survived as Jews both because they wanted to, and because they were not given much choice in the matter by their neighbours. There was, of course, the option of conversion to Christianity or to Islam, and some did take that course. But family and community pressures, and the need to belong, usually made conversion to another faith difficult. Conversion to the religion of a majority culture is rarely the result of religious revelation. More usually it is an act of opportunism, and often it is an expression of hostility to one's background.

There were of course, just as there are today, Jews who wished quietly to give up their Judaism through integration into the non-Jewish world and inter-marriage. Without converting, they merged into the majority environment. Instead of being Jews they became 'persons of Jewish origin'. The more tolerant the host nation, the easier this process became, and their children and grandchildren became Christians or freethinkers. The greater the tolerance of Gentile society, the more likely became the process of assimilation. The paradox thus emerges that, although physical persecution threatened the individual lives and well-being of Jews, it very much assisted the survival of the Jewish people. With their backs to the wall, Jews fought for survival.

To withstand the forces of persecution over centuries, Jews developed additional lines of defence. One agent in the process was the belief in chosenness. Ancient prophets taught that Jews were persecuted because they were special to God, and this became part of their survival armour. The Prophet Amos has God saying to Israel, 'You only have I known of all the families of the earth; therefore, I will punish you for all your iniquities.' The more they were persecuted, the more Jews viewed themselves as the Suffering Servant of God depicted by Isaiah, whom Christians, incidentally, interpret as being Jesus.

Despite this, the survival of Jews to the present day is not due to their religiosity or piety. While Judaism is first and foremost a religion, strangely enough Jews today are not a particularly religious people. Half the world's Jewish population may belong to synagogues, but only 10 per cent will be observant, in the sense that they engage in daily prayer, attend synagogue regularly, and keep the Sabbath and Jewish festivals. It is natural for Gentiles to assume that all Jews are religious, because Jews are perceived as a people united by their religious beliefs, and it is true that these were the original reason for their persecution.

Jewish life in the State of Israel sheds light on the subject of Jewish religiosity. Israeli citizens define themselves either as *Dati*, 'religious', or *Chiloni*, 'secularist'. Significantly, even in a Jewish state in which the Sabbath is an official day of rest, in which all hotels are required to serve Kosher food, and in which there are no civil marriages, only 10 per cent are religious. Secularists will on occasion attend synagogue, will have religious marriages and funerals, and even celebrate Bar Mitzvah, but they consider these observances to be ethnic or national customs. It is important to remember, however, that by 'religious' the secularists mean the Orthodox, and not followers of a Progressive religious movement.

Secularists may indeed acknowledge the value of religious forms. When pressed for the significance of their beliefs, they will confess to some form of belief in God or some mysterious role for the Jewish people in the divine scheme, but usually little more than this. Even most atheist Jews refrain from finally cutting their ties with the Jewish community and will want their children to be Jewish. They will insist on Jewish weddings to prove the Jewishness of their children.

This half-understood pride in Jewish religious forms contrasts interestingly with the trend during the 'Enlightenment' for some Jews in Western Europe to convert to Christianity for the sake of advancement. Other Jews of that period rejected all forms of religion and converted to some form of the Socialist message. For instance, while one section of Russian Jewry created a secular Jewish mission to reinhabit the Holy Land, another group formed an atheistic Socialist Bund to improve economic and political conditions in their native Russia.

Atheism, therefore, in the modern period, has been as much a part of Jewish life as theism. Even today atheists who cling to their Jewish identity will usually make no excuse for it. Their historical origins, and the challenges of anti-Semitism to create an independent Jewish destiny, are good enough reasons for them to be Jewish, even if they feel there is no God.

Jewish history itself has threatened Jewish religiosity. The Bible describes how the Israelites made a covenant with God: they would worship and obey Him because He liberated them from Egypt and brought them to the Promised Land. Until the second century CE they attributed their triumphs to God's favour and their defeats to his punishing hand. Since the destruction of the Second Temple and the defeat of the Bar Kochba rebellion in 137 CE, Jewish history has been one of humiliation and degradation. The apogee of this suffering was the Holocaust. As one post-Holocaust theologian eloquently put it, the Jews have kept their side of the Covenant, but God has not kept his.

The horrors perpetrated by the Nazis against Jews, while the rest of the world remained silent or co-operated with them, convinced many Jews that the Jewish God had either never existed, or that He had been killed along with his children in the extermination camps. If these feelings are right, then the fact that so many Jews are still religious is perhaps more remarkable than that so many are not!

Part of the secret of Jewish survival is the religiosity of a small percentage of

Jews, and the tacit acceptance by many of the non-religious that this religion plays an important role in their lives. Respecting the old customs is one way of making certain that Hitler's ambition to rid the world of Jews is never fulfilled.

And finally, as in many secrets, there are the elements of imagination and love. Jewish survival owes much to love of roots, and to the human imagination which takes pleasure in looking backwards as well as forwards. A person who feels part of a society with some four thousand years of history behind it may well have a greater romantic attachment to it than one without such an affiliation. Jews can attach themselves to a time-machine which can take them back in history as well as forward into the future, should they wish it.

The secret of Jewish survival therefore lies to a great extent in the mysterious combination of the realities of Jewish and world history, and in the faith and imagination of the individual Jewish heart and soul.

I heard from the elders who came out of Spain that one of the boats was infested with the Plague, and the captain of the boat disembarked the passengers ashore at an uninhabited place. Most died there from starvation. Some of them gathered up their strength to search for some habitation.

There was one Jew among them who struggled together with his wife and two children. The wife died. The man carried his children until they all fainted from hunger. When he awoke, he discovered that his two children were dead.

In great grief he rose to his feet and declared: 'Lord of all the world, you are doing a great deal that I may desert my faith. But know you for certain that – even against the will of heaven – a Jew I am and a Jew I shall remain. And nothing – neither what you have done to me until now or that which you will do to me in the future will be of any use.'

The Jew buried the boys, and went in search of a settlement.

Solomon Ibn Verga, Historian, 15th –16th cent.

Kingdoms arise and kingdoms pass away, but Israel endures for evermore.

Midrash

The survival of Israel through six great empires of the ancient world into our modern civilization is the outstanding proof that faith can control events by giving them ever new meanings, and so creating new facts. The story of the Jews through the Christian centuries deserves to be better known by us than it is, not only as a rebuke to our pride and to our conscience, but also to show that if history makes men, men make history. There is a Yiddish tale of starving children in a Jewish cellar, whose cry for bread is suddenly stilled when their penniless father declares that this day is a fast unto the Lord. Thus has Israel's spiritual consciousness transformed the material factors of her strange history.

H.W. Robinson, English Bible Scholar

JEWISH RACE
ARE ALL JEWS RELATED?

5 The Jewish Race

'Are all Jews related?'

A convert to Judaism receives a Hebrew first name which is followed by *ben*, 'son', or *bat*, 'daughter' of Abraham, to signify that by becoming Jewish, the convert becomes the spiritual descendant of Abraham, who was the first Jew.

It is more than likely that most born Jews are also no more than spiritual descendants of Abraham. The Bible itself tells us that Abraham circumcised all the males in his household, which means that his servants and followers too had entered into Abraham's covenant with God and thus became Jewish, and it is also clear that Abraham had an enormous household. Several times the Bible mentions the increase in his wealth and servants. When Abraham learns that his nephew, Lot, has been made a captive of war, 'he armed 318 trained men who were born in his household' to go in hot pursuit of the enemy. This figure would indicate a household of thousands.

Isaac, his son, inherited his father's enormous wealth, and he in turn chose Jacob to succeed him as head of the tribe. Whether Jacob ever took possession of his father's inheritance in Canaan (which would by then have included thousands of souls) after his return from his father-in-law's country is an interesting question. Jacob himself had accumulated great wealth and servants. No doubt when he and his eleven other sons joined Joseph in Egypt, though the Bible numbers the family as seventy, their households must have been much larger.

The famine which brought Jacob to Egypt may have destroyed part of the tribe, and many servants may also have been left behind in Canaan to fend for themselves. But whatever happened, the biblical account of the Exodus from Egypt, 430 years later, set the number of the Israelites as '600,000 men on foot besides women and children' as well as a 'mixed multitude' of slaves who took the opportunity to flee from Egypt with the Israelites. What happened to the mixed multitude when, after forty years of preparation, the Israelites conquered Canaan? Were they perhaps joined by the descendants of those from the Hebrew tribes who had not gone down to Egypt? It is hard to imagine that some of the invaders rejected the God who had delivered the Israelites from the Egyptian Pharaohs and brought them to the Promised Land as conquering heroes.

These facts provide weighty arguments against the pure Abrahamic ancestry of those who settled in Canaan after the Egyptian period; and if this is so, then the possibility of racial purity becomes more and more remote as Jewish history unfolds. For the Israelites showed themselves very open-minded about non-Israelite settlers who were prepared to accept their customs and live in peace with them.

Only two non-Israelite tribes, Amon and Moab, who were ironically descendants of Abraham's nephew Lot, behaved badly to the Israelites on their return from Egypt, and were forbidden by Moses ever to enter the Israelite covenant with God. But even so, the Bible records that Ruth, a Moabite woman, joined the Judaeans and became the great-grandmother of King David.

During their 2500 years since the Babylonian Exile many Jews assimilated, but many must have been added to their numbers by conversion. When the Jews enjoyed a brief period of independent sovereignty, just before the Roman period of rule, they forcibly converted the Idumaeans to Judaism. The awful Herod, who became the King of the Jews, was an Idumaean.

So the popular belief that Jews wish to keep their racial stock pure is without historical evidence. The Pharisees, indeed, were keen to convert others to their God. A talmudic tale of a scholar who purchased, at enormous cost, the sexual company of a beautiful non-Jewish courtesan is illustrative of the rabbinic attitude: at the last moment the scholar had moral reservations and, leaving his money behind, kept his virtue intact. The courtesan, overwhelmed by the man, tracked him down to the academy where he studied, introduced herself to its head, and expressed her desire to convert in order to win him as her husband and lover. The evidence for a Jewish racial mix is plain to see today: the black, brown and varying hues of 'white' complexions making up the Jewish population of the State of Israel prove that the insistence on racial purity is a myth. But the opposite belief persists, and perhaps has its origins in three factors. Firstly, and most importantly, is the disapproval of Jews who marry out of the community. The intolerance of out-marriage leads certain individuals to assume that Jews have a racist attitude; but in fact this intolerance derives from the fact that Jews make a priority of keeping the family as a functional, integrated unit.

Non-Jews may not be aware that there have been periods in Jewish life when, because of snobbery or national rivalries, Lithuanian Jews would disapprove of their children marrying Galician Jews, or German Jews would be discouraged from marrying Eastern European Jews; Jews originating from Spain would, for centuries, not marry anyone from outside their own group. Even in modern times, parents of European settlers in Israel were for a period unhappy when their children married children from Morocco or Yemen, and vice versa. The desire to keep a specific cultural life intact was the key to this sense of particularness. It was certainly not a fetish for racial purity.

Secondly, Jews living in any one country will tend to be the products of one or two periods of migration, and will thus share characteristics derived not only from their Jewish origins but also from their national background. As a minority in a strange country, Jews from specific regions clung together not only for security but for support, marrying within the group for socio-economic as well as religious reasons. Jews in many countries present a look-alike image, which would foster the view of a common racial stock, but should be attributed not to environmental circumstances but to the Jewish will for separateness.

Finally, anti-Semitic racists have an interest in promoting the concept that the Jews are and act like a race, albeit an inferior one.

The ongoing bitter controversy in the Jewish community on 'Who is a Jew?' also does not centre on race or genetics but is a matter of legal definition. The importance of this issue derives from the anxiety of Orthodox Jews concerning those individuals who are not Jewish according to their rules, but who marry those who are. The matter at issue here is not racial in the least, but legal.

The evidence, therefore, shows that Jews are a social and religious group, but not a racial one. There may be those, including Jews and non-Jews, who would wish to argue otherwise, but they do so for their own reasons, and their views have no foundation in fact.

Jews differ from one another in mind as in face.

Talmud: Berakhot

Here in Israel they are killing the myth that there is a physical type of Jew. The thing that is so startling here is that Jews from India are so Indian and Jews from Persia so Persian.

D. A. Schmidt, N.Y. Times 1951

In China the Jews are hardly to be distinguished from the Chinese, in Africa they resemble the Negroes, in Germanic North Europe they look like the Nordic type, in Russia, the Russian.

Race and Civilization, Friedrich Hertz

Dark Syriod Jews are often taken for Spaniards or Italians, Armenoids for South Slavs or other Alpines, and blond blue-eyed Jews for Northwest Europeans.

Aryans and Non Aryans, Franz Boas

There is not even a standardized German Jewish type. The Swabian Jew is different from the Jew of Hamburg or Lübeck – not because Jews are peculiarly adaptable, but because the influence of the environment has always proven more effective than imported traditions.

Weltbuhne, 1932, Carl von Ossietzky

There is no Jewish type, although there are Jewish types…this comes about through isolation in the ghetto and the prohibition of mixed marriage.

Le Judaisme comme Race et Religion, Ernest Renan

JEWISH CONVERSION —
It's IN THE BLOOD...

6 Jewish Conversion

'You can't become Jewish,
it's in the blood'

For those who believe that Jews are a nation, becoming Jewish through conversion seems as impossible as for an Anglo-Saxon to become an Italian. Obtaining Italian citizenship does not make one genuinely an Italian, of course, but some people think Jews do have a generally unwelcoming attitude towards those who want to join the religious family life of an adhering Jew. People who have little contact with Jews may suspect that this is a secret society which no outsider could possibly enter. It seems to be felt that there is something called 'Jewishness' that you cannot obtain either through instruction or association. It is a feeling. Like blood, it flows only through the veins and arteries of Jews.

One cannot deny that there is a shared feeling, the product of a common inheritance, centuries of looking inward, and the consolidation of certain traits, values and emotions. What is interesting is the number of Jews who no longer have this 'Jewish' feeling, and how quickly it can disappear altogether. It is very easy in a Western country for a Jew to say of himself that although he was born Jewish, he no longer is so except by birth. A choice having been made to drop out, his children might be raised without a religion, and go neither to synagogue nor to church, and celebrate Christmas as a national holiday with the usual adjuncts. Naturally, the circumstances have to be favourable for such assimilation to take place, and the grandparents would have to be irreligious Jews or to be rejected as role models by the second generation.

But if Jews can lose that Jewish feeling, surely non-Jews can equally achieve it? I know converts to Judaism who are indistinguishable from born Jews. Some have not even been converted but have lived and been accepted as Jews. It has happened more than once in my experience that a non-Jewish woman has come anxiously to a rabbi with her husband before their child's forthcoming synagogue wedding. In one case the rabbi was told that the mother for some reason never got around to converting, and that after a civil marriage they had joined the Liberal Synagogue. Their children had never been told that their mother was not Jewish and had no reason to believe she was not. Their home was no different from other Jewish homes they knew. The family ate together on Friday night. She prepared traditional Jewish dishes. Her children had celebrated their Bar Mitzvah or had been confirmed or both. But now that she had to stand under the wedding canopy during the ceremony, she felt she was living a lie: so what should they do?

The woman had opened up a Pandora's box not only about her own status but the Jewishness of her children and the danger that the future in-laws would not accept the Jewish status of their new daughter-in-law. While sparing you the details, I will tell you it had a happy ending. The wedding took place and happiness reigned. The point I am making is that this woman, due to her association with Jews, had been able through sympathy to absorb the Jewish feeling. All sincere converts who wish to make Judaism a part of their life, and have the cooperation of their Jewish spouses, can in the same way become as 'Jewish' as they like.

What must also be stated categorically is that while Judaism is not a missionary religion, it does accept converts. Even the Orthodox, who in certain countries make extraordinary demands of candidates, still make it possible. The neo-Orthodox, the Conservative and Progressive wings are far less demanding and therefore appear more welcoming.

There is no racial objection to Jews marrying converts. How could there be, when there are black Jews in Ethiopia, dark-skinned Jews in Yemen and blond Jews in Scandinavia? Some Jews, it is true, are a little wary about converts. This might begin with the Jewish parents' disappointment that their child could not find a Jew to marry. Again the reason is not racial, for particularly in Jewish life marriage between two individuals is also a marriage between their families, and the lack of that cultural bond with the non-Jewish in-laws will be missed. Parents will also be anxious over the success of a relationship that lacks a common background.

Attitudes towards converts mostly depend therefore on the individual families into which they marry, the balance between the comparative strength of character of parents and children, and the quality of the love between them. In the modern world, where the fulfilment of the individual has become the greatest goal, family ties have become increasingly unstable, and many people will regard national or religious differences as secondary to the hope that they have found a person with whom they can share the rest of their lives.

The process involved in becoming Jewish varies from country to country. The required course of instruction and exposure to the Jewish rituals and observances can last as a little as a month or as long as five years. This will depend on the orthodoxy or severity of the religious grouping to which the candidate is applying. Since marriage to a Jew is the usual motive for wishing to become Jewish, identification with the Jewish people and way of life, and some knowledge of Jewish thought and practice, are required. It is not surprising that different sections should have different requirements. But what is unfortunate is that converts who have completed the process may be accepted by one rabbinic authority but not by another. This has led to the 'Who is a Jew' controversy, which has been complicated and confused since the establishment of Israel. When the Prime Minister David Ben Gurion formed his first government, to avoid civil division between Orthodox and secular Israelis he handed authority over all matters of religious status, marriage and divorce to the Orthodox rabbinical authorities. It was they who determined who was a Jew, and the consequence was that only their recognition of Jewish status enabled a person to marry in Israel. Because Israel was keen to encourage immigration from the West, and these included large numbers of non-Orthodox Jewish converts, the Israeli government allowed any individual automatic immigrant rights under 'the Law of

Return', provided their Jewish status was confirmed by any external religious authority, Progressive or Conservative as well as Orthodox. This led to the paradox that Progressive Jewish converts or their children could enter Israel as Jews under the Law of Return, yet not be considered as Jewish by the authorities who were in charge of marriage, divorce and Jewish burial.

As the militant Orthodox are formed into religious political parties, and represent 20 per cent of the voting public, they have sought to use their political leverage in the formation of coalition governments to change the Law of Return to admit only those who are Jews according to their own legal standards. The 'Who is a Jew debate', therefore, is at its fiercest before Israeli elections and during the bargaining and 'trade-offs' that go on when the larger political parties seek to win the participation of the minority Orthodox parties in order to achieve a coalition. The strong American-Jewish lobby, which represents a community in which the Progressives and Conservatives are in the majority, prevents the Israeli government from caving in to the Orthodox, so the Law of Return, in spite of many attempts to change it, creates the anomalous situation of two classes of Israeli Jews.

Beyond the refusal to recognize any converts but their own, the stringency of the Israeli Orthodox law in demanding written proof of Jewish status creates other problems which are shared by the Orthodox in other countries. Unless a religious marriage certificate of each set of parents' weddings can be produced, Jews will find it impossible to have a Jewish marriage before a full investigation can be made into their background. The determination that no questionable Jew should slip through the net sometimes leads to terrible consequences. Survivors of the Holocaust and their children may not be able to prove that they are Jewish because their birth certificates or the religious marriage contracts of their parents have been lost or destroyed. One can imagine the fury of people whose parents have been in Nazi concentration camps finding their Jewish status challenged or denied.

The situation of such Jews – whom Hitler considered Jewish but an Orthodox court does not – is one manifestation of the problem. The status of many Jews from the former Soviet Union can also not be proven, as so many did not have Jewish weddings. The political desire within Israel for a large 'Soviet' emigration made the government crack down on the Orthodox authorities, who had no choice but to accept their Jewishness with little or no evidence.

The Ethiopian Black Jews are another example. Because these Jews have been so long out of touch with Judaism that they were unaware of Talmudic law, and their practice of 'normative' Judaism was minimal, the Orthodox would not have accepted them had not the Prime Minister of the day, Menahem Begin, insisted that these souls, who considered themselves Jewish, must have the right to refuge from persecution in the country they had always considered their homeland. Again, the Orthodox buckled under pressure from the government and made the necessary compromises. At first their rabbis performed quick conversions, but they then suspended even this when the Ethiopians protested that this was an insult to their history as Jews.

It should be remembered that the battle on 'Who is a Jew' is an internal conflict, but it does not reflect an exclusivistic approach to the outside world. Each religious community is prepared to accept converts if they meet their standards of sincerity and observance. The refusal to accept the convert of other sections is a conflict of authorities and not of attitudes.

On the matter of accepting converts to Judaism we should let the Bible have the last word and set the norm for Jewish behaviour. In the story of Ruth, her mother-in-law sets out to return to Judaea from Moab, where her husband and two sons had died. Both her widowed daughters-in-law see the bitter woman on her way and volunteer to join her. But only Ruth persists: 'Whither you go, I will go, where you lodge, I will lodge, your people will be my people and your God my God.' There is no record of her converting to Judaism, but a Judaean she surely became, because she later married Boaz, a rich farmer, and her grandson was Jesse, the father of King David, a beloved King of Israel and one of the greatest of biblical characters.

There are good reasons for believing that the story of Ruth is a merely legendary account of David's ancestry. But the fact that it was accepted by the Rabbinic Masters as part of the Bible reveals a universalism which lies at the heart of classic Judaism. This essential teaching insists not only on the acceptance of all individuals who sincerely wish to attach themselves to the Jewish people, but affirms that they are worthy of becoming the ancestors of such illustrious heroes as David, King of Israel, whose House was designated to establish an Eternal Kingdom.

'Behold, surely thus shall a man be blessed who fears the Lord' (*Psalms 128:4*) teaches us that even as we find that Abraham and Sarah became converts and were blessed, so shall all converts who follow their example be blessed.

Midrash

At the time the Gibeonites sent to Joshua with the plea, 'Come up to us quickly, and save us, and help us; for all the Kings of the Amorites that dwell in the hill country are gathered against us' (*Joshua 10:6*). Joshua asked himself, 'Shall we trouble ourselves for the sake of these converts?' The Holy One said to him: 'Joshua, if you keep away those who have been far off, you will finish by keeping away those who are near. Also, consider your own origin – is it not from converts?' (Joshua was a descendant of Joseph who married Asenath, an Egyptian.)

Midrash

God scattered Israel among the nations to ensure that converts be numerous among them.

Talmud

7 A Jewish Rule Book

'Jews treat Gentiles differently'

A Jewish friend told me of a farewell business luncheon he had organized for one of his associates. The person to whom he delegated the task chose a Chinese restaurant, owned and frequented by Jews in the suburbs of Montreal. The meal was good and the conversation lively. My friend expressed surprise when he heard one of the diners remark that the restaurant was a meeting place for the town's most beautiful prostitutes, as it did not seem to be in the part of town conducive to such activity. His informant lowered his voice and explained: 'You know, all Jews have money and they have a special rule book which lets them sleep with Gentile women, so the best hookers come here where the pickings are rich.'

Many people – except for those who regularly interact with them – believe that Jews have one set of rules for themselves and another set for others. Clifford Longley, writing for *The Times*, commenting on the fact that all four defendants in the Guinness trial were Jews, blamed this on the 'outsider' perspectives of minority groups. While praising the 'highly creative tension leading to good art and literature', he pointed to the negative side, 'creating a climate of "us" against "them" in which the rules applying to the way "we" treat each other do not quite apply to the treatment of "them"'. This is a prejudice against Jews based not on malice but on ignorance, as will be shown later.

Ernest Saunders, the man who sought to expand the Guinness empire, was the son of a Jewish Viennese gynaecologist, but a Christian churchgoer. The first person to come to his defence was his vicar. He received professional advice from non-Jewish merchant bankers. Those Jews who were convicted had originally been invited to participate by a stockbroker who, because he was Jewish, turned first to individuals whom he knew; and these happened to be Jews. But they themselves felt that they were coming to the assistance of an established and respected Gentile business at the request of a highly regarded Chairman and Chief Executive. If they broke the rules, it was not because they were Jews taking advantage of non-Jews, but because they were acting in the hope of joining the winning side in a takeover battle, and of making a profit out of the victory. The fact that the trials of the three non-Jewish professional advisers to Guinness were suspended with no verdict (and on appeal one of them was exonerated) made many Jews feel that *they* had been treated by a different set of rules.

The Guinness shareholders, the majority of whom are not Jewish, made amends to their rival bidders by a payment of some £90 million. They have little cause for anguish over an affair which imprisoned and humiliated individual Jews, whose greed was probably no greater than that of other businessmen of any religion or nationality. Their undoing was that they acted on the wrong side of the law. They did not attribute their wrong-doing to being Jewish – and nor should others.

What is most instructive here is the response of the Jewish community to the high profile of Jewish businessmen in the Guinness scandal. Many Jewish leaders, such as Lords Sieff and Young, gave Gerald Ronson unswerving moral support because he had been a byword in the community for charitable contributions. He was not to be disowned until proven guilty. After completing his prison sentence he was rehabilitated on the basis that he had paid for his crime, and, indeed, that others who had acted similarly had got away with it.

Other leading Jews discreetly took an opposing view. They could not understand the support the community leaders were giving him. For them his crime brought discredit on the Jewish community, and leaders were compounding the felony by not distancing themselves from him. The fact that members of the British Royal family maintained their association with him did not mitigate their discomfort.

I am aware that many non-Jewish readers will say, 'Yes, but surely Jews close ranks when it comes to business. They will behave differently towards each other than towards Gentiles with whom they are doing a deal.' This is also a misconception. Personally, I am aware of two transactions involving Jews who sought to out-manoeuvre other Jews. In one case the Jews on opposing sides were even close acquaintances. While there was some initial bitterness at the sense of betrayal, once the dust settled they remained on friendly terms. The other ended in a settlement out of court but after causing great personal distress.

There may be Jews who are more comfortable doing business with other Jews, but they will be people who lead lives totally separate from the non-Jewish world, and there are very few of these. Even in occupations where Jews predominate, such as the diamond polishing and distribution trades, they will deal no differently with non-Jews than with Jews, though they might feel it easier to relate to individuals with whom they share a 'language' and some social empathy.

The assumption that Jews have special rules for relations with non-Jews is particularly ironic, as for centuries those Jews living in Christian and Muslim countries suffered from special rules being imposed upon *them*. In most places before the nineteenth century, Jews were not allowed to own land or belong to trade guilds, but were compelled to work in the non-productive areas of selling, bartering and money-lending.

In 1750, King Frederick II of Prussia issued a charter for Jews in which the number of Jews allowed in Berlin was defined. 'In order that in the future … secret and forbidden increase of the number of families may be more carefully avoided, no Jews shall be allowed to marry…until a careful investigation has been made by the War and Domains offices together with the aid of the Treasury.' According to this charter, which was in no way unusual for the period, Jewish 'male and female servants and other domestics are not allowed to marry. Should they attempt to do this they are not to be tolerated any longer.' Equally all Jews could only work with a special licence. Children could not set up their own businesses, but had to work for other licensed Jews.

Not only had all Jews to be registered, but in certain places they could not leave their homes on Christian festivals, and were obliged to wear identifying badges or special hats. They were aware of being religious outsiders, but these laws made them into social pariahs.

It seemed logical, perhaps, to those who put them beyond the pale, to assume that Jews had their own rules to enable them to combat their peculiar situation. But while it might not be surprising if Jews had indeed developed the means for attacking their enemies, in fact they did not. On the contrary, they believed that by being loyal to their patrons and by looking after their own needs without disturbing their host societies, they might be left alone. They became accustomed to penal taxation and gratuitous fines, imposed on the whim of their oppressors. An illustration of this is the letter of Leopold, of the House of Hapsburg, which declared in 1703 that Samson Wertheimer was to have special privileges as a Court Jew. In view of his services, neither he nor his family would suffer the penalties imposed on other Jews. 'He will have to pay neither protection-money [*Schutzgeld*] nor tolerance-money [*Toleranzgeld*], nor will he have to pay any duties, whether they be regular or irregular, or however they may be designated.'

Court Jews received great privileges, others were grateful for small favours. But all, however much they were provoked, perceived their collective interests to be best served by being subservient, and constantly on their best behaviour. Of course there were men or women who were not able to control their righteous anger, but these courageous individuals were rare, because there was no one to applaud their courage, and there were many to exact a price for it. Seen in this perspective, Shylock in *The Merchant of Venice* is a hero, defending his challenged right to the pain, anger and yearning for justice which are the natural entitlement of humanity. In a moving speech, bound to win the sympathy of any fair-minded person, Shylock declares:

> I am a Jew. Hath not a Jew eyes? hath not a Jew hands, organs, dimensions, senses, affections, passions? fed with the same food, hurt with the same weapons, subject to the same diseases, heal'd by the same means, warm'd and cool'd by the same winter and summer, as a Christian is? if you prick us, do we not bleed? If you tickle us, do we not laugh? if you poison us do we not die? and if you wrong us, shall we not revenge?

On the other hand, evidence has been presented by some people that the Jewish Law, the Torah and the Talmud have different rules for Jews and Gentiles. There is truth in this, but these varying rules have to be understood in their historical context.

When Near Eastern society was developing, some 5000 years ago, every nomadic tribe, city or nation created codes of behaviour in order to create order within their own ranks. But beyond the call for hospitality – a sign of virtue in more civilized individuals, but not required of them – there were no rules of conduct towards foreigners except in war. Societies in which fathers were permitted to kill their sons and sell their daughters, or where cities had distinct classes of freemen and slaves, could not be expected to be concerned about the welfare of strangers.

The Laws attributed to Moses were in advance of the codes of others, but they are still a product of their time. In an age when starvation was the only alternative, submitting oneself to slavery did not seem a bad thing. The civilizing processes were the laws which protected the slave and his family from maltreatment.

In addition to the Golden Rule – the command to 'love your neighbour as yourself' – the Torah orders one to love the stranger. A Hebrew slave brought to slavery by ill-fortune had a limited period of servitude, and on the Sabbatical year (each seventh year) he would go free. But the foreigner enslaved as the result of war had no such right.

There is, however, an incorrect assumption, current even among Jews, which must be nailed once and for all. And that is that Jews are allowed by Jewish law to treat non-Jews less ethically than fellows of their own faith. This is an anti-Semitic stereotype rooted in medieval times, when Jews were encouraged by Canon Law to lend money for commercial and military adventurism and militarism. As Jews were forbidden to lend money with interest to other Jews, the myth of unfair behaviour toward Gentiles developed. It is of interest that biblical law forbade interest-bearing loans not only to Israelites but to non-Israelites living in the lands of Israel and Judaea. Loans in biblical law were intended as a form of charity to those in desperate need, and in such cases interest was considered immoral. It would appear that interest for commercial reasons would have been allowed, and this would be the reason for allowing interest on loans to foreigners.

Clifford Longley puts it well when he writes, 'So the despised Jewish money-lender was the creation of Christianity, despised because he was rich; despised, above all, because lending money at interest was regarded as a sin. That he was also necessary is where a good measure of Christian hypocrisy came in. But, human nature being what it is, despising someone hypocritically is a reason for despising him even more.'

The fact that Christians were at one time not allowed to take interest from other Christians indicates the prevailing attitudes in the past, that the concept of right and wrong only operated within national borders and perhaps even within the limits of a religious community.

The experience of Jewish businessmen in the ruthless marketplace of unwelcome take-overs and fierce competitive practices is that they receive no different treatment from Jews than non-Jews. Jews, like other ethnic or national groups, may try to rationalize acting less favourably to those who are not kith and kin, especially if in the past they were victims of their hostility. Jews should be on guard themselves against this self-justification: 'Love the stranger as yourself' is as much the heart and soul of the Jewish law as is 'Love your neighbour as yourself'. If Jews act unethically against non-Jews, their sin is as great as if they had wronged a fellow Jew.

Living as we do in an international community with reciprocal trade agreements and International Courts, it is hard to imagine oneself in a time when all social organizations were closed shops and for whom the foreigner was the 'barbarian' – as Greeks referred to them. He was outside the law, even if he had his own laws and even if they were objectively better than those of the home-born.

An innovative merchant travelling to foreign shores or cities was risking his very life, for he could be killed for his merchandise. He could only survive on his eloquence and wits, his ability to entertain his host and persuade him that his survival was of greater benefit than his death. He could also hope that the host would be influenced by the unwritten law of hospitality to strangers. The foreigner might also gain from the curiosity he might arouse by telling tales from a strange land, to break the monotony endemic to any closed society.

In business practice there was no fair price. The market price was simply the most a person could get. American Indians sold Manhattan Island for trinkets which were estimated to have a value of $22. (Did the Pilgrim fathers feel that they had behaved as good Christians when making such a deal?) Within any community, there is the need to conform to certain norms, if only out of the need for reciprocity. Outside the community, anything goes. There would be no point in risking one's life if one did not come home a rich man. 'Go west and make your fortune' was not only the American dream. It is the dream from which trade and empires are built.

The laws which influenced economic life within the Jewish community also affected marriage and sexual relationships. Laws were designed to protect the potential victim without sacrificing the rights of those who made the rules. In a male-dominated society, the victim was the woman. As a married woman she would be given the rights of food, shelter, clothing and sex. Failure to meet these obligations would lead to the imposition of a divorce on the husband, with a financial settlement for the wife by the elders of the city. Concubines and captive women also enjoyed some protection.

What was missing was any proscription of non-marital sexual relationships with foreigners. Adultery was a capital crime, and in a polygamous society, this meant that any married woman proved to have slept with another man was subject to execution together with her accomplice, but only if her illicit partner was an Israelite. A foreigner had no legal standing in the community and to this extent did not really exist. Thus, while the children of an adulterous relationship in which both partners are Jews are according to Orthodoxy illegitimate, and are in a sense penalized for their parents' sins, a child born to a married woman who was raped by a foreign soldier is not considered illegitimate and has all the rights of other Jews.

There will be other opportunities to discuss the Jewish attitude to women and sex, but my purpose here is to show the absurd results of applying laws formulated for one ancient society to modern times, when people of different nations and religions come into regular contact. It was not that the law book had one set of rules for Jews (or whatever they were called at the time) and another set for the others. There simply were no laws for the others at all.

Some Jewish men may be especially stimulated by non-Jewish women, or may be attracted to opposites. In the past Jewish families created a greater protective shell around their daughters, which made their sons look for experience elsewhere. The permissive age in which we live has changed all this. Casual sexual relations are now as likely between Jews as between individuals of other faiths.

The fact that Jewish laws regarding commerce and sexual relationships might be subject to change may have been foreseen by the Talmud, when it ruled that 'the Law of the land is the Law'. Jews were expected to abide by the principles of their own laws, but they had to accept the restrictions of the laws of the land in which they lived.

There still are pockets of ultra-Orthodox Jews who seek to live in isolation. Like the Amish sect in the USA they do this to protect themselves from assimilation. They refuse to go to the civil courts in matters of dispute with other Jews and prefer to set up their own courts of rabbinic scholars, but this involves tiny numbers of people, even though they have increased in recent years with the rising tide of fundamentalism. There are two startling examples of this. One was the case of an Orthodox Jewish woman living in London who employed a teenage boy to sit with her young children. When it was discovered that the children had been sexually abused, the teenager, also ultra-Orthodox, was arrested and brought to trial. The mother was then criticized for using the civil courts, and she and her family were hounded out of the neighbourhood, after riots and threats of violence.

The other was the son of the Sosover Rebbe, leader of a Hasidic sect in London, who persuaded friends and relations to invest their money in a business which gave huge returns. Initial success led to other Jewish investors from the USA as well as Great Britain and the Continent. The business collapsed and he owed millions. A declaration of bankruptcy would not have satisfied his Orthodox Jewish investors. He shaved off his beard to achieve anonymity and fled. The Orthodox investors, believing that they had been swindled, never sought legal redress but tracked him down in Brussels. His beatings and torture required weeks of hospitalization. Happily, these are extraordinary exceptions.

Generally Jews are fully integrated into non-Jewish communities outside Israel, or into the modern lifestyle and ideology of the Jewish State of Israel, and behave very much like members of other communities and faiths. In business, they will keep or break the laws of the land very much like everyone else, motivated by their own personal inclinations and ambitions. In sex, when society is permissive they will follow suit, even if they are rather slower to do so. They will join the popular movements of the day, be they feminism, tolerance of homosexuality or whatever.

Jews, like members of other communities, have rule books. They are designed to improve and regulate their own behaviour, but do not encourage a different standard of behaviour towards outsiders. Humanity being what it is, laws will be broken. Often other individuals will be victims of law-breaking. Leaving aside war and racial rioting, members of any one community are as likely to suffer from each other as from members of another group.

He has showed you, O Man, what is good:
and what the Lord does require of you,
but to do justice, and to love kindness,
and to work humbly with your God.

Bible, Micah 6

8 Jewish Solidarity

'Jews stick together'

The impression shared by Jews and Gentiles is that the Jews are a united people who look after their own. The extent of Jewish unity is exaggerated. Jews may on occasion seek to give this impression because 'unity' seems to be a good thing and the Gentile might think better of them if they appear to be united. Also, 'unity is strength', and a persecuted people require cohesion to ward off political opponents. Non-Jews may be justified in feeling that loyalty to a common cause and a sense of collective responsibility have been the key to Jewish survival: 'They survive because they stick together.'

Non-Jews have another reason for believing that Jews are closely linked to each other: it makes it easier to relate to individuals you don't know if you can lump them together. When someone says, 'The Jews do this' or 'The Jews believe this', he becomes an expert on Jews. The person who reacts to such generalizations by pointing out differences, and suggesting that Jews should be considered individually, may be written off as a bore. Distinctions which are either completely black or entirely white are more interesting and easier to understand than the grey areas between.

In truth, Jews must be among the most divided ethnic entities (if that is what they are) in the world. For example, in Israel, there is a group of ultra-Orthodox Jews living in Jerusalem known as 'Guardians of the City', who do not recognize the legitimacy of the State of Israel and support its enemies. Why? Because the creation of the Jewish State by Jewish secularists and not by the awaited Messiah is regarded as a desecration of God's name.

While one speaks glibly of the strength of the American Jewish lobby and assumes that all Jews are Zionists, there is deep division among the Jewish mainstream even about Israeli politics. While every attempt is made to present a united front on behalf of Israel, the cracks cannot be hidden. Jews are divided now about what concessions Israel should make to achieve peace, as they were when Israel invaded Lebanon in 1982.

It goes without saying that, outside Israel, Jews divide between the political parties according to how they perceive their individual interests. In Britain, as an immigrant community, the large proportion felt sympathy for the Labour Party. As that party inclined to the left and the Jews became more prosperous, many moved their allegiance to the Tories. The same could be said in regard to American politics. It is true that as a large proportion of Jews support Israel, a political party's policy on Israel will influence Jewish voting.

Even in regard to other issues of mutual concern, Jews will be divided. Before the dissolution of the Soviet Empire, when Jewish life was repressed and Zionism was considered to be an Imperialist and anti-Soviet doctrine, Jews were debating priorities: was it more important to persuade the Soviet authorities to let their Jews go to Israel or to let Jews lead unhampered lives in the USSR? The lack of religious unity within the Jewish community is the subject of another chapter.

In regard to looking after their own, my experience as a fund-raiser indicates that some do and some do not. For every Jew who gives charity to Jewish causes there are at least ten who do not. It is the successful businessman who will be most likely to contribute to Jewish welfare, education and Israel. But they will do this only after securing the financial future of their children and grandchildren. In this they will not be unlike wealthy Gentile families. The ratio of their support for non-Jewish causes will be in direct proportion to their integration into the host society. A study of charitable distributions of leading Jewish family foundations will show a large variance between those who contribute 75 per cent to Jewish causes and those who give 90 per cent to general causes.

I would like to think that as a matter of course Jews do care for their own, but honesty makes me qualify this assertion. In certain countries they did so because they had to, since their rulers did not wish the Jewish poor or elderly to be a drain on their own purse. In democratic countries making welfare provision for all citizens, Jewish hospitals or homes for the elderly or the mentally ill are relics of pre-enlightened times. Also, Jews had special dietary and other religious and social needs which gave those institutions continued validity even when the state began to provide the selfsame services.

Sometimes, looking after their own was a defensive mechanism on the part of the established Jewish community in the face of new waves of immigration from other countries. The first waves of immigration, who had succeeded economically and socially in the host society, were nervous that an influx of poor illiterate refugees would embarrass them. But it was with a generous spirit that they created Jewish institutions to look after the needs of the poor immigrants.

All this is not to say that Jews from abroad are not invited to Jewish homes for a Sabbath meal when they appear in synagogue on a Friday evening. Though with the increase of student travel, Jewish youths have begun to complain that a free meal ticket is no longer guaranteed when they march into some ancient synagogue during their travels. Perhaps there are too many of them; and anyway their worn jeans reveal fashion trends rather than that the wearer has fallen on hard times.

Support for educational institutions is very large, but can barely be considered as charity because it is designed, not to provide education for poor Jews, but to promote Judaism and Jewish identification through specialized instruction.

Of all causes, the State of Israel ranks foremost in capturing the imagination of the Jewish community, and contributions towards the absorption of refugees into Israel runs into millions. Sadly, home-based welfare charities have taken a poor second place in the scale of priorities to Israel's needs. The Jewish community in the United States has resolved the conflict of interests between Israeli and local Jewish charities by setting up the United Jewish Appeal, whose boards of governors in different states and cities agree the allocation of funds between Israel and home needs.

Three elements reinforce the desire of Jewish communities to look after their own and Israel. One is the pride natural to every minority community. The second is the long Jewish experience of having to organize self-help in Muslim and in Eastern and Central European countries. In Poland, for example, the Jews were almost self-governing in the towns in which they outnumbered Gentiles, and ran their own courts, schools, synagogues, hospitals and institutions for the handicapped. They funded these by taxing themselves in addition to paying state taxes, and elected officers and councils to administer the needs of the community. Wherever they went, they brought this experience and applied it. The final element is the emphasis in Judaism on the primacy of charitable works. 'Charity' is a derivative of *charis* which is the Greek word for 'grace' or 'favour'. The etymology of the word suggests the concept of voluntary giving. The Hebrew word used to describe charitable deeds is *tzedakah*, which means 'justice'. Biblical laws prescribe charity as an obligatory act. A corner of the field *had* to be left for the poor; during the harvest, all fallen grains and forgotten sheaves had to be left for the poor; twice in every seven-year cycle, there was a tithe for the poor.

The medieval Jewish philosopher, Maimonides, encapsulated the Jewish attitude to charity by citing seven degrees in ascending level. The lowest level of giving is when the donor knows to whom he is giving and the recipient from whom the gift comes. One of the higher levels is when neither the donor nor the recipient know each other. But the highest is the interest-free loan to enable a poor people to establish themselves so that they no longer require charity.

One cannot generalize about generosity towards those in need; it is a very individual matter. Even among a people for whom charity was considered the highest virtue, there will be mean individuals who will withhold support from their closest relatives and friends. Still, my personal experience suggests that Jews, because of their background, have a greater sense of obligation than others to help each other and also those outside their community.

A study of charitable giving would doubtless indicate that Jews are among the leading donors and voluntary organizers of many causes. They support university-building campaigns, research into the cure of diseases, care for the handicapped, Third World relief, the arts and every other cause under the sun. Most who involve themselves in charitable giving and work do not congratulate themselves, but there will always be those who take pleasure in the recognition that their generosity can bring them. In the United Kingdom, a knighthood or other royal honours occasionally provide an incentive. For the most part, however, prosperous Jews consider it a blessing that they are in the position to help others. The habit of doing so for generations, and the expectation from their peers that they continue to do so, keeps this most excellent of Jewish traditions very much alive.

Behold, how good it is and how pleasant when brothers live together in unity.

Bible, Psalms 133

SUCCESS — ALL JEWS ARE RICH...

9 Jewish Success

'All Jews are rich'

Whenever I am asked to explain the success rate of Jews and why all Jews are rich, I think of my unsuccessful Jewish relatives, friends and acquaintances – they include some who are unemployed and even unemployable. The large numbers of small shopkeepers, salesmen, clerks and cab drivers are neither rich nor stories of success. The majority of Jews are ordinary people without any distinction.

But nevertheless, many Jewish success stories do blare out at us from the media and many more are hidden in the annals of history. Even in those areas which are not the focus of public attention, the number of Jews in res–ponsible and influential positions is out of proportion to their numbers. This applies particularly to the medical, professional, scientific and academic worlds, although Jews in business and politics receive more publicity than the others, perhaps because riches and power create greater interest as well as envy.

As I write this, I am aware that of the thirty-two British Lord Justices of Appeal, three are Jewish, whereas only one out of 157 members of the population is a Jew. Together with a Jewish Lord Chief Justice, this means that 12·5 per cent of the Court of Appeal is Jewish compared to 0·64 per cent typical of the total population. Of course this could be a coincidence, and a survey of all judges might show a smaller percentage, but even so, like the number of Jewish Nobel Prize winners, the number is well out of proportion to their population size.

If non-Jews are surprised at the Jewish success rate, so are Jews. A typical dialogue among Jews is:

'Did you know that Michael Douglas was Jewish?'

'No, are you sure?'

'Yeah, his father is Kirk Douglas who was Jewish.'

'I didn't know that he was Jewish. It seems that everybody is Jewish.'

Jews are ambivalent about the success of Jews. There is the element of pride – 'another one of us has made good' – and then there is the anxiety of being overexposed. This was especially noticeable when there were four Jews in Margaret Thatcher's cabinet, one of them Home Secretary and another Chancellor of the Exchequer, the two most sensitive positions in government, that intrude in the lives of every individual. Some Jews felt that if the economy were to fail, or if there were uncontrollable race or labour riots, 'the Jews' would be blamed. And as evidence to support this anxiety, they noted that the Chancellor was dubbed 'Lawson the *Litvak*'. Since *Litvak* is

Yiddish for 'Lithuanian', the nickname did indeed have an anti-Semitic flavour. They felt it was wrong for their co-religionists to accept high office, because they were raising not only their own heads but those of the entire community over the parapet and might be shot at. Ex-defence minister Alan Clark records in his diary that there was talk at 'eminent Tory dinner tables' of there being 'too many Jew-boys in Margaret Thatcher's cabinet'. Most Jews, however, took great pride in such success and believed that it both reinforced the integration of the Jewish minority in British society and proved that Jews were making a worthwhile contribution to the country that had given them so much freedom of opportunity.

Jews find it as difficult as non-Jews to know how to respond or explain the success stories, and they spend more time looking for the answer than do non-Jews. One explanation that does not work is the power of the so-called Jewish network system. Networking among Jews, like all networking, is based on who you know, to the extent that Jews tend to know more Jews – because most minorities huddle together for increased security, they will help each other when they can. But in a competitive world based on the Market Economy and the 'Search for Excellence', no Jew, unless he is joining a family business, can expect special treatment. A Jew, like anyone, must prove his ability to land the job and keep it.

Similarly, although social contacts could be valuable in getting started in business, law or accountancy, in the areas of academia, the arts, sciences, medicine and politics, they will be worthless. Government, the Civil Service, the Judiciary and the academic, medical and other bureaucracies may recruit to a limited extent on an 'old boy' system based on schooling and background, but this will not be biased in favour of Jews as such.

In a public company established by Jews, it can be as much of a disadvantage as an advantage to be a member of the founding family. A son or nephew might have to prove himself better in order to escape the accusation of nepotism. Incredible as it may seem, some Jews prefer not to employ other Jews, especially their relatives and friends, because of the embarrassment if it does not prove satisfactory. Of course, in Jewish circles closed off from external influences, such as the ultra-Orthodox, there is a greater tendency to employ one's own, but then the consideration of loyalty and of Sabbath and Festival observances and dietary restrictions also come into play.

In general, therefore, personal ambition will motivate Jews to cultivate those contacts likely to enhance their opportunities for success, and ignore their being Jewish or not. They share this attitude with the ambitious go-getters of any religion or nation.

So what is the basis for the success story of Jews at the top? Survival of the fittest is the most popular answer, and to be more precise, survival of the most intelligent, and of those prepared to take risks to improve their situation. Joseph Heller touches on this amazing ability in *Good as Gold* when a Jewish brother talks to his sister about their parent's generation:

Imagine those old people ... leaving with children from a small town in

Russia more than sixty years ago and coming all the way here. How did they do it? They knew they would never go back. I can't go anywhere without hotel reservations and I can't go out of town two days without losing some laundry or luggage or having a plane connection cancelled.

Jews have had to live by their wits. Migrating in search of a better future from one country to another, they had little they could take with them. They survived because of their brains, tenacity and optimism. (When one praises the 'genius' that made Jewish immigrants so successful, one should not forget the many more who remained impoverished and oppressed in the 'old' countries and were wiped out by the Holocaust.) They valued the intellect as a life-preserving force and invested in it by educating and training their children. Not all became doctors, professors or lawyers, but many did. Jews were steeped in the struggle for survival. They encouraged many of the less academic to become risk entrepreneurs. Some made millions, while others became shopkeepers. The sons and daughters of both rose in the professions, finance or commerce.

Jewish eugenics also provides a partial answer. Jews traditionally respect education, and the rich and successful aimed to marry their daughters not just to the sons of rich families but often to Talmudic scholars. This blending of learning and success through marriage led to the intensification of Jewish qualities and ambitions – the desire for education, success and security and the wish of parents that their children should outstrip them. Yet with the ever-increasing rate of out-marriage this phenomenon has dramatically changed, and the consequences are yet to be assessed.

Human experience indicates that the need to 'prove' oneself is in inverse ratio to one's security. In today's world, women are expected to be better than men if they are to succeed at the same jobs; and so too do Jews, in many cases, have to be better than non-Jews to overcome prejudice and to 'justify' their own preferment. Political pundits charting the meteoric rise of David Young, elevated to the House of Lords and the Cabinet, did not tire of telling their readers that Margaret Thatcher said of him, 'Others bring me problems, he brings me solutions'. Members of minorities tend to work harder and to have a greater need to please and to succeed. But while Gentile labourers may be content with their pay packets and have no regrets if their children follow in their footsteps, Jewish labourers will feel the need for their children to go beyond that level and to achieve what they perceive to be a secure future. This may also apply to other immigrant minorities.

A final thought on the reasons of Jewish success, particularly in the arts, science and industry. Jews as outsiders seek to make a virtue of uniqueness; they will not be fixed in traditional structures or ways of doing things. They often blaze new trails and make constructive changes in society. Clifford Longley, a perceptive commentator on religious minorities, says that the effect of the 'outsider' perspective 'generates a highly creative tension, leading to good art and literature' – and he could have added good business. As I have written before, it is the curse of the Jew to have had a history of separateness.

The success of Jews is the positive result of that separateness, making their achievements in many instances a benefit to others as well as to themselves.

The Jews generally give value. They make you pay, but they deliver the goods. In my experience, the men who want something for nothing are invariably Christians.

Saint Joan, G. B. Shaw

Thinking became just as characteristic a feature of Jews as suffering.

History of the Jews, Heinrich Graetz

It was not the publican nor the financier whom the Sons of Israel honoured and aspired to emulate; it was the rabbi, the interpreter of the law, the scribe, the scholar, the wise man.

Israel Among the Nations, Leroy-Beaulieu

10   Jewish Materialism

'Jews drive a hard bargain'

In this age of consumerism, when saving is considered almost criminal, accusation that Jews are materialistic is not as prevalent as it used to be. But the feeling that Jews are especially interested in money and in displaying their possessions is still popular. My own personal experience is that Jews' attitude to money and what it can buy will vary according to the society in which they live. They will behave like those of similar means among non-Jews. *Nouveau-riche* Jews will behave like *nouveau-riche* Gentiles, and old Jewish wealth will behave like old Gentile wealth.

All the same, it is fair to say that Jews value wealth and do not feel it is in conflict with spiritual or moral values. Jesus' statement about the unlikelihood of the rich entering heaven does not reflect mainstream Jewish sentiment. The Hebrew Bible and rabbinic literature begin with the premise that God gave the world to humanity for its enjoyment, and that laws were made to create harmony so that all could enjoy his bounty.

The Essenes, a group who lived in the time of Jesus, did disavow the pleasures of the flesh for the life of the spirit, but normative Judaism has always discouraged ascetic practices. The rabbinic admonition, 'Do not separate yourself from the community', is interpreted as a ban on chastity and asceticism. The rabbis insisted that each man should marry and have children; and family responsibilities make it essential to line one's nest, and to secure or increase the comforts of life.

Judaism has never separated the material from the spiritual, and thus has not put the latter on a higher moral plain. The fact is that the spirituality which is identified with other-worldliness is not a Jewish value, and there is little trace of it in Jewish thought. The morality of the Hebrew prophets rested not on their spirituality but in their dedication to the improvement of moral conduct. They did not deny wealth, but denounced the abuse of it. They applauded the 'good life', but condemned the human exploitation which prevented the weak and poor from participating in it.

Because Judaism is a life-affirming religion, all conventional pleasures are also affirmed. High value is placed on home comforts, clothing and cosmetics which not only protect but enhance human life. The poor are objects of sympathy requiring assistance but never admiration.

The life of the spirit in Judaism is identified with the study of Torah, which is the ongoing attempt to understand God's relationship to Mankind and the Jewish people. Scholarship, rather than mysticism, is the way Jews express their non-materialistic aspirations, and since Jewish scholars have always been held in the highest regard, they tend to be well supported. For generations, rich Jews have married their daughters to scholars and have been proud to finance their studies and teaching according to their means.

But these scholars are anything but other-worldly. Depending on their fame or reputation, ordinary Jews would come to them for advice or to have them adjudicate in their disputes with fellow Jews. Some Jews elevate their scholars to almost saintly stature. The leaders of some Hasidic groups, for instance, are accredited with a special relationship to God, and live in luxury provided by the voluntary self-taxation of loyal disciples.

So materialism as such has never been despised by Judaism, and art and culture have been viewed as integral parts of this value system. Jews would lavish care and funds on beautiful ritual goblets, candlesticks and manuscripts to express their love of Judaism. They would also provide handsome dowries to attract the best matches for their daughters, in order to enhance the learning and refinement of their families. Material comfort and beauty were therefore a natural part of the Jewish belief that life is supposed to be good, in spite of the misery occasionally inflicted on them by their enemies.

Economic deprivation has incidentally contributed to the idea that Jews are intoxicated by wealth. Since Jews were for centuries not permitted to own land or to join the Guilds of craftsmen and were subject to arbitrary exile from their towns, regions or countries, it was a merely practical precaution to hold some or most of one's wealth in the form of money or easily transportable commodities such as jewellery which one could gather up in a hurry if one had to flee.

The generalization that Jews are selfish materialists still thrives in some areas. *The Shorter Oxford Dictionary* defines the word 'Jew' in several ways. But among its descriptions are 'As a name of opprobrium or reprobation, applied to a grasping or extortionate usurer, or a trader who drives hard bargains or deals craftily'. For the sake of fairness, the dictionary seeks to explain how 'In medieval England, Jews, though honourably engaged in many pursuits, were particularly familiar as money-lenders, a profession closed by Canon Law to Christians. Thus the name of Jew came to be associated in the popular mind with usury and any extortionist practices that might be supposed to accompany it ...'

Old images never die, and to this day Jews are accused of driving hard bargains, and more – that they are mean and penny-pinching. I met a Christian who told me that he believed that he had a Jewish great-grandmother because she was always called the 'old Jew'. Upon questioning, I discovered that this 'old Jew' had a reputation of being very careful with her money. More likely than not, she was simply called this by her disapproving relations.

The perception of Jews as mean happens to be in clear contradiction to their reputation for ostentation. For if Jews are liberal in their spending habits, they can hardly be mean. Yet while Jews may have a tendency that has developed over centuries to be careful with their money and to seek value for money, the difference between contemporary Jews and other groups is only a matter of degree. If Jews are more careful, it may well be due to an inherited sense of insecurity. Today, individuals who are in fear of losing their jobs will draw in their horns and save; for centuries Jews have had good reason to put money aside for rainy days. In their case, such days were more like tidal waves.

An impartial look at the matter of driving hard bargains leads one to the conclusion that most people like a bargain, indeed the entire advertising industry works on that premise. All sorts of people are prepared to camp out for hours in front of large stores to capture a great bargain on the first day of the sales.

A non-Jewish house painter once told me that Jews have this reputation merely because they bargain better than most. Their approach is more subtle. A non-Jew might either exclaim that such-and-such is an outrageous price, or that he had not realized that costs had gone up so much. In either case the value of the item or the service is rejected, and the possibility of negotiation is closed. A Jew, however, might knit his brows, purse his lips and say, 'I had not really expected to pay so much.' The sympathy aroused by the potential customer in the vendor could lead to a compromise in price. If the seller later discovers that he has been too generous, he might then blame the Jew, even though the negotiations had been straightforward and honourable.

It is true that Jews have been over the centuries – through no fault of their own – a commercial rather than a land-based people, and that this has made them more sensitive to pricing and the possibility of saving without losing quality.

Curiously, my impression is that it is Jews who are more disturbed by this trait than the non-Jews with whom they do business. The latter usually welcome it, and may remark on Jews' high degree of loyalty to people who give them good service, continuing to use them whenever possible and passing on the warmest recommendations to friends and neighbours and almost becoming their unpaid agents. Although this is not to suggest that there are no Jews who do not renege on a deal or leave debts unpaid. The stereotype of the grasping Jew, represented by Shakespeare in the character of Shylock or by Dickens in the person of Fagin, was born out of persecution, and today seems to be disappearing. Since Jews now enter all the businesses and professions of their own free will, their inherited anxieties fade.

So it seems that Jews traditionally see no reason to deny their wealth. But can it be said that they like to display their material success ostentatiously? This will be argued particularly in communities where it is considered good manners to be discreet about wealth. It is appropriate for a duchess to be decked in diamonds but not a fishwife. Bad manners and lack of style are contemptible, but are not the monopoly of any one people or nation. Jewish thinking is also that materialism which enhances life is admirable, while the materialism which is a reflection of greed, or delight in the relative deprivation of others, is contemptible.

I would say that Jews share a down-to-earth quality which enables them to enjoy the wealth they have earned. This is not done selfishly, for most of those who have had the good fortune to acquire wealth share it through charitable giving. Few glory in their riches, and those who do, of whatever religion and race, are not among my friends, nor, I imagine, among those of anyone who values good taste.

JEWISH SEX —
OVER SEXED . . .

11 Jewish Sex

'Jews are oversexed'

It is common for sexual images and fantasies to revolve around men and women of other nations and races. Are Italian men as passionate as they appear in the imagination of British women? Are black men more virile and better endowed than white men? Are the French more subtle in love-making than Americans? The wisest response to such questions is probably to examine why the question was asked in the first place. If the evidence for these generalizations is based on extra-marital sexual flings, it would be distorted by the excitement of novelty and of indulging in the forbidden.

Lady Chatterley's lover, in D.H. Lawrence's novel, was a British gamekeeper who had learnt from nature that sex could give great pleasure. Without charm or refinement he was able to liberate the sexual feelings of a repressed aristocratic woman. Much of the ability to enjoy sex, like all things, depends on a lively use of the imagination. Fantasies and reality often blend in sex, as love transforms dreams into reality and makes reality magical.

Like all such fantasies, the image of Jews as salacious oversexed males or seductive black-eyed beauties is far from reality. There may be such Jewish individuals but as a stereotype it is a hopeless failure.

Jewish attitudes towards sexuality may, however, have played a role in creating it. I have already suggested that the lack of an emphasis on spirituality in Judaism, as opposed to physicality, may be one reason why non-Jews perceive Jews as materialistic. The fact that Jews place marriage on a higher pedestal than celibacy is another aspect of the nature of Judaism. Making marriage the ideal state for human relationships implicitly accepts the value of sexual intercourse.

The importance of sexual fulfilment is, however, more than implicit. The marriage ceremony, with its hyperbolic celebration of love between man and woman, leaves little doubt that sex is the most intoxicating and tempting dish on the marital menu. The Torah lists sexual relations as one of the three obligations that a man owes to his wife, the other two being to supply food and clothing; and sexual abstinence on the husband's part was grounds for divorce and a financial settlement.

The rabbis quantified the obligation according to occupation. Thus, a seaman could meet his obligations by performing twice a year, while a scholar of the Law, basically a man of leisure, must satisfy his wife weekly, according to some, or daily according to others. It was considered especially meritorious to make love on the Sabbath. The rabbis' enthusiasm for sex is illustrated by their description of heavenly bliss: three things are intimations of the delight of the World-to-Come – Sabbath, sunshine and sex.

They also specified the obligation of a man to his wife. 'A man is obligated to make his wife happy during intercourse', was the view of a leading rabbi. As sons were considered of greater economic value than daughters, the following prescription would certainly lead to increased female pleasure. Rabbi Joshua said, 'What should a man do to have sons. Let him gladden his wife during intercourse!' The Master Raba taught that the secret to engendering sons was intercourse twice in succession. They also took the view that if a woman has her orgasm first, she will bear a son, and that if the man has his first, she will bear a daughter.

Within the marital bond, all sexual positions were allowed and inhibitions discouraged. A woman could divorce her husband if he made love in the 'manner of the Persians' – who did so with their clothes on. Because of the pleasure motive, one is discouraged from making love in the light of day because the sight of a blemish might be off-putting.

The power of the sexual urge was feared and respected. The rabbinic view was that the only way to escape sexual promiscuity was to avoid temptation. The Talmud is full of tales of rabbis who, having boasted of their ability to withstand temptation, are brought down by Satan in the guise of beautiful women. A charming story is told of a rabbi known as Amram the Pious. When some women were redeemed from captivity and came to his town, they were taken to his house and given lodging in his loft, from which the ladder was removed. As one of them was walking about, her form was revealed to him by the skylight which illuminated the loft. Amram seized the ladder which ten men could not normally lift, set it up and began to ascend. When he was half-way up, he took control of himself and cried in a loud voice: 'There is a fire at the House of Amram.' When the neighbours came running, the only fire they witnessed was his unfulfilled passion. Amram's rabbinic colleagues came and said to him: 'You have shamed us.' He replied: 'Better you should be ashamed of Amram in this world than that you should be ashamed of him in the next world.'

The sexual urge was referred to as the 'Evil Inclination', but far from being regarded intrinsically as evil, it was the source of all constructive human activity. The Talmud contains an allegorical tale of how the personification of the Evil Inclination was captured. While it was in prison, chickens ceased to lay eggs. The conclusion of the Rabbinic Masters was that, without the Evil Inclination, Man would not build a house, take a wife, beget a child or engage in business. Two thousand years ago, therefore, Jews had recognized that the sexual urge was synonymous with a life force, which modern psychologists now refer to as the libido.

During the centuries, attitudes to sex have changed and Jewish communities scattered throughout the world have developed different approaches to sexual behaviour. Some will be more restrictive than others, even puritanical. But what can be safely said is that Jews have no reason to have any hang-ups about sex.

Individual Jews, like everyone, will have their attitudes primarily influenced by parental upbringing. As a result they have their share of sexual repression as well as sexual liberation, assimilating the prevailing attitudes of the host society to a larger or lesser degree. If Jews, however, are true to the Jewish philosophy of life, they will treat sex as one of God's most delight-giving gifts, to be enjoyed to its full. They need no greater encouragement to do this than the rabbinic dictum that, on Judgement Day, every person will be held accountable for every permitted pleasure he chose to resist.

From the Talmud

Rabbi Kahana placed himself under the bed of Rab. He heard his master talk, laugh and satisfy his needs. Rabbi Kahana said to him: 'My master acts as though he never before tasted a dish of food.' Rab exclaimed in surprise: 'Kahana! You here? Depart, for this is not the way to act.' He replied: 'It is Torah and I must study.'

Why does the Torah say that a menstruant is ritually unclean for seven days? Lest he get used to her and become disgusted with her. Therefore the Torah says: 'Let her be unclean for seven days in order that she may be as beloved to her husband as she was when she entered the bridal canopy.'

'Who makes us wise by the fowls of the heaven,' (*Job 35:11*) refers to the rooster who first coaxes the hen and then mates. Rabbi Johanan said: 'If the Torah had not been given to us we could have learned . . . good manners from the rooster, for first he coaxes and then mates.' How does he coax her? Rabbi Judah quoted Rab: 'He tells her this: "I will buy you a cloak that will reach to your feet." After the event he tells her, "May the cat tear off my crest if I have any money and do not buy you one."'

The Evil Inclination attacks the Sages most of all. Abaye overheard a man say to a woman: 'Come, let us arise and go together.' He thought: 'I will go and keep them from sin.' He followed them across a meadow for three parasangs. When they parted, they said: 'The way has been long, but the company sweet.' Abaye thought: 'If He-Who-Hates-Me [The Evil Inclination] had thus encountered me, I could not have withstood him.' He went and leaned in deep anguish against a doorpost. A certain old man came up to him and taught him: 'As a man is greater than his fellow, so too is his Evil Inclination greater.'

When Rabbi Judah the Patriarch came to the city of Rabbi Eliezer son of Simeon, he asked 'Did that righteous man leave a son?' They replied: 'He left a son and every harlot who hires herself out for two coins hires him for eight coins.' He was brought before Rabbi who ordained him a Rabbi.

When Rabbi Ishmael son of Josi met Rabbi Eliezer son of Simeon, a team of oxen could easily pass under the arch formed by the underside of their protuding bellies. A matron teased them: 'Your children could not be yours.' They replied: 'Our wives' bellies are larger than ours.' She retorted: 'That proves what I say all the more.' To which they replied: 'Love forces back the flesh.'

12 Jewish Paranoia

*'Jews never stop talking about
the Holocaust'*

'Why are Jews so fixated on the Holocaust?' was one of the questions asked of me by a Catholic about to marry a Jew. Before attempting to provide an answer it has to be acknowledged that many Jews in fact prefer to ignore the Holocaust and avoid discussing it. They are as likely to switch TV channels as are non-Jews when a film on the Holocaust appears on their screen. Even some of those Jews who have been its victims wish to blot out the experience.

While it is understandable that many should prefer to forget such events – and one might even say that this is a healthy reaction – for Jews it could also be dangerous. It is common for individuals and groups who have suffered disasters to take precautions to prevent them occurring again. And for this reason, it is merely sensible for Jews to analyse the Holocaust. But preventing its recurrence is not easy. Some groups who have been butchered in wars may be able to increase their defences, make new allies and keep a wary watch on their traditional enemies.

Jews, however, are spread over the world, cannot easily join forces for defensive action – and anyway, against whom? Should it be against Germany, for that was the country which spawned the Nazis and engineered the rounding up of Jews, their transport to camps, their destruction in ghettos, their extermination in gas chambers and all the other horrific manifestations of human depravity? How can it be right to identify Germans alone as the enemies of the Jews? What of the nations of Central and Eastern Europe who co-operated in the mass deportation and slaughter? What of the French who surrendered to the Nazis and implemented their policy with little protest? Some French Jews have described how, when they were rounded up and sent off to the camps, they never saw a German until they reached their final destination. Even the Allies did little to halt the slaughter, despite the fact that Hitler had told them what he intended to do to the Jews. Ships filled with refugee Jews were sent back to Germany by Allied authorities.

One could go on to analyse the actions of every government during the Holocaust and pinpoint levels of responsibility, but this is not necessary to make the point: it is simply impossible to identify the enemy of the Jews against whom they as individuals or communities should build up their defences .

Some Jews have come to believe that, if the enemy is the world, there is little one can do, except perhaps to accommodate one's enemy. But this too is impossible, for the only crime committed by victims of anti-Semitism is their birth as Jews. In order to help non-Jews understand the full meaning of the Holocaust for Jews, it is usually enough to ask them to imagine that all individuals with a surname such as 'Black' had been deported to Eastern Europe and killed, and that even those who had changed their names or who had had a great-grandfather called 'Black' suffered the same fate. Imagine also that all those with the name 'Black' had been stigmatized and persecuted for centuries. Would you not, if you were called 'Black', fear that you and your children, because of it, could be future victims of this irrational hatred?

Most Jews do not wish to be reminded of the implications of the Holocaust, but Jewish leaders and many of those who have confronted the issue for themselves feel that it must be studied and explored – precisely so that it will not happen again. But, as I have just written, how can one defend oneself against the entire world? And if not, against whom in particular? Is it the governments? Is it the neighbour next door? Are some enemies more dangerous than others? Can you trust those who claim to be your friends? Is this not close to paranoia?

The fear of recurrence is, however, justified and heightened by two other almost incredible ingredients. First, the revisionist theory that the Holocaust never happened, and was a fiction of the Jews designed to exploit Christian guilt in order to obtain the land of Israel! And secondly, that the Israelis themselves are pursuing a policy of genocide against the Palestinians (a thesis current during the Israeli invasion of Lebanon), a myth that seems retroactively to justify the Nazi attempt to wipe out all Jews. Arab and Communist cartoons following its Six Day victory in 1967 caricatured Moshe Dayan as Hitler, with the Star of David on his armband in place of the swastika and Palestinians as the victims.

Both these slanders attempt to stand the Holocaust on its head, but the second is designed specifically to identify the victim with the persecutor, and thus to whitewash what is probably the greatest crime in human history by asserting that the Jews not only brought it all on themselves, but are no better than the Nazis. This view achieved credibility when the United Nations Assembly resolved that Zionism was 'a form of racism', a resolution which was nullified only in 1992. The enthusiastic reception by Israel of thousands of black Ethiopian Jews who could not conceivably make a contribution to her economy made even Israel's most virulent enemies realize the absurdity of such a monstrous contention.

In the light of the anti-Semitic distortions of the Holocaust – and they are widespread – how are Jews to respond to the accusation that they are paranoid? Since they are constantly vulnerable to persecution, they feel that to behave consistently within this reality is far from paranoid! Non-Jews should try to understand the dilemma Jews face when they confront the Holocaust. Equally, Jews should seek to disentangle the emotional knots they get into when they either ignore or try to deal with the issues which arise from this tragedy which affected virtually their whole people within living memory.

Generally, Jews view the Holocaust as an isolated event, even though they accept that anti-Semitic encounters are fairly commonplace and to be expected. While most will assert that the Holocaust could not have happened in the English-speaking world, a vociferous and articulate minority will attack this view as wishful thinking, and maintain that given the right economic and political circumstances, it could happen anywhere. The fact that Germany, a particularly cultured country, was hospitable to Nazism indicates that the vast majority of humans will indeed co-operate or stay silent in order to save their own skins. If the victims happen to be Jewish, the anti-Semitism rooted in Christian culture for centuries will make the silent ones feel less guilty, and make those who co-operate feel that they are doing good. Jews who take a sanguine view of human nature are condemned by others for refusing to look at these objective facts.

But even Jews who believe that another Holocaust *is* possible none the less continue to relate to members of other faiths, to do business with them, and often to become their friends. If asked to explain this inconsistency, they will say that anti-Semitism becomes virulent only in specific situations, or that to perceive every non-Jew as an enemy would make life unbearable! They argue, I believe rightly, that Jews must try to relate to non-Jews without hatred or bitterness, for these are feelings which stunt emotional and personal growth. Hatred, like fear, does more harm to the hater than the hated.

As part of a people, however, Jews cannot afford to forget the Holocaust, but must learn to apply its lessons. This they have done admirably; for now, as a people, they have taken their destiny into their own hands. The Jewish State was established as a haven for persecuted Jews, and has expressed willingness if necessary to fight for the rights of Jewish citizens everywhere.

But the time must be drawing near when the international community or regional alliances will prevent a tyrannical and oppressive government from destroying its own citizens, and will not plead the doctrine of non-interference as a moral justification for inactivity. It is sad to think that, had Hitler not gone to war but had limited himself to wiping out the Jews in Germany, no nation would have declared war on the Third Reich because it was an 'internal matter'. If the Holocaust has a lesson for all mankind, and not just Jews, it is this: that one cannot stand by and allow fellow humans to be callously destroyed for no other reason but their national history, race or religion.

As part of a collective identity, Jews should be on guard everywhere not only against anti-Semitism, but any form of racial hatred. They, like others, should not minimize the dangers of racist remarks and the targeting of any group as the cause of a nation's misfortunes.

Unfortunately, Jews have by and large not yet been able to digest the universal teaching of the Holocaust, which is that within humanity there is an unfathomable capacity for evil. It is understandable that Jews have been so traumatized by their wholesale degradation and destruction, that they should feel singled out for special victimization. But is it not equally to be expected that rabbis, Jewish leaders and historians will be upset when they are told that they make too much of the Holocaust, and that others have suffered too?

In fact the tendency to regard the Holocaust as just another national tragedy has led many Jews to claim it as uniquely Jewish. To non-Jewish ears, it sounds as pathetic as though they were saying that 'there is no suffering like Jewish suffering'. But the intention of those Jews is only to assert the existential situation which made them the likeliest candidates for the horrors perpetrated by the Nazis and their sympathizers. As a volcano does not erupt without pressure building up underground, so the human horror which enveloped the Jews as its primary victim did not happen without warning. The study of why it happened should not be discounted by comparisons to other horrors such as the nuclear bombing of Hiroshima and Nagasaki, the blanket bombing of Coventry and Dresden, the slaughter of Armenians, Kurds, Bosnians and Croats, or even the Nazi treatment of other minorities.

Of course, the quality of the evil is much the same: the hatred and sadism which spills out over Jews is no different from that which destroys other individuals and groups; and if Jews forget this, they will lose the sensitivity to universal human suffering which is the very essence of their Torah. Since historic circumstances have made Jews the perfect scapegoat for human failures, the Holocaust is not so much a Jewish problem as a human one. Only the healing of the human soul can prevent future holocausts against Jews, or any other unfortunate and defenceless people.

Jews often ask whether the Holocaust could have begun anywhere other than Germany, and I believe that the answer, subject to the appropriate circumstances, must be yes. To deny the validity of the question involves regarding Germans as congenitally evil, which would also be racist. Yet the teaching of the Holocaust and the memorialization of those thousands of Jewish communities eradicated without a trace must be applauded, but not in order to pursue the issue of blame.

The symbolic power of the Holocaust is encapsulated in the admonition of the philosopher Emil Fackenheim, who stated that there is now an eleventh Commandment: 'Thou shalt not give Hitler a posthumous victory.' He also gave 'Thou shalt survive' as the positive affirmation. Professor Fackenheim is a friend of mine whose writing I admire, and whose oratory leaves me spellbound, but I find the application of his admonition troubling. Jewish leaders have tended to use it to make the Holocaust the major reason for Jewish survival. Jews are asked to live as Jews and transmit Judaism to their children because of the killing camps of Hitler. But surely, Judaism's survival cannot be justified on the grounds that Jews have been massacred. Is there some reluctance to perceive that Judaism improves and enhances life for those who live by its moral code and share its insights?

I wince when Jews are told to be loyal to their community only in order to avoid betraying their dead ancestors. Jewish survival should rather be based on the need to fulfil the divine purpose which motivated Abraham to go into a strange land at the command of a God, who demanded justice rather than sacrifices, and compassion rather than fasting and prayer.

One aspect of the tragedy of Hitler's camps was indeed that so many of the Jewish inmates had never been religious or believers, but were only there because of their identity. But surely, only by understanding the roots of the Jewish faith and by attempting to meet its spiritual demands do we give Jewish survival a purpose.

Jewish leaders may equally point to the Holocaust as a major reason for rallying behind the State of Israel in its struggle to defend itself. But the Jewish State no longer requires that its legitimacy be dependent on the guilt of non-Jews for their role in the Holocaust. Nor should Israelis or Diaspora Jews justify their own moral shortcomings by comparing them to the unparalleled crimes of others.

Jews who become morally insensitive and despair over the potential for human mercy also give Hitler a posthumous victory, because his desire was not merely to destroy the Jews physically, but to undermine and ridicule the very civilization to which Judaism contributed so much.

The roots of the Holocaust must be revealed and analysed, not just by Jews but by all men and women who want them eradicated. Jews will always have a special interest in the Holocaust not only because it brought the destruction of a third of their people, but because it was the climax of centuries of unlimited hatred. All the world, however, should realize that the men who invented the 'Final Solution of the Jewish Problem' were but steps away from inventing the final destruction of human civilization. 'Never Again' must, therefore, be the watchword not only of Jews but of all decent men and women, when they look at the evil face of the Holocaust.

The Jews are the chosen people of the world's hatred.

Auto Emancipation, Leo Pinsker

It lifts forty sins from the soul to kill a Jew.

Ukrainian Proverbs; New Dictionary of Quotations, H. L. Mencken

A nation's attitude towards the Jews is the measure of its cultural maturity.

Thomas G. Masaryk

Men find the bad among us easily enough. They take the worst of us as samples of the best; they take the lowest of us as presentations of the highest; and they say, 'All Jews are alike'.

Our Mutual Friend, Charles Dickens

Anti-Semitism is a mad passion, akin to the lowest perversities of diseased human nature. It is the will to hate.

The Emperor Hadrian was an honest anti-Semite. One day, the Talmud records, on his journey to the East, a Jew passed the Imperial train and saluted the Emperor. He was beside himself with rage, 'You, a Jew, dare to greet the Emperor! You shall pay for this with your life.' In the course of the day another Jew passed him and warned by example, he did not greet Hadrian. 'You, a Jew, dare to pass the Emperor without a greeting,' he angrily exclaimed, 'you have forfeited your life.' To his astonished courtiers he replied, 'I hate the Jews. Whatever they do, I find intolerable. I therefore make use of any pretext to destroy them.'

So are all anti-Semites.

Leo Tolstoy
Quoted in Book of Jewish Thoughts, J.H. Hertz

JEWISH PREJUDICE . . .

13 Jewish Prejudice

'On Goyim, Shvartzes and Shiksehs'

This is a chapter I hate writing. Very few people are courageous enough to accept their own faults, and even those who have the capacity may wish to be tactful about the shortcomings of their families or communities. Just as self-acceptance is a sign of mental stability in the individual, so the attempt to spread an honest understanding of a people indicates its own security in the larger community. I must confess, therefore, with sadness bordering on shame, that among the Jewish people, as among other religions, communities and nations, there are individuals – far too many – who are prejudiced against others.

For generations there have been Jews who refer to non-Jews as 'Goyim'. While the word in Hebrew means nothing more than 'nations' – the English equivalent is 'Gentiles', from the Latin *gens* meaning 'nation' – Jews tend to employ the word with distaste or contempt. I am glad to say that the expression seems to have lost its nastiness, as non-Jews will occasionally introduce themselves to me with the words: 'Rabbi, I am a Goy.' But more liberal Jews still wince at the word and condemn Jews who employ it.

More objectionable than the word itself are the sentiments that go with it. One still hears expressions such as: 'You can't trust a goy'; 'What can you expect from a goy?' or 'As stupid as a goy!' Their origin is not difficult to understand. When I voice my dismay at these views I am expected to understand their history: 'Surely it is natural for Jews, who have suffered as victims for centuries, to get back at the Gentiles.' In addition, the contemptuous dismissal of non-Jews as dumb or unworthy of trust is wholly harmless, I am told.

To understand, however, is not to forgive. The prejudice which begins with words can end with violence. The old schoolboy adage, 'sticks and stones will break my bones but names will never hurt me', misses the reality. Just as Jews believe that God created the world with a word, malicious words eventually become the sticks and stones to beat the innocent.

Jews may also take pleasure in condemning other groups as inferior to themselves in order to gain some solace for their own position of insecurity. I remember my father speaking with contempt of the poor 'Shvartzes' (Yiddish for black people) who loitered about his place of employment. This made me uncomfortable even as a child of eight. And I was relieved when in my teens I was able to discover that in spite of this prejudice he still believed that black people had equal rights to dignity and self-respect. On the Boardwalk in Atlantic City, NJ, before it became the gambling centre of the American East Coast, black men would push cushioned wicker wheelchairs for individuals or couples to enjoy the sea on one side and the hotel gardens and shops on the other. The pushing bar was no more than a foot from the back of the chair, so the occupants literally had the black men breathing down their necks. But to his credit, my father felt this work demeaning and condemned it: 'If people were decent human beings they wouldn't agree to be pushed like this and the black people would find better ways to make a living.'

A definition of a racist current in the USA is one who not only wishes to discriminate but is capable of doing so. According to this definition there would be very few racist Jews, because not only would they not be capable of discriminating, they would not even wish to do so. 'Racist' Jews are those who enjoy boasting of their own superiority over others, but they do not do anything about it. None the less, it is a dangerous phenomenon, for it seems to encourage Jews to stand by while other minorities are oppressed and persecuted.

Fortunately the prejudice of the few is more than compensated for by the work of Jewish organizations in the struggle against racism and any form of prejudice. The American National Association for the Advancement of Coloured People had leading Jews among its founders. To this very day, the Anti-Defamation League, a leading American Jewish organization, is the source for the most detailed information on the activities of the Ku Klux Klan, and the FBI turns to it for assistance in tracking down these inciters of hatred against Southern black people.

And, the reader will ask, what about the Israeli treatment of Palestinians? Are they not treated as second-class citizens, and made to suffer enormous discrimination? The years of enmity between Jew and Arab in Israel and the Occupied Territories have indeed brutalized the sensibilities of many Jewish Israelis, who have come to regard 'all' Arabs as less than themselves, but these are still a minority even if, sadly, they are a growing one. I remember hearing Golda Meir as Israel's Prime Minister telling a largely Jewish audience at the Royal Albert Hall in London, 'I can forgive the Arabs for hating us, but I cannot forgive them for making us hate them.'

The Palestinians were not originally considered inferior by Israeli Jews, but they have indeed come to be viewed as a threat to security and safety and thus to be denigrated as 'the enemy'. This is not the occasion either to defend or to attack Israeli policy towards the Palestinians; only to affirm that the distrust and hatred between the two communities is based on a struggle for political power and national rights, so may produce racist feelings but not based on them.

Returning to the Diaspora, where Jews are in the minority, calling a non-Jewish woman 'Shikseh', the Yiddish for 'abomination', is common when referring with disapproval to someone a Jewish man is dating. It is, for the most part, a 'put-down' for the Jew rather than the non-Jew, a less than subtle way of reminding him that his place in life is next to a 'nice' Jewish girl. Parents would console themselves when their sons were seeing 'Shiksehs' because these would provide the pleasures that Jewish girls were reputed to reserve for the marital bed. But today, when so many 'nice' Jewish boys marry out, the term 'Shikseh' is rarely used, partly because one would offend the spouse of a Jewish associate, but also because the antipathy is being broken down. Also, like the name 'goy', it has become common for non-Jewish girls in Jewish circles to refer to themselves as such – more to the embarrassment of the Jews they are addressing than to themselves.

Readers may be surprised to learn that greater than the Jewish prejudice towards others is the perception of prejudice between different groups of Jews. Jews from different regions of Eastern Europe – doubtless neighbouring villages too – would believe the other to be capable of almost any misdemeanour. 'Galizianers' (from southern Poland) were 'unreliable'; Rumanians were 'robbers'; 'Litvaks' (Lithuanians) were 'sophistic intellectuals'; and 'Yekkes' (Germans) were 'unbending snobs'. As many jokes are based on such distinctions as on the classic 'Englishman, Irishman and Scotsman', and ultimately have about as much significance, which is very little indeed. But this chapter does remain necessary; because Jews, no less than others, have poor defences against the temptation to hate their neighbours. Suffering – to reverse an old motto – does not ennoble; Jews have emerged remarkably little tainted from their centuries of degradation.

A gentile who observes the Torah is as good as a High Priest.

Talmud

If you talk against your fellow Gentile, you will come also to slander your fellow Jew.

Midrash

Righteous Gentiles have a place in the World to Come.

Tosefta

To promote peace, poor Gentiles (like Israelites) may not be denied the gleanings, the forgotten sheaves and the corners of the field.

Mishna

If you know that a Jew robbed a Gentile, it is your duty to testify it in Court.

The Sherira Gaon, 10th century, A Responsum

I call heaven and earth to witness that whether it be a Jew or heathen, man or woman, free or bondman – only according to their acts does the Divine spirit rest upon them.

Midrash

To rob a gentile is worse than robbing a Jew because it also desecrates the name of the God of Israel.

Tosefta

14 Jewish Loyalties

'Jews have double loyalties'

One of the most exciting and dramatic events of this century, seen by millions of people glued to their television sets, was astronaut Neil Armstrong's 'small step for a man but one giant leap for mankind'. Yet I very much doubt that many of us would wish to follow in his footsteps. The creation of a Jewish state after 2000 years of homelessness and persecution should, I feel, be seen in the same light. Most Jews felt they were experiencing a miracle, but only a few decided to make Israel their home.

There was a relentless build-up towards the fulfilment of national sovereignty. The stunned and deafening silence when Allied troops entered the Nazi concentration camps in 1945 and witnessed the scale of human destruction; the living skeletons, the heaps of unburned corpses and the stench of burning flesh would have been unbelievable had they not been seen. So, after only a short period of Jewish opposition to the British Mandatory Power over Palestine, Britain withdrew, and the Jewish people won support in the United Nations Assembly, for a state in a tiny part of Palestine – but only if they could fight for its survival.

As tens of thousands of displaced European Jews, freed from concentration camps but incarcerated in British camps in Cyprus, were released to immigrate to their new home, the Jewish Defence Corps, the *Hagana*, prepared to defend the state against seven neighbouring Arab countries, all ready to mount their own genocidal campaign against the Jews as soon as the British forces left.

As a child of eleven I listened to the radio and heard the announcement of the UN vote cast by Colombia, which guaranteed the necessary majority in favour of a Jewish State. It was electrifying. There were radio reports of dancing in the streets of New York City as well as in Tel Aviv and Jerusalem. The prayers of two millennia had been answered. The Messianic Age seemed to have begun. Jews could rule themselves in the land of their ancestors. Against the bright flame of this new reality was the grim knowledge that, had there been a Jewish State a decade earlier, at least two million Jews – who had been denied entry to Palestine under the British Mandate – might have been saved from the Nazi inferno.

Only the most hardened and unsympathetic Gentile would fail to see that it was natural for Jews to make the survival of their tiny State their highest priority, even if they chose to remain in the countries which had offered their parents refuge from earlier persecutions.

Let me be frank about this. Next to my family, I feel that Israel enjoys my first loyalty. I do not feel this fact makes me any less loyal to the welfare of the USA, where I was born and of which I am a citizen, or to Great Britain, the country of my residence. There is no contradiction because Israel's interests could never threaten the existence or security of the USA or the United Kingdom, in the way that these countries' perception of their own self-interests could undoubtedly pose a real threat to the physical survival of Israel and its inhabitants. It is in this context that I lend my unswerving support to a tiny state of Jews, which since its creation has been the subject of attack and vilification, and whose enemies have sworn to wipe it off the map.

My priorities do not imply the suspension of ethical judgements concerning Israel. Just as British citizens demonstrated against the joint expedition of their own military forces with those of France and Israel against Egypt in 1956 without being accused of disloyalty, so did Jews, and especially Israelis, have the right to criticize the Israeli government when it invaded Lebanon. The 400,000 Israelis who demonstrated against the Israeli siege of Beirut were not disloyal. They were simply exercising the right to make moral judgements and to demand standards of ethical behaviour from those with the power to rule.

If, as an American, I am asked why I support US foreign aid to Israel at times of economic recession, my reply must be that, without this aid, Israel's future could be endangered, and that the difference this aid makes to the American economy is negligible. It has been remarked that the United States could remove its total budget deficit were it to increase the taxes on petrol by some 20 cents on the gallon. In a situation with such opportunities to remedy its problems, I feel it as no sign of disloyalty to make Israel's security my major priority.

Yet the question with which I started, why Jews living in the Diaspora (the word means the 'land of dispersion' and is applied to any country outside Israel) do not go and live in Israel and join in its struggle for survival, is valid. Many young and old Jews have indeed gone on *Aliyah* (meaning 'going up', the expression for immigration to Israel). Others do not do so because they lack the idealism or commitment to make the State of Israel a priority over all other personal interests. Prosperity at home, proximity to friends and relations, the need to learn Hebrew, the challenge of moving to a strange if Jewish environment, lack of commercial or professional opportunities, the danger of war, the requirement that young men spend three years, and young women two years, in military service and thereafter up to two months a year on reserve duty, are all factors which must make even the highly committed supporters of Israel hesitate before making the decision to emigrate.

Political Zionism was initiated by a Viennese journalist named Theodor Herzl. Shock ripples of anti-Semitism had been caused by the framing in 1894 of an innocent Jewish French army captain named Dreyfus for selling secrets to the Germans. After he was found guilty and imprisoned, Emile Zola, among many other Frenchmen, came to his defence with his book *J'accuse*, which finally led to his exoneration. Meanwhile Herzl, an assimilated Jew who had been reporting on the trial for his newspapers, had a revelation which was to change Jewish history. The only defence against anti-Semitism, he argued, was an independent Jewish State.

Until Herzl, the idea of a Jewish return to Zion had been a religious fantasy. But the publication of *Judenstaat* ('The Jewish State') began a movement to turn a pious dream into practical reality. Herzl's own lack of religious and historical sentiment is revealed by his willingness to achieve statehood in Uganda or Colombia when the Turkish Empire did not appear ready to agree to establishing one in Israel. The Holy Land, however, was a more evocative location even to secular Jews, who made up the largest part of the World Zionist Congress which met periodically to formulate policy and implement the plan for national sovereignty.

Many at these conferences had additional goals besides that of returning to their historical homeland. For some Zionists it also meant a return to the land – to the honest labour of farming denied them since their exile from Judaea. For others, it meant the creation of socialist communes. But for all it was the right to be in charge of their own destiny, to be a country like other countries, a nation with a government, courts, a police force and an army.

There were religious Jews who for this very reason were opposed to the creation of a Jewish State. The ultra-Orthodox rejected the Return to Zion with the argument that such a move could only be achieved by means of divine intervention. Other religious leaders feared that Judaism would be sacrificed on the altar of nationalism, and that the dispersion of the Jews had a messianic moral dimension which would be lost if all Jews were centred in one country and were corrupted by *realpolitik* like other nations.

Assimilated Jews in government and industry – particularly in Great Britain, though not all – were concerned that a Jewish State would call into question their loyalty to the country of their citizenship. Some even openly opposed Zionism and the formation of a Jewish national homeland. These reservations began to disappear when news of the scale of the Nazi implementation of its genocidal policy began to come through. But even when the Jewish State announced its independence and was engaged in combat for survival, there were still Jews who were unhappy about the concept of a Jewish nation.

The Six Day War in 1967 had a more significant impact on the Jewish world than did Israel's war for independence. In 1948 Jews were still reeling from the Second World War, the scything of its people by one-third from 18 million to 12 million souls, and the almost messianic fulfilment of a dream of millennia with the rebirth of a Jewish commonwealth. In May 1967, however, the Jewish world was expecting another Holocaust. The United Nations International Peace Force agreed to the Egyptian demand to leave the Straits of Tiran, thus blocking one of Israel's economic life-lines. Egypt was preparing its vast army for an invasion of Israel which, it was later confirmed by Egyptian military manuals, would have inaugurated the destruction not only of the State, but of its Jewish inhabitants. Jews had nightmares that the USA would not come to its support and that Israel on its own could not repel the hundreds of planes and thousands of tanks preparing to cross its borders.

Israel's pre-emptive strike on 5 June wiped out the Egyptian Air Force in one day, and made possible the rapid conquest of the Sinai Peninsula. Also captured were the West Bank (when Jordan ignored Israel's warning against joining the war) and the Golan Heights (from Syria). This victory, achieved in six days, had a miraculous quality; even non-Jews were swept up by its drama.

Awareness of the potential consequences of defeat converted even the most doubtful Jew into a Zionist. It also confirmed that Gentiles perceive Jews, whether they like it or not, as in part Israeli. American Jews were bussed to Washington DC to call for American intervention to save Israel. They discovered en route that intervention was no longer required, so instead asked Congress not to call for a cease-fire until Israel had finished the job. But when they arrived, proud fifth-generation American Jews were awe-struck when their Congressmen addressed them concerning *their* great generals and said how proud they could be of *their* army.

The identification of Jews with Israel is only partly a matter of choice. It is equally due to the perception of non-Jews. It is ironic that Jews tend to be mistrusted because they are assumed to have dual loyalties, but equally would not be respected if they were disloyal to the Jewish State. This assumption of Jewish loyalty, as well as their active support, makes non-Jews raise the same question as they did about Germans or Italians living in Great Britain, or Japanese living in the USA, during the Second World War. Then, because of this suspicion of these 'resident aliens', they were incarcerated. I have little doubt that in the case of a war between a Western country and Israel, Jews could suffer the same fate, even if they protested that their primary loyalty was to the land of their residence. Fortunately, the likelihood of war between Israel and a Western nation is extremely small. It is far more likely that Israel will have to battle for survival against its enemies with no support other than from fellow Jews.

It is this sense of Israel's potential isolation, despite the support it has been able to muster from the USA, which makes world Jewry contribute so generously to Israel's programme of accepting refugees from all parts of the world. Israel's Law of Return gives every Jew who wishes it automatic citizenship when he goes to live in Israel. It is suggested that this is discriminatory and even racist. Racist it is not, but it is certainly discriminatory. It is an example of positive discrimination similar to that practised in the USA in favour of Blacks. Jews have lost their lives over the centuries for the lack of a haven of refuge, but now have one country where their admission is guaranteed without the need for special immigration legislation.

When the United Nations established a commission of inquiry after the Second World War to determine what should be done with the thousands of displaced Jews, they carried out interviews in camps in Germany. According to one of the two Jewish escorts to the Commission, David Horowitz,

> When they questioned the inmates, they could not find one person whose dream, whose concept of rehabilitation, was not tied to Israel. Both individually and collectively everyone had only one answer: 'After everything we suffered at Treblinka, Bergen-Belsen and Auschwitz we cannot be rehabilitated anywhere but in Palestine.'

David Horowitz reports on two interviews he had with Paul Mohn, the Swedish deputy chairman of the Commission.

> He came and told me, 'I understand that you will need the young, the strong, the healthy whom you will take, but the others, those who are spiritually and

physically ruined, will remain behind. None the less', he added, 'perhaps you will also absorb some of the tragic cases?' When I told him that we would take every last Jew regardless of his or her condition, I could see disbelief in his eyes despite his friendship for us. Only at a later date, when he came as a member of the Bernadotte delegation to Israel, did he visit me at my home and told me, 'You were even better than your word'.

(*Holocaust and Rebirth,* Yad Vashem, Jerusalem, 1974, pp. 148-9.)

This report highlights why a Law of Return is necessary. It also explains why the world's Jewish population feels obliged to meet the economic strains that the absorption of these Jews would place on the native Jewish population of Israel, especially when so large a part of the GNP has to be spent on defence. The Jewish State is a safety net for every Jew, and most of them help sustain it. The sad fact is that there are many who do not.

Theodor Herzl had hoped that the creation of a Jewish State would resolve the Jewish problem, and in one sense it did. All Jews now have the right to be part of a majority culture and to determine their own destiny without fear of anti-Semitism. But in another major sense it did not. Just as Jews could be potential victims in each country of dispersion, so the State of Israel could be the victim of a hostile or indifferent world, wanting or willing to see it destroyed.

When the State of Israel is allowed to be like all other nation states of the world, in that its right to exist is not questioned, Israel will not excite the same degree of Jewish loyalty. Until then, it is natural that the continuation of Jewish life, of which the existence of Israel is such an important component, will be a major priority of Jews in whatever country they live.

His Majesty''s Government view with favour the establishment in Palestine of a national home for the Jewish People, and will use their best endeavour to facilitate the achievement of this project, it being clearly understood that nothing shall be done which may prejudice the civil and religious rights of existing non-Jewish communities in Palestine, or the rights and political status enjoyed by Jews in any other country.

The Balfour Declaration, 1917

The Land of Israel was the birthplace of the Jewish people. Here their spiritual, religious and national identity was formed. Here they achieved independence and created a culture of national and universal significance... Impelled by this historic association, Jews strove throughout the centuries to go back to the land of their fathers and regain their statehood.

Israeli Declaration of Independence

The State of Israel represents and speaks only on behalf of its own citizens, and in no way presumes to represent or speak in the name of Jews who are citizens of any other country.

David Ben-Gurion, First Prime Minister of Israel

15   Jewish Vengeance

'Jews believe in an eye for an eye'

Some Gentiles may be full of disbelief to learn that Judaism not only rejects the concept of vengeance, but considers the taking of revenge as unacceptable human behaviour. Why then do we constantly hear that Israel is 'taking revenge' on its enemies – revenge being the term used by the media for Israeli retaliation. While extreme right-wing Israelis may demonstrate for vengeance after a terrorist attack, the call for vengeance has never been part of Israeli terminology or practice.

The media's responsibility for promoting this image was illustrated by a recent radio news programme, when a presenter introduced his story by saying that, after a captured Israeli sergeant-major had been murdered by the Hamas (Islamic Fundamentalists), Israel's Prime Minister had called for vengeance. But when the statement was quoted in full it contradicted the original headline. While promising to 'pound the Hamas mercilessly', the Prime Minister also called on people to show restraint so that the country would not fall into chaos.

The message was clear: the Israeli military would seek to destroy the source of Islamic terrorism, but Israelis must not take out their anger against innocent Arabs. Israel asserted its right to use retaliation as a deterrent, but rejected vengeance as non-strategic violence.

Revenge is an irrational reaction, and leads to ever-escalating murderous responses. Vendettas destroy entire families, until so much innocent blood is shed that one or both parties call a halt to it. The emotional basis of revenge is the concept of 'honour', but Israel has never operated on this basis. Her failure to react to the Iraqi Scud attacks during the Gulf War is evidence of this; Israel was congratulated for her military restraint. While it was pleasing for Jews to see Israel praised, she did not, in this instance, deserve it. The Generals had decided pragmatically that there was nothing to be gained by joining the war. The loss of life and property as a result of attacks could not be compensated for by retaliating against Saddam Hussein. As to defending herself, the Americans had given their Patriot anti-missiles system, and as to adding her weight to the pounding of the Iraqis, the Western Allies did not need Israeli assistance.

Were revenge part of Israeli policy, she could even now, without fear of reprisal, attack Iraq, but there is no military advantage in doing so. Yet when Israel realized that the West was ignoring Iraq's nuclear ambition in the 1980s, she mounted a lightning strike to destroy Iraq's nuclear reactors; and she might do so again if the UN is unsuccessful in destroying Iraq's nuclear potential. But this would still not be an act of revenge; only a well-considered implementation of Israel's defence strategy. Israel's response to attack is always reported, but not her failure to retaliate.

Israel's retaliation has only one purpose, to limit the effectiveness of her enemies. Her critics may maintain that all Israel is doing is continuing the cycle of violence; but this is not accurate, even though the violence does not always end after an act of retaliation. Violence will not end until terrorist organizations, which are currently funded to kill, are starved of support. The scale of their operations *can* be limited. By this strategy, Israel has over the years succeeded in ridding herself of the terrorist threat on three of her borders, Jordan, Syria and Egypt. These countries have suppressed the terrorists within their borders in order to protect themselves from Israeli raids.

Israel has behaved no differently from the USA when she bombarded Libya for harbouring and supporting terrorism (after which the US government was also accused of acting like a 'Terrorist State', by shedding innocent blood and causing a cycle of violence). There were warnings of doom from all sections of the media that Libya would retaliate, but the opposite in fact occurred. President Ghadaffi of Libya has retreated into his shell and now even denies the role of his government in the Lockerbie disaster and is negotiating over the surrender of the two Libyans held responsible, although previously he would have taken credit for it as an appropriate attack against Western imperialists supporting Israel.

I am not seeking to defend Israel's policy of retaliation, but only to argue that her reaction against terrorist activities is not motivated by the desire for vengeance. It is possible to recognize this and still to condemn the Israeli army for suppressing the Intifada in a way that has led to the deaths of youths and children, as well as the blowing up of houses and the deportation of Palestinian leaders. Injustices should be condemned wherever they occur. But critics should keep in mind that Israel argues that, if youths are killed at demonstrations, it is because they are the ones *in front* of others throwing boulders and cement blocks at Israeli soldiers. Why youths and not adults are put in the front lines of violent demonstrations is a question worth pondering; but not here.

The persistence of the media in describing Israel's retaliatory strikes as vengeance may derive from an ancient misunderstanding of what was seen as the 'Jewish' morality of 'a life for a life, an eye for an eye and a tooth for a tooth'. The bold imagery of this biblical law of retaliation, *lex talionis*, has led people to believe that the command is to seek revenge. Its intention, however, is the very opposite. The Bible tells of Cain's great-great-great-grandson Lamech who said to his two wives:

> Adah and Silla hear my voice.
> You wives of Lamech, harken to what I say.
> I have slain a man for wounding me,
> a young man for striking me.
> If Cain is avenged sevenfold
> Truly Lamech seventy-sevenfold.
> (Genesis: 4:23–4)

Much later, Simeon and Levi, the sons of the Patriarch Jacob, wiped out the entire male population of the town belonging to the Prince of Shehem because he had seduced their sister Dinah. When Jacob reprimanded them, they replied,

'Should he treat our sister as a whore?' These are indeed tales of vengeance! But the *lex talionis* is a call for *just* retribution. It is human nature to consider one's own family or possessions more precious than those of another. It is natural for a father, for example, to want to tear apart a man who molests his child, but the biblical law sets limitations.

In the Talmud, the Rabbinic Masters explain that the biblical law was never meant to be applied literally, except in the case of wilful murder. The rationale for their argument is that there would be no benefit for an armless man if the perpetrator suffered a similar fate. The Masters agreed that the Bible intended that there be monetary retribution to the value of the arm. In addition to the material damage, they added penalties for the suffering, the humiliation of being without a limb, and the income lost.

Despite this, the image of the vengeful Jew has stuck. Christians are still taught that while Jesus taught his disciples to love their enemies and turn the other cheek, Jews affirmed *lex talionis*, the divine law of vengeance.

The State of Israel places as high a value on human life, including the lives of their enemies, as do most civilized nations. At its very formation in 1948, years before similar legislation in the USA and England, Israel banned capital punishment, except for those found guilty of genocide.

On 13 September 1993 the absence of the vengeance motive was conclusively proved when Prime Minister Yitzhak Rabin shook hands with the PLO President Yasser Arafat. For the sake of peace, memories of forty-five years of terrible conflict were laid to rest. The Israeli government accepted that while the evil that had been done could never be undone, only the cessation of hatred could end the cycle of violence, bereavement and bitterness for the living and those yet to be born.

Israel's government can be justifiably criticized for many actions; but to say that it even had a policy of revenge reveals that the speaker has failed to shake off a mistaken concept which owes much to the ignorance of Jewish attitudes. Perpetuating this error leads to prejudice, and then to the souring of relations between Jews and their neighbours.

You will not take vengeance, nor bear a grudge.

Bible, Leviticus 19

Say not, 'I will do to him as he has done to me.'

Bible, Proverbs 24

He who takes vengeance destroys his own house.

Talmud

16 Judaism and Christianity

'Should Jews become Christians?'

Judaism and Christianity have a great deal in common but also much which divides them. It is sad that few believers in either community know enough about their respective religions to appreciate, let alone to enjoy, the fascination of their similarities and differences.

At the outset it must be said that what keeps them apart is far greater than that which unites them. It is extraordinary that two religions whose sources in the ancient world appear almost identical should come up with such different solutions to human needs and problems. I shall begin with a broad brush and risk over-generalization in order to make the distinctions clear, and then show how the variety of beliefs in both faiths allows on occasion a blurring of the frontiers between them.

Let's begin with the uniting features. Both religions believe in one God, although there are Jews who will question the unity of the Christian God since it consists of the Trinity. But this challenge can be dismissed because Judaism and Christianity both differ from paganism in the affirmation of God's uniqueness: He rules alone. Pagans, on the other hand, believed in a number of powers whom they deified. Since pagan gods were often in conflict, human worshippers could determine which to propitiate in order to achieve their desires. Paganism is comparable with belief in the influence of planets and constellations, many of which bear the names of gods, and there were other gods and demi-gods in mountains and in rivers. Gods were everywhere. But before anyone scoffs at the absurdity of such beliefs, it is as well to consider the number of people who still read their stars daily in the newspaper horoscopes.

The Talmud was aware that Christianity is not as purely monotheistic as Judaism, and that Christians prayed to the Virgin Mary, Mother of God, and to patron saints as well as to the Trinity; but it none the less maintained that Christians should not be confused with pagans because they were not 'worshippers of stars and constellations'. The God of the Jews and Christians (and his agents – we will deal with Satan later) was to be the sole object of worship. He alone could influence events in favour of his petitioners. Unlike pagan gods, He was neither arbitrary nor subject to the power of other gods.

Not only was God uniquely supreme, He was also benevolent, and the only demand He made of humans was that they be good and treat each other with kindness and charity. The command uttered by Micah sums it all up: 'Do justice, love kindness and walk humbly with God.' Sacrifices and prayer for Micah were not an attempt at bribery but a means of coming closer to God and bringing his influence into the lives of his supplicants. The portrayal of God may vary within and between the Old and New Testaments, but it remains the same just and loving God.

God also has an objective for humanity. Pagans believed in a *Moire*, a fate which limited their lives. They were encircled by external influences which governed their lives, and finally met the common fate of death. The after-life was a shadowy place in which one could hope at best for eternal rest.

The God of whom the Hebrew Prophets spoke, on the other hand, had a vision of a human society in which all would dwell in peace and brotherhood. This would come about when the laws given by God and the love He put into their hearts would together transform the human spirit. The strong would care for the weak, the rich would feed the poor, and no one would go to war. This would be the Messianic Age. Jeremiah imagined a divine anarchy in which each and every individual would be good almost by instinct. Isaiah went further and believed in an age so wonderful that the lamb would lie down with the lion and a child would 'play with the asp'. This prophetic vision was also emphasized in Christianity. Expressed poetically, the Jewish and Christian faiths hold that humanity has no fate, only a destiny.

These are some of the similarities between the two religions. But the spiritual divisions are equally profound and fascinating. To begin with, Christians believe that the life and death of Christ were a climax for humanity, and that the world changed irrevocably when God sent his Son to die so that all his children could achieve eternal life.

This event passed the Jews by. Jews who believed Jesus was their Messiah formed a sect of Jewish Messianists, tolerated but largely ignored by the broad Jewish culture under the tyranny of Rome. There was a multiplication of Jewish factions seeking solace for their oppression.

Christianity's annulling of the Mosaic law, and the cessation of circumcision as the sign of the covenant between God and Israel, perhaps made it easier to win male converts. These, and the change of the Sabbath from Saturday to Sunday, helped give Christians a separate identity, while the affirmation that Jesus was the Son of God effectively put them beyond the pale of Judaism. With the conversion of the Roman Empire to the Christian faith, Jews could no longer ignore what had now become a threat. For Christians, the Jewish people had turned a blind eye to one whom they had deified. Now Christianity, the child of Judaism, would take revenge, rejecting the mother faith which had spurned the child whom they worshipped as the Son of God. The Gospels would remove all blame for the crucifixion of Jesus from the Romans, and place it on the Jews. So began Christian anti-Semitism; and so began the closing of the doors to any dialogue. Polemics flourished, and a vast literature developed to propagate and defend the positions of each faith against the other. The profound psychological and moral reasons for the different paths were rediscovered only in recent, more enlightened, decades .

The fact that the Jewish Bible is called by Christians the 'Old Testament', while the Christian supplement is the 'New Testament', reflects the Christians' belief that they are the 'New Israel', who have received testimonies greater than those received at Mount Sinai. What is nearly always forgotten is that the Jewish Bible, even by the time of Jesus, had been augmented and to some extent superseded by an Oral Law which, while it claimed to be no more than an interpretation of the Mosaic Law, had developed and even altered it. The authority to interpret the Law had been transferred from the priesthood to an educated laity, the Rabbinate. This transfer had enormous significance, for these Rabbis (literally 'masters') became the judges and transmitters of the Law, and their right to office was a matter of learning and not of wealth or inheritance. The downgrading of the inherited priesthood and the emergence of a highly educated laity enabled Judaism to develop beyond a sacrificial cult when the Second Temple was destroyed under Vespasian, the Roman emperor.

Yet while Jewish worship became fully participatory, requiring no rank or office for those who lead the congregations in prayer, Christianity continues to use the sacrificial service as the basis for its worship. Jesus is conceived as the sacrificial lamb of God, killed as a 'sin offering' for the human race. By eating his flesh and drinking his blood through the Mass, the faithful take on his spiritual power to die and be reborn, purified and free of sin. The Mass has to be administered by appointed priests, while the laity are onlookers at a sacrificial service, their participation being restricted to the eating of the wafer dipped in wine.

The belief in such a scenario – Jesus as God's sacrifice on behalf of humanity – is impossible for a Jew who wishes to remain within Judaism. In the same way, any Catholics and Protestants unable to have faith in Christ's power to renew life bear a spiritual blemish which deprives them of grace and salvation.

If the Christian belief in a dying God is the first major divide between the two religions, the second is the differing approaches to Mission. Christians believe that by sharing their 'good news' and instilling faith into others, they are saving the souls, indeed the lives, of these people, for eternity. From its inception under Paul, Christianity became a universal religion .

Judaism also believed in a Mission, for the nations of the earth were to be blessed through Abraham and the God who sent him on his journey. But this end would be attained only when each nation would obey universal laws of justice and compassion, and when individuals and nations would live in harmony. Each individual and nation could maintain its own faith and rituals and even its own Gods, as long as the objective of everyone was a moral ordering of human society.

The histories of Judaism and Christianity have certain ironic twists. One of them is that, at the period of Jesus' birth, the Jewish people's party, known as the Pharisees, were seeking to impress their neighbours with the truth of their religion. Jesus himself was dismayed by their evangelism, and condemned them for, as he put it, crossing the seas to win one convert, while by implication, neglecting the lost sheep of Israel.

The time when Jews were able to share their faith came to an end when the Nicaean Council of bishops in 325 made it a capital crime for Jews to convert others to their faith. In biblical times, however, there seems to have been no ambition for the Israelite faith to be thrust on others as a key to salvation.

The differing attitudes towards Mission can best be understood in the context of human sin. The disobedience of Adam and Eve in the Garden of Eden is the common scenario of both traditions for the origin of sin in the world. The story is clear. Our ancestors were immortal dwellers in paradise, but their immortality came to an end when they sacrificed it for divine knowledge. God had said to Adam and Eve that if they ate from the Tree of the Knowledge of Good and Evil they would die. They were tempted by the wily serpent, and almost against their will ate of the fruit of the forbidden tree. When God became fearful that Man would become like Him, having both knowledge and immortality, He expelled them from the Garden of Eden and blocked the way to the Tree of Life.

That sin of disobedience had certain other logical consequences. Firstly, the acquisition of knowledge included an awareness of sex, which led to childbirth. Secondly, the expulsion from paradise also led to the need to work in order to survive from day to day. As a result, the pain of a woman in childbirth and that of a man working to feed his family are the two curses which, in addition to death, are the results of the first sin.

Although the story is clear, the interpretations of this grand myth are not, and require some explanation. Jewish and Christian commentators recognize the inherent sinfulness of human nature. The Jews, however, had a more positive attitude towards this evil disposition. They called it the *Yetser Ha-Rah*, 'the Evil Inclination'. It entered a child at birth, and ruled supreme until the *Yetser Ha-Tov*, 'the Good Inclination', entered at the age of puberty. But it was recognized that without the Evil Inclination human society could not survive. As mentioned in the chapter on Jewish sexuality, the Rabbinic Masters recount a legend concerning the captivity and imprisonment of the Evil Inclination. As a result, they reported, chickens stopped laying eggs. They concluded that without the Evil Inclination people would not marry, enter business or build homes. The adjective 'evil' is usually also dropped from the phrase, suggesting that its opposite, the Good Inclination, is less an inclination than an effort. The Jewish view is that the 'Inclination' is equivalent to the sexual drive, the life force, the vitality, without which human life would not continue. The task of each individual, however, is to sublimate the power of this Inclination into creative and good works. It would be quite wrong to destroy it by abandoning natural activities such as sex, food, drink or society.

Asceticism was therefore strongly discouraged by the Jewish Masters. They were instructed to marry, and criticized bachelors and recluses. Not to marry, according to the Masters, was to lead oneself into sin. Only one of their colleagues, Simeon ben Azzai, was forgiven for not marrying, on the basis that his soul was joined to the Torah.

The code of law gives expression to this desire to control the Inclination, and to give order to social behaviour, by limiting the power of the wealthy and protecting the weak and disadvantaged. The ethical standards expected of both the weak and the strong are identical, and favour is to be shown to neither in dispensing justice. The law for one – from king to beggar – is the law for all.

To summarize the Jewish attitude towards sin, it is believed that humans suffer the consequences of Adam and Eve's disobedience, but that they also enjoy the benefits. According to the story of Eden, our primal ancestors sacrificed innocence and immortality for knowledge – sexual, scientific and moral. Without that, we would not be alive to love or hate, to lust or cherish, to create or destroy. The loss of innocence is the price we pay for the possibilities of culture and civilization. In Jewish thought, it is a price worth paying.

The Christian view of Eden, on the contrary, is that Adam's Original Sin condemned him and his descendants to the loss of grace and to perpetual punishment. The serpent was identical to Satan, the fallen Angel, and it was he who persuaded Adam and Eve to sin, separating Man from God and nature. The sin could be expiated only by faith in the Son of God, who died that the children of God might live. According to such an interpretation, the sexual drive is sinful, and chastity and abstinence virtues. While the Jewish tradition requires marriage, Christianity merely tolerates it because it is better to marry than to burn with passions that could lead to perdition in Hell's fires. All human evil is the result of original sin, and cannot be atoned for merely by acts of goodness. Sublimating the Inclination into constructive behaviour is good, but not good enough. The evil in man, which separates him from his Creator, can be removed only by grace and the love of God.

This contrast between the Jewish and Christian attitudes towards sin leads to another basic division: law versus love. For Jews, obedience to the Law is the way to overcome Sin, while for Christians, law is a trap, a further temptation to sinfulness. Christians believe that only by an utter change in human nature can one escape from the shackles of sin, a freedom achieved by human faith in God, and God's love and grace for humanity. It is for this reason that Jews seek to emulate God primarily through the practice of justice and righteousness, supplemented by compassion; while Christians emulate their Saviour through love and charity, supported by the belief in law and order.

The difference between the Jewish and Christian God will be explored more fully in the next chapter, but for the moment one can conclude that the God of the Jews is visualized primarily as a Judge and King, although the Hebrew Prophets often refer to Him as the husband of the people of Israel. In worship, God is referred to as 'Our Father our King'. The paternal image, unlike the maternal one which gives unconditional love, demands obedience in return for approval. For Christians, however, God is a lover, a mother figure who would draw her beloved children into her bosom if only they believe and free themselves from their sinful nature.

Despite these differences, it is important to acknowledge that both religions respond to the spiritual needs of their believers, and both offer basic truths that can move even non-believers at certain moments in their lives.

What is striking is that the Jewish goal for humanity does not differ from that of its daughter religion, Christianity. The Prophet Moses said to the people of Israel in the wilderness before they entered the Promised Land:

> The Law which I give you this day is not too difficult for you, nor is it beyond your reach. It is not in the heavens that you should say, 'Who among us can go up to the heavens and get it for us and impart it to us that we may do it?' Neither is it beyond the sea, that you should say, 'Who among us can cross the sea and get it for us and impart it to us, that we may do it?' No, the thing is

very close to you, in your mouth and in your heart, to do it.
(Deuteronomy 30: 11–13)

The Prophet Jeremiah had a vision of a time when even laws would not be necessary – the verses are declared in Liberal synagogues after the Holy Law is returned to the Ark: 'No longer shall every man have to teach his neighbour and his brother saying, "Know the Lord", for they shall all know me from the least of them to the greatest.'

Jews and Christians share the same hope for the future: the freedom from human sins which separate people from God and from each other. Christians believe that their Saviour has come and that they need only take hold of him through faith for earth to become heaven. For Jews, the Messiah has not yet come, and the Messianic age will have to be won by the triumph of good over evil in each individual and in society. One can say that Judaism is more practical and Christianity more spiritual, but it is basically all a matter of perspective.

What is sad is that most Christians and Jews do so little according to their faith to make that time come for which all good people pray and work: the day when nations will 'beat their swords into ploughshares, and their spears into pruning hooks: nation shall not lift up sword against nation, neither shall they learn war any more. But they shall sit every man under his vine and under his fig tree; and none shall make them afraid. For the mouth of the Lord of Hosts has spoken it' (Micah 4: 3–4).

I do not regard a Christian as a stranger, because he believes in divine creation and providence.
Solomon Ibn Verga, Historian, 15th–16th century

Christians are not heathens. They believe in God and do not tolerate bloodshed…We must pray for their welfare.
Isaac Lampronti, Rabbi, Physician, 1679–1756

Not long ago I was reading the Sermon on the Mount with a rabbi. At nearly each verse he showed me very similar passages in the Hebrew Bible and Talmud. When we reached the words, 'Resist not evil', he did not say, 'This too is in the Talmud,' but asked, with a smile, 'Do the Christians obey this command?' I had nothing to say in reply, especially as at that particular time, Christians, far from turning the other cheek, were smiting the Jews on both cheeks.
My Religion, Leo Tolstoy

JEWISH & CHRISTIAN GODS
HOT LINE TO GOD...

17 Jewish and Christian Gods

'We all worship the same God'

The most important Jewish prayer begins with the affirmation of God as 'God of Abraham, God of Isaac and God of Jacob'. Rabbinic Masters asked why God was mentioned separately with each Patriarch rather than, more laconically, 'God of Abraham, Isaac and Jacob', and the answer is significant. The God of Abraham was not the same as the God of Isaac, and the God of Isaac was not the same as the God of Jacob. He revealed Himself differently to each of the Patriarchs; or, more accurately, each of them perceived God according to his own capacity and needs.

So, in considering the God that Christians and Jews worship, we are looking at a structure of faith within which individuals will find for themselves the God they worship.

Christians are given wide scope for answering their spiritual outpourings. Of the possible avenues of worship which the Trinity affords, Christians may concentrate on Christ, the Son of God. The need to have communion with the feminine aspect of life, the Mother, made Mary a major object of worship, and in order to emphasize her sanctity, immaculate conception was attributed to her as well as to Jesus. Visits to cathedrals in Catholic countries make us appreciate the power also of saints over the souls of many Christians. Each Catholic may have a patron saint, depending on their birthday, as well as the choice of others with special powers to protect them according to circumstances. Just as a foxhole atheist may cry out to his mother for help as he is about to breathe his last breath, the Christian may call on Mary, Mother of God. Believers choose their objects of devotion to meet their emotional needs.

Judaism does not have the benefit of a Trinity or saints. The Jewish God is indivisibly One, but it would be wrong to believe that all religious Jews relate to God only in his image as a ruling king and a demanding father. Although a rose by any other name would smell as sweet, the same cannot be said of God. The names given to God in Jewish literature and liturgy manifest his different aspects and the ways in which He may be encountered. The Rabbinic Masters explain why there are two Hebrew names of God in common use throughout Israel's history in the following way: the name *Yahweh* reflects God the Merciful, the feminine element, and *Elohim* the God of Justice, the masculine element. But God is also referred to as 'the Infinite One', *Ein Sof;* 'the Holy Spirit', *Ruah ha Kodesh;* 'the Presence', *Shechinah;* or 'the Place', *ha Makom.* These names are in addition applied to varying degrees of divinity in the Cabbalistic literature. If Christians see echoes of the Trinity in these different names, they will not be far wrong, but it does no more than reveal that the need for God is rooted in a human temperament shared by all of us.

The most popular name in Rabbinic writings, and the one which for me indicates the true nature of the Jewish relationship to God, is 'the Holy One Blessed be He', *ha Kadosh Barukh Hu*. Under this name he reveals himself as the Jewish confidant, the caring father and loving husband.

Judaism recognizes no order of saints, and no intermediaries between the individual and God. Nevertheless, very Orthodox Jews may visit the burial places of the Patriarchs and Matriarchs in Israel, or of revered Rabbinic Sages and Mystics, to recite psalms and prayers, and will believe that this will have a beneficial effect on them. Indeed, prayer is the natural outpouring of the human heart attempting to influence the spiritual world. It might take the form of an effort to free ourselves from the consequences of our sins, a petition for special favours, or a thanksgiving for blessings received. Whatever the intention, during prayer Christian and Jewish believers have an image of whom they are addressing.

Overall, I think Jews identify their God as a benevolent king who out of his inscrutable will, or even by the limits of his own power, will often not give a positive response to a petitional prayer. In Jewish history there have been painful moments when the prayers of martyrs alone affirmed the existence of God in what appeared to be a Godless world. A major aspect of Jewish prayer, which also indicates the nature of the God Jews worship, is the longing for justice and compassion. For in Judaism, God represents the guarantor of moral values and of the promise of the ultimate victory of good over evil.

A vital element in the Jewish view of God is the belief that a special relationship exists, based on a binding contract between Him and Israel. Jews declare daily the cornerstone of Jewish faith: 'Hear O Israel, Yahweh is our God, Yahweh alone.' In response to this declaration, God undertakes to care for Israel and to be their God. One of the many implications of this belief in the 'Chosenness' of the Jewish people is that Jews who pray regularly feel that they have a hotline to God. How this feeling can survive intact, when Jews have been perhaps more forsaken than any other people, remains an enigma. The failure to understand the paradox of Jewish suffering is one reason that so many Jews have lost their religious faith, even if they continue to identify as Jews.

Christians also believe that they have a special relationship to God. It is based not on direct contact with Him, but on a faith in Christ as Messiah and Son of God, whose coming to earth enables all believers to attain eternal salvation through Him. Christianity welcomes all new believers into the Christian Communion, but many sections assert that those who do not join are deprived of this saving relationship. In this sense they feel that they have an even hotter line to God.

The Christian God is perhaps more personal if only because He is in part a human figure: churches abound in crosses, crucifixes and pictorial representation of the Holy Family. The emotional response evoked by this religious art is very powerful and is completely missing in Jewish worship.

The power of Christian worship became a religious reality to me after a dinner my wife and I enjoyed at an Italian restaurant in London with friends of ours. Our host was called to the phone. On his return, he announced that due to a cancellation he had a spare seat on a private jet which had been hired to take him and his team from London to Florence to order fabrics. They would be leaving at eight the next morning and returning the same night. My wife hesitated, but I jumped at the opportunity to see some of the greatest art in the world for the first time.

It was a sunny day, and after we landed I made my way to the city by taxi, spending the morning walking over the cobbles by the Ponte Vecchio, seeing statues by the unbelievably powerful Michelangelo, gasping at the glories of the Uffizi Gallery and enjoying lunch in a simple restaurant. Next I walked to the Duomo, but as I entered that great cathedral I was overwhelmed with emotion. Normally I visit churches as a tourist. This time, I sat in one of the side chapels and looked in amazement at the crucifixes, images and sacred stories depicted in stained-glass windows, watching petitioners lighting candles which, clustered in their hundreds, glowed eerily in the darkened cathedral. People kneeled in prayer, to the sound of Gregorian chanting.

All I could think of at this moment was my sudden overwhelming awareness of human suffering, and it occurred to me that no synagogue, no matter how ancient, could convey such a sense of the tragedy of existence. I imagined the millions who in the course of history had poured out their hearts to images of Jesus and Mary, pleading for salvation from their grief, and for a sign that they were forgiven. I could barely believe the tears that were running down my cheeks, and knelt inwardly at the altar of human suffering and of the evil that caused it. I asked myself how people could be evil to others, or could kill people with faces as human as their own.

Perhaps the Christians are right, I felt, and humanity's sinfulness is so great that it is irredeemable except by miraculous intervention and divine transformation. Could the laws of Judaism ever hope to change the human heart, or are they merely a palliative, keeping evil in check? Is it like a police force detecting only a small percentage of the crimes committed?

The paradox struck me. Here I was, one of a people for whom suffering is not merely a matter of individual fate but also a consequence of being Jewish; for over centuries, this accident of birth has been an invitation for persecution, humiliation and even death. Yet Judaism has no prominent symbols of suffering or sinfulness. Christians, however, have eloquent images for the feeling that life is a vale of tears from which the only refuge is faith: they have a God, a Mother of God and even saints to understand and share their suffering.

I tell you this to show that there are aspects of Christian faith which can touch Jews, just as there are aspects of Jewish faith which may touch Christians. It is fair to say that those Christian groups which emphasize Jesus the man, with his exemplary life and teaching, rather than Christ, the dying God, come closer to the Jewish affirmation that life can be changed in this world, that humanity can improve itself even without supernatural intervention. The faces of the Jewish and Christian Gods may be different, but their hearts are the same. The heart of God with which we all seek to commune wants a happier world which all of us can enjoy.

Jews and Christians, and members of all religious faiths, should discuss their belief in God within their own communities and with the believers of other religions, simply because this is a challenge to their self-understanding and their religious goals. This would perform a greater service than any attempts to pay lip service to God, by people who do not live as though He were a reality and never discuss what they mean by God or the impact of his existence. Individuals' belief in God reflects their personalities and goals. Differences in faith between people are as natural as other differences between individuals, even within a shared system of religious beliefs.

That central declaration in the Bible, 'Hear O Israel, Yahweh is our God, Yahweh alone,' is followed by this statement: 'You shall love Yahweh, your God with all your heart, with all your soul and with all your might.' I heard of a rabbi who remarked on this, 'Anything a person loves in this way is his God.' What Judaism and Christianity, and all moral religions, teach is that the worship of wealth, power or position impoverishes us, while the worship of a transcendent and moral God carries us beyond our basic nature and elevates us towards those divine attributes of love, justice and mercy.

I cannot resist the temptation of quoting from an essay by my own teacher and mentor, Henry Slonimsky, whose radical theology enabled me to keep my faith in a living God. His belief that both God and man are the tragic partners in the struggle for human and world reconciliation suggests the deepest spiritual bridge between Judaism and Christianity.

The earth is soaked with the tears of humanity from its crust to its centre is the reasoned opinion of Dostoyevsky's profoundest character in *The Brothers Karamazov*. And Schelling in his profoundest essay speaks of the veil of sadness which is spread over all nature, the deep ineffaceable melancholy of all life.

It isn't merely the fact of suffering, where that is an inevitable incident in the process of growth, or where it is compensated by fruit and flower of richer and deeper life. Such things we could understand and accept. Nor could we object to suffering which comes as inevitable retribution for foolish and wicked behaviour. But where the suffering is out of all proportion to the spiritual results which ensue; and above all, where the suffering falls to the lot of those who do not deserve to suffer, first the innocent, and secondly the good and true, that becomes the most stunning and paralysing experience of the human soul, the most awesome paradox of the whole spiritual life.

Transfiguration of suffering therefore looms as the most pressing task imposed on the thinking mind, and, if successful, would be the rescuing of God, the restoring of God to the place he claims in our reverence.

The Greeks met the problem by inventing the art-forms of tragedy, the highest of all art-forms as dealing with the deepest of all problems.

The Jews faced it on an even higher plane: in the Bible by the invention of the supreme images of the human race, the Suffering Servant and Job; in the Rabbinic period by the coining and phrasing of supreme categories in which a sublime solution is compressed and enshrined, in the 'sufferings of love' and finally in their history, with their own body, with their own living person, as the most signal and paradigmatic sufferer. They are protagonists in the most august drama, the making of man. They are the people whose actual course of life furnishes the material for the apotheosis in Isaiah 53, and the image there conceived is so supreme that it was borrowed and used to invest the central figure of the Christian religion.

Now what does transfiguration mean? Is it a word or a reality? What does it come to? What do the good achieve in taking over the sins and sorrows of the world, in a word by doing God's work for him?

The assertion of God in a godless world is the supreme act of religion. It is a continuing of the act of creation. It adds slowly to the area and substance of the Kingdom of God, the translation of God as ideal into the God of empirical power. Man in whom God's creative effort had achieved a provisional pinnacle, so to speak God's own self-consciousness of his aims, becomes, from now on, God's confronting partner, and the two together a re-enforcing polarity of give and take. They are inevitably lovers, and both of them tragic heroes. But in a very real sense the fate of God and of the future rests on the heroism of man, on what he elects to do, for he is the manifesting God and the focus of decision.

The enormously difficult idea of growth, the idea that the reality of a thing can be still in the making and is to be found only in its fullness and completion, only at the end, not at the beginning; the difficult idea of the reality of time in which something genuinely new can come into being, that is, something not explicable merely in terms of what preceded – these lead to the thought that God cannot possibly be anywhere but at the end, the culmination or consummation. And a change in the very character of God must take place. This is due to the re-entrance into himself of the saints and heroes who have lived and died for the sanctification of His name, so that he becomes more and more like the best whom he has inspired, more and more a lover, from being at first primarily artist and dramatist. Without such an enrichment and deepening in the character of God himself there can be no intelligent religion for future mankind.

From 'The Philosophy implicit in the Midrash',
Hebrew Union College Annual 1956

JEWISH WORSHIP —
TOO EMBARRASSED . . .

18 Jewish Worship

*'I was too embarrassed to go
to the synagogue'*

I have a strange feeling when I go into someone else's place of worship. The strangeness of the feeling is due simply to the fact that I am a stranger. I do not know the people in the congregation or the minister. If I feel this way in other synagogues, the feeling will be compounded in the places of worship of other faiths.

Christians should not wonder at their sense of alienation when they visit Jewish services, nor should it make them feel that Jews are peculiar because they worship so differently. An explanation of the Jewish service will never make a non-Jew feel at home in a synagogue, but it should give a better understanding of what Judaism means to Jews: because the synagogue is the centre of Jewish communal life. Let me explain with an abbreviated history of the origins of the synagogue.

The third and last patriarch, Jacob, had his name changed to 'Israel'. He had twelve sons who were the ancestors of the tribes of Israel. Because of the importance of one of them, Joseph, who as ruler of Egypt saved his family from starvation, *his* two sons became the heads of tribes as well, making thirteen tribes in all. Moses and Aaron were of the tribe of Levi, the third son of Israel: Moses, the prophet appointed by God to redeem the Israelites from Egypt, and Aaron, his brother, spokesman and High Priest. The sons and descendants of Aaron inherited the priesthood, while the other families of the tribe of Levi became the 'Levites', the assistants to the priests. The tribe of Levi was given no portion in the Promised Land conquered by the Israelites, but were maintained by a system of tithes and first offerings from the fruit and grain given by the other tribes. The priests were the religious interpreters of God's will to his people, and it was through their sacrifices on behalf of the people that sins against God were expiated and thanks to God were offered.

Until King Solomon built the Temple in Jerusalem, the priests offered sacrifices to God at a succession of designated places, usually on hilltops, which were more inspiring than valleys or plains. The Temple then became the centre of the sacrificial cult. Animals were offered daily and on festivals, while individuals also brought personal sacrifices according to specific rules.

Solomon's ambitious building programme required a policy of labour levies and heavy taxation. The tribes suffered under this oppressive regime, and rebelled after Solomon's death. Ten tribes in the north of the country declared themselves independent, leaving only the tribes of Judah and Benjamin in the south loyal to the royal house of David. Solomon's son Rehoboam ruled over Judaea, while King Jeroboam ruled over the ten tribes of Israel. Not prepared to have his subjects go to the Temple in Jerusalem to offer their sacrifices, he established his own place of worship in Beth El, meaning 'House of God'.

In 722 BCE, Sennacherib, the Assyrian potentate, ransacked the kingdom of Israel, took its leaders into exile and dispersed its inhabitants. The defeat was so total that the population disappeared, remembered only as the Ten Lost Tribes of Israel. A similar fate almost befell the kingdom of Judaea; it too was defeated by the Babylonians, its Temple destroyed and leading citizens taken into exile. But they were soon to return and rebuild the Temple under the protection of Cyrus, King of Persia. This Second Temple existed for 600 years, and was destroyed by Romans in 70 CE.

It is generally assumed that while the Second Temple stood, this was the only Israelite place of worship, but at the very time that these daily sacrifices were performed in Jerusalem, prayers were recited simultaneously by local priests in villages and towns. It is also assumed that during their fifty years in exile, the Judaeans met for religious worship, to repeat the religious formulae once uttered by the priests. This was intended to keep alive their hope for a return to Judaea. The *synagogue*, the Greek word meaning 'place of meeting', must have started in Babylonia. The central act of worship would have been a reading from a Scroll of the Torah followed by a message from the Prophets and a description of the Temple sacrificial service.

I have outlined the origins of the synagogue in this way in order to show the enormous change that took place in Jewish life once the Temple and the order of sacrifices had ended. In Temple times the priests had performed the sacrifices, while the laity watched and joined in with responsive chants. When the synagogue took its place, the priests lost their major role. The service became more democratic; all the worshippers participated, while learned and respected laymen could lead the service as well as members of the hereditary priesthood. The only automatic privileges remaining to the priests, and their assistants the Levites, were to be the first to be called to the central platform to read from the sacred scroll, and to bless the congregation with the words of the priestly blessing as recorded in chapter 6 of the biblical book of Numbers.

In the absence of sacrificial offerings, the Rabbinic Masters devised other prayers which now form the essence of Jewish prayer. Religious Jews still pray three times a day – morning, afternoon and evening – but for pragmatic reasons synagogue worship is usually organized twice daily, morning and evening, the afternoon prayers being said immediately before sunset, and the night prayers thirty minutes later when night has fallen.

The central prayer is petitional and recited standing. It is divided into various petitions, for example for healing, for rain in its proper season, and for the restoration of the Temple. It follows the call to the community to praise God, and the solemn affirmations that He is the creator of the universe and the God of Jewish history. Following the petitional prayer is the *Alaynu* – the affirmation of God as King and the prayer for the day when He will reign alone and supreme. Another important prayer is that recited by mourners. It is called the *Kaddish*, which means 'sanctification', and comes at the conclusion of certain sections of prayer and at the end of the service. The prayer glorifies God and concludes by calling on Him to make peace on earth as He makes it in heaven.

At the Sabbath morning service, which will be the occasion when most non-Jews would visit a synagogue, perhaps for the Bar Mitzvah of a friend's child, the centre of the service will feature the removal of the Scroll of the Torah from the Ark in the south-east wall (facing Jerusalem), the readings from it, and then a second reading, the equivalent and origin of the Christian Second Lesson, from the historical or prophetic parts of the Bible. These readings follow a prescribed schedule which relates them to the Torah section that has just been read. The readings from the Torah are divided so as to be read sequentially over the span of a year.

The use of Hebrew, and the responsive readings of the cantor and the congregation will make the traditional service difficult for an outsider to follow. It will be easier in non-Orthodox synagogues, where many of the prayers are in English and the leader often announces the page numbers. In Orthodox synagogues the services are also longer, because there have been accretions over the ages with little editing. In addition, some Jews only arrive in synagogue after the service has begun, and read to themselves those prayers they missed, until they catch up with the congregation. In most cases the leader of the service will begin reading each prayer, and the congregation join in until its conclusion. The leader will then either repeat the whole prayer, or the last sentence, which will provide the cue for the congregation to begin the next prayer.

The separation of the sexes in Orthodox synagogues may be off-putting to non-Jewish couples. They would be advised to meet their Jewish friends before the service so that both the man and woman will have companions to guide them as to where to sit and on the service. The origin of the separation of men and women dates back to the days of Temple worship, when for the sake of decorum and to avoid sexual harassment during periods of festive joy, separate courtyards for the different sexes were considered appropriate.

What may also surprise non-Jews is that men will wear their hats or 'kapuls' (caps) in synagogue, as in Jewish life the covering of the head was an act of piety, an expression of humility before God. In Orthodox synagogues, adult women will also normally wear hats.

On entering the synagogue, the visitor will find bookcases containing prayer-books and *Humashim*, which contain the printed Torah divided into sections for weekly readings supplemented by the weekly reading from the Prophetical books. Jewish men may carry velvet bags in which the *Tallit*, the prayer shawl with fringes, is kept. This is worn to remind them of God's commandments.

Modern Orthodox synagogues will usually have prayer-books with the English translation on facing pages. Non-Jewish visitors should realize that a large majority of worshipping Jews do not understand the Hebrew themselves and therefore require such translations. The Hebrew is used because it was the original language of Jewish prayer, and the maintaining of past traditions is seen as more important than the increase in sincerity which might come from a fuller understanding of the prayers being recited.

The fact that Hebrew is not generally understood should not lead the visitor to believe that the prayers are secret, any more than they would have thought so of Latin prayers when it was the language of prayer in Catholic churches. It is worth noting also that the use of Hebrew makes the contents of the prayers less important than their form. While observing my coreligionists at worship, I am struck that their participation in a synagogue service tends to function more as an affirmation of their belonging to the Jewish people and loyalty to their traditions, than as an act of worship. The vernacular language began to be used instead of and alongside Hebrew prayers with the reformation of the synagogue by 'Enlightened' Jews at the beginning of the nineteenth century. Reformers justified this by citing the Talmudic assertion that prayers could be recited in any language; and also the rabbinic emphasis on sincerity in worship. How could there be sincerity without comprehension? The Orthodox rejected these arguments because they viewed these innovations as imitations of the Christian world.

Synagogue worship reveals some of Judaism's stronger and weaker points. A strength is that the Service is a rallying point for Jews to affirm faith in the God of history, in spite of his frequent failures to defeat the forces of evil. This reinforces the collective fortitude of Jews and has enabled them to survive as a religious community. But a weakness is that there appears to be little room for personal prayer – the outpouring of the individual soul desperate for help or consolation. This is a shortcoming of the synagogue, and I must confess that the only days on which I feel a real opportunity for personal religious expression are the Jewish New Year and the Day of Atonement. On these holiest days of the Jewish calendar, when Jews are called on to review their personal achievements and failures, there is a spiritual excitement in the synagogue, evoking an individual inwardness notably lacking in Sabbath and daily prayers in the synagogue.

Overall, the synagogue experience is more collective than personal. The three Hebrew names for synagogue indicate their collective functions: 'House of Meeting', 'House of Study', 'House of Prayer'. This is highlighted by the fact that Jews never visit a synagogue for personal meditation or prayer. The synagogue and public Jewish worship, however, give the Jew an enormous sense of belonging.

The large majority of Jews, even those who subscribe to synagogues, do not attend daily or Sabbath services unless there is a special personal reason, such as a family or friend's child's Bar Mitzvah, or a bereavement. Jews may attend after the death of a parent in order to say the *Kaddish*, the memorial prayer, daily. Erratic attenders tend to go to synagogue on the High Holy Days, but even then may feel slightly out of place. They will be unfamiliar with the heightened elaborateness of the prayers, and their Hebrew may be inadequate for following the texts being recited. For them it will serve primarily as a reminder of their Jewish roots, and may stir up nostalgia for the times when they went to synagogue with parents or grandparents.

The power of the synagogue and the main function of public prayer lies, therefore, less in the fulfilment of spiritual needs, than in maintaining the direct relationship between God and the Jewish people, as the Temple once did when it stood in Jerusalem.

With the Synagogue began a new type of worship in the history of humanity, the type of con-gregational worship without priest or ritual, still maintained substantially with ancient form in the modern synagogue, and still to be traced in the forms of Christian worship, though overlaid and distorted by many non-Jewish elements. In all their long history, the Jewish people have done scarcely anything more wonderful than to create the synagogue. No human institution has a longer continuous history, and none has done more for the uplifting of the human race.

Pharisaism, R. T. Herford

The Tzanzer Rebbe was asked by a Hasid: 'What does the Rebbe do before praying?' 'I pray', was the reply, 'that I may be able to pray properly.'

Hasidic Anthology, ed. Louis I. Newman

From the Talmud

"To love the Lord your God and to serve him with all your heart" *(Deuteronomy 11:13)*. What service is that which you render with your heart? It is prayer.

Prayers are more efficacious than sacrifices.

The 'Holy One Blessed be He' yearns for the prayers of the righteous.

Rabbi Eleazer would first give a coin to a poor man and then pray, because it is written, 'through righteousness I shall behold your face' *(Psalms 17:15)*.

When you pray, know before whom you stand.

Rabbi Helbo said in the name of Rabbi Huna: 'When a man leaves the synagogue, he should not take big steps." Abbaye added: 'only when one comes from the synagogue: but when he goes to it, it is his duty to run, as it is written, "Let us know and pursue after the Lord."' *(Hosea 6:3)*.

He who goes out in the spring and sees the trees in blossom should pray, Blessed be He who has left nothing missing from the world but has created in it beautiful creatures and beautiful trees for the enjoyment of Man.

When you pray for your own ill, pray for all who are ill!

CIRCUMCISION —
PRIMITIVE CUSTOMS? . . .

19 Jewish Circumcision and Ritual Killings

'Do Jews have primitive customs?'

Much as Jewish parents will want to have a son (although as often as not they will want a daughter), they may dread the event because of the circumcision that will follow.

According to Jewish Law, males have their foreskins removed when they are eight days old in the presence of relatives and friends, after which drinks and cakes may be served. The operation, performed by an expertly trained *Mohel*, lasts less than half a minute. The child may not even cry following it, but the mohel's thumb soaked in sweet Kosher wine will be in his mouth to comfort him. Within a few more seconds a bandage is applied and the child is returned to his mother, more for her comfort than for his. If the operation has been done expertly there will be no infection, and when in two days the bandage falls off, the child is as good as new but minus a foreskin. If the child is jaundiced or unwell in any way, the circumcision will be delayed until it is well. If the child bleeds too easily, the operation will be postponed until there is no danger of excessive loss of blood. The health of the child is more important than performance of the ritual.

Before the circumcision most mothers are frightened, as for that matter are the fathers. No matter how many successful operations one has heard of, one cannot help but fear the possibility of something going wrong. I have had three sons circumcised and have held two other boys during the operation, and in every case, except one, I closed my eyes to be spared the sight. I made an exception with my grandson, and can say that it was over so quickly that I hardly saw it!

The organization of the surgical instruments and dressings, the agreement as to who is to hold the child before and during the circumcision, the recitation of the prayers naming the child and invoking blessings for his future are what takes time and may provoke anxiety, especially for the mother, who traditionally does not hold the child and suffers the anxiety of waiting.

Circumcision is so rooted in Jewish life that even irreligious and secular Jews insist on it for their children. It is obvious that the disadvantages of the operation are not sufficient to provoke its rejection.

Why do Jews do it? According to biblical tradition God commanded Abraham to make circumcision the sign of the covenant between God and his descendants. The rite of circumcision is known to Jews as the *Brit*, the Hebrew word for 'covenant'.

Most Jewish traditions, however, are adaptations and refinements of rituals already practised in the lands of their origins. Circumcision was a religious rite in Egypt as early as 4000 BCE, when the Egyptian tomb at Saqqara was decorated with an image of a boy with his hands held behind his back being circumcised by a priest. The scholarly view is that the operation was at first performed only on the priestly class, perhaps as a mark of self-sacrifice or sanctity, and later on on warriors and the nobility.

Historically speaking, Abraham may have been impressed by the practice during his visit to Egypt; or, as is more likely, circumcision became common among the Israelites during their long sojourn in Egypt. This is borne out by a strange story told in the book of Exodus. In it we are told that Moses was commanded by God to persuade Pharaoh to free the Israelites, but on his way to do God's bidding, 'Yahweh met him and sought to kill him. Then Zipporah [his wife] took a flint and cut off the foreskin of her son and cast it at his feet ... so He [God] left him [Moses] alone.'

This tale would suggest that the sacrifice of a foreskin was required to save Moses' life. Only after the rite was adopted by the Israelites in Egypt was its origin ascribed to Abraham while he lived in Canaan. Interestingly, when Abraham was commanded to circumcise himself and all the members of his household, the narrator informs us that Ishmael, his son, was thirteen years old. As in some African tribes today, circumcision may have been part of the rites of passage to manhood at puberty.

Since circumcision was practised in Egypt originally among the priesthood, and because the Israelites were God's 'Kingdom of Priests', so the custom was given a religious significance – the physical mark of the bond between God and Israel. When prophets reprimanded the people of Israel for their immorality, they pleaded with them to 'circumcise the foreskins of their heart', for the heart was a seat of moral feelings.

Judaism, however, prescribed that the operation be performed when the child was too young to suffer anxiety, and when the healing powers were at their strongest, rather than making it an ordeal when he was thirteen. Also, unlike other traditions which require the ceremony to remain just as it was thousands of years ago, the circumcision is performed not with a flint, but with the most modern instruments designed to minimize pain. The operation, therefore, can no longer be considered barbaric. Although it is the mark of a male Jew, one can be Jewish without it. It is more a symbolic rite than an initiation. Also, many non-Jewish families, including the British royal family, practise it as a matter of hygiene; under the double-layered foreskin there are glands which secrete a substance which can cause discomfort and lead to inflammation.

Evidence has been put forward on its hygienic aspects based on the fact that Indian Muslims, who are circumcised, suffer cancer of the penis less frequently than Hindus who are uncircumcised. Jews hardly every suffer cancer of the penis. It is also maintained that women with circumcised husbands are less likely to contract cervical cancer. In many hospitals in the United States it is a matter of routine to circumcise all new-born males.

In view of the medical evidence in favour of it, why does Jewish circumcision attract criticism as a barbarous practice? Perhaps it is the celebration that sometimes accompanies the operation, combined with the anxiety of the mothers, which makes the *Brit* seem barbaric. While it is natural to celebrate the birth and naming of a child, and even praiseworthy to give his birth a religious significance by welcoming him into the Jewish community, to make a social event of a surgical operation may strike a person as unseemly.

But it is the birth of a healthy child into the Jewish community and not his suffering which is the cause for joy. Indeed, the pain, we can only hope, is soon forgotten even by the afflicted child.

On the Jewish method of animal slaughter, I am something of an expert one generation removed. My father killed chickens for kosher consumption. He had been trained in Jerusalem in this skill, because America, which was his destination in 1930, was in deep depression, as was Palestine, and there were not many jobs available for non-English-speaking immigrants. Killing chickens was one job that was available.

As a child I was embarrassed when I had to explain to my school friends what my Dad did; I could not describe him as anything other than a ritual slaughterer of chickens. I even now smile when I imagine what pictures must have come before my classmates' eyes when I told them what my father's job was. Did they imagine him dancing around a bound chicken chanting voodoo incantations? I sometimes think that one reason I was not beaten up more often for being Jewish was that I inspired respect and fear in them. It could be dangerous to mess around with a kid whose father was a ritual slaughterer!

However, there is little that is ritualistic about the way Jews kill animals for consumption. They are merely using what their lawgiver and teacher considered the most humane method of preparing animals for their consumption. My father would spend hours sharpening his knife so that there was not even the smallest nick in it. When a chicken's jugular vein was cut, the defenceless bird would hardly feel anything. My father's training had consisted in learning how to hold the chicken's head still so that when the vein was cut, it would be a clean cut, and the chicken would lose consciousness immediately. If the head had moved or the chicken wrestled before it died, it could not be eaten by Jews. There was an enormous incentive for the slaughterer to kill painlessly.

While there may be still more painless ways of killing animals, it is completely unquestionable that the rules for Jewish slaughter are motivated purely by sensitivity to animal suffering. For the same reason Jews are not allowed to eat birds or animals which have been hunted, because the animals would have suffered by being wounded and might not have died immediately. It would, of course, be the height of hypocrisy to ban the Jewish method of killing animals on the grounds that it is inhumane, if blood sports were to be permitted.

But for Orthodox Jews who believe that God gave them the law, such comparisons are irrelevant, and would imply that others knew better than God the best method for killing animals. Liberal Jews, like myself, would need to be convinced that other methods are consistently more humane before breaking with our Orthodox colleagues in defending *Shehitah*, the Hebrew word for slaughtering, against political moves to ban it.

This chapter is intended not to argue the validity of *Shehitah* but only to assure readers that it is motivated by humanitarian concerns. But how does it work? While a clean cut of the animal's jugular vein is the least painful way of slaughtering it, the need to put it into an immovable position can be terrifying. Chickens, turkeys or ducks can be held by the slaughterer and the matter does not arise, although any creature being led to slaughter, by whatever method, must have a sense of panic. But keeping a cow immobile involves putting it into a revolving drum – a form of strait-jacket – which is still perhaps better than the conventional method of putting its head into a metal helmet from which a bolt is shot to stun it before slaughtering. Defendants of *Shehitah* maintain that the suffering is a matter of degree, and also that the bolting method is uncertain, leaving some animals fully conscious at the moment when their heads are violently cut off.

In the end the whole matter, by whatever method, is bloodcurdling, and this has led many, including Jews, to join the ranks of the vegetarians. Killing in any fashion, they argue, is cruel, and anyone who is prepared to eat meat must justify the view that it is acceptable to do so.

So long, however, as there are humans who enjoy chicken Kiev and Filet Mignon, it is right that the most humane way of dispatching their victims should be found. Jewish tradition has taken great pains to find the way. If they are wrong, it is not for lack of concern; kindness to animals is an essential ingredient of Jewish law and tradition.

And God said to Abraham, 'As for you, you shall keep my covenant, you and your descendants after you throughout their generations. Every male among you shall be circumcised. You shall be circumcised in the flesh of your foreskins, and it shall be sign of the covenant between me and you. He that is eight days old among you, every male throughout your generations, whether born in your house, or bought with your money from any foreigner shall be circumcised. So shall my covenant be in your flesh an everlasting covenant.'

Bible, Genesis 17

You shall not muzzle the ox when it treads out the grain.

Bible, Deuteronomy 25

Six days shall you do your work, but on the seventh day you shall rest; that your ox and your ass may have rest.

Bible, Exodus 23

Scripture prohibits inflicting pain on dumb creatures.

Talmud

A man may eat nothing until he has fed his animal, as it is written, 'And I will give grass in your fields for your cattle' *(Deuteronomy 11:15)* and only after that, 'You shall eat and be satisfied' *(ibid.)*.

Talmud

The man who is cruel to animals will have to answer for it on Judgement Day.

Judah the Pious, 12th century

20 Jewish Family Life

'All Jewish families are close'

Judaism is a home-based religion. Jews express their religiosity at home with daily prayers, the observance of the Sabbath and the Holy Days. One of the high points in the religious calendar, the Passover ritual, is celebrated not in the synagogue but in the home. It is significant that the event celebrated at Passover – the liberation of the Israelites from slavery – began in humble homes as the former captives ate the paschal lamb and unleavened bread before their hasty departure from Egypt.

Rituals do bind people together. Childhood memories of one's mother lighting the Sabbath candles with her eyes covered, of joining one's father in the blessing over wine before the Sabbath meal, or of saying the blessing over specially plaited bread have a cohesive effect on family life. The custom of family togetherness every Sabbath eve (Friday) also helps. The importance in so many Jewish homes of keeping the home *Kosher* puts further emphasis on the home as the Jewish sanctuary.

But the synagogue is also important. Only there, in the presence of a congregation, can one participate in the central Jewish rite of reading from a sacred scroll containing the Torah – the Five Books of Moses. But for most Jews, the synagogue acts as an adjunct to family life. Before and after the reading from the scroll, new babies and marriages might be blessed and prayers for the sick recited. Young boys, and in many synagogues young girls as well, will mark their coming of age by reading sections from the hand-written parchment scroll. It is also only in synagogue that the Kaddish prayer can be recited by those mourning recently deceased members of their family, or on the anniversaries of their deaths.

With the exception of the High Holy Days, the synagogue will be most frequently attended on family occasions – to celebrate a *simha* such as a baby naming, Bar Mitzvah or wedding. Jews will attend because family loyalty beckons them. The tendency for family members to support each other will be reinforced by these religious practices. Also, since Jews for centuries have perceived the world as hostile or potentially hostile, Jewish parents tend to be more protective of their children, perhaps, than the home-born citizens of the majority culture. But a child's marriage is also a cause for common concern. While most families will be happy so long as they are convinced of the wisdom of their child's choice and like the proposed fiancé, a Jewish family will have other desiderata. An in-marriage is a matter for self-congratulation, while an out-marriage a threat to the fabric of the family's integrity. In either event, the role of the family in the process of choosing a mate is another uniting factor.

Acknowledging these binding influences, I still believe that the image of the Jewish family as a united, close and warm unit is exaggerated. Jewish families are not free from division or strife, and this often leads to separation or divorce and to the estrangement of children and parents. It could be that the cult of the individual has caused more tension in the Jewish family than in others. Jews have always tended to be individualistic, mainly because large institutions, such as the state and government offices, have been experienced as oppressive, and because Jews in larger business enterprises have often felt thwarted by anti-Semitism. So Jews have traditionally found independence the most productive avenue for success; but when this cultural tendency is intensified by the modern demand that each person must seek their own fulfilment, the Jewish family unit comes under special threat.

Parent–child relationships can equally suffer from expectations which may not be fulfilled, especially as the mother is often as demanding as the father in raising a child to become successful and a source of pride to them. I may be guilty of over-simplification, but I believe that non-Jewish mothers tend to be less conditional in the love they give to their children, and non-Jewish fathers less ambitious for their children to surpass their achievements. How many successful second-generation immigrant men have said to their 'lazy' sons whom they have sent to the best schools, 'If I had had your education, how much more I could have achieved!'?

Children are naturally rebellious, but there is often an additional edge to the rebellion of Jewish children, based on the desire to escape the 'lack of emotional space'. Many feel suffocated by what they perceive as the intrusive Jewish family atmosphere and long to break away entirely. At the same time, however, they may expect moral and even financial support in going their own way. Areas of emotional tension come to the surface as fathers are asked to support their children in a life of which they do not approve. The enlightened expectations of modern society will often come into conflict with the traditional Jewish perceptions of life.

I am not saying that Jewish family life is less healthy than others; indeed, in many respects it is more supportive. But the emotions which are the source of this closeness can work against it. When love's expectations are disappointed, the result will not be apathy or indifference; it may be bitterness and even hatred.

So although Jewish families may start with a firmer basis, this is no guarantee, especially in an open democratic society, that they will withstand the outward pressures suffered by every family. What should never be discounted is the desire of individual members of any family for personal freedom. There will always be some who are deeply influenced by their families and are able to find security within them, and others who feel confined and break away, to start afresh with new ideas and values, and with different objectives.

Even matters that have no substance – even the small talk a man has with his wife – is written down in the heavenly ledgers and is read to him at the time of his death and judgement.

Midrash

From the Talmud

Rab said: 'Let a man always be careful not to offend his wife for since her tears are always ready to flow, she is quick to feel oppressed.'

'All the days of the poor are evil.' *(Proverbs 15:15)*. This is the man with a bad wife. 'But he that is of a mercy heart hath a continual feast' *(ibid.)*. This is the man with a good wife.

Rab's wife tortured him. If he asked for lentils, she would make him peas. If he asked for peas, she would make him lentils. When his son Hiyya grew up, he gave her his father's instructions in the reverse order. 'Your mother has improved,' he remarked to his son. His son replied: 'It was I who reversed your order to her.'

R. Judah was learning with his son, R. Isaac, the verse: 'And I find bitterer than death the woman.' His son asked him for an illustration. He answered: 'Your mother, for example.' But did he not also teach his son that no man finds contentment except with his first wife, as it is written: 'Let your fountain be blessed and enjoy the wife of your youth.' And when his son asked him for an illustration, he answered: 'Your mother.' Is this not a contradiction? No, she was the angry type, but she could be assuaged with kind words.

When love was strong, we could sleep on a sword's broadside. Now that love is not strong, a bed sixty armlengths wide is not big enough.

The sanctuary Altar weeps for him who has sent his first wife away.

Our masters taught: he who loves his wife as his own person, who honours her more than his own person, who directs his sons and daughters onto the right path and marries them off at puberty – of him Scripture says: 'And you will know that your tent is in peace' *(Job 5:24)*.

21 Jewish Husbands and Wives

'Mother knows best'

James Thurber has a cartoon of a frightened little man with a briefcase approaching his home, which is drawn as a threatening woman. In Western society, both henpecked husbands and terrified wives abound. The battle between the sexes is first fought in the arena of family life, as affections, loyalties and sibling rivalries challenge the authority of parents who make the daily decisions and determine their family's future. Cultures without clearly demarcated sexual roles may provide greater opportunities for individual fulfilment, but personal pain is the price paid for the resolution of these creative tensions.

The feminist movement, in its quest for sexual equality, naturally underplays the real power that women in the West have had in the decision-making process in the home. It may have been a man's world, but women often directed the men.

Western civilization is rooted in the Hebrew and Greek cultures, and their greatest literatures, the Bible and the histories of the Trojan wars, prove the influence of women. If they were not given equal status with men, it was not because they were viewed as inferior beings, but because of their vulnerability, the consequence of their monthly cycle and periods of pregnancy and nursing.

Traditional Jewish law treats women as a group in need of protection. They have civil rights and responsibilities but no legal authority. Fathers must train their children to earn a livelihood, but mothers are responsible for their broader education. The superiority of male status is indicated in the Bible by the facts that Eve is created to meet Adam's needs, and that God speaks only to men. Yet it is woman who opens the way to civilization by giving Adam the fruit of the Tree of Knowledge. It is she, abetted by the serpent, who like Prometheus gives 'fire' to Man.

Later in biblical history, it is the childless Sarah who first compels the Patriarch Abraham to take her handmaiden Hagar to bed to give him a son – Ishmael, who is the legendary head of the Arab people – and later forces Abraham to dispossess him in favour of Isaac, the child of their old age. Similarly, it is Rebecca who decides that, of her two sons, it is her favourite, Jacob, and not Isaac's favourite, Esau, who will lead the clan.

These tales have been told and read for millennia in Jewish homes and synagogues and must have made an impact on the mentality of Jewish husbands and wives. How many Jewish mothers were given a sense of power – and how many Jewish sons and husbands a feeling of *déjà vu* – as they had to acknowledge that 'mother knows best'. Look at the description they still read of how mother and son collaborate in deceiving their blind husband and father into blessing the younger rather than the elder son. Isaac has just asked Esau to prepare a meal for him over which the blessing will be made:

> Now Rebekah was listening when Isaac spoke to his son Esau. So when Esau went to the field to hunt for game and bring it, Rebekah said to her son Jacob, 'I heard your father speak to your brother Esau, "Bring me game and prepare for me savoury food, that I may eat it, and bless you before Yahweh before I die." Now therefore, my son, obey my word as I command you. Go to the flock, and fetch me two good kids, that I may prepare from them savoury food for your father, such as he loves; and you shall bring it to your father to eat, so that he may bless you before he dies.' But Jacob said to Rebekah his mother, 'Behold, my brother Esau is a hairy man, and I am a smooth man. Perhaps my father will feel me, and I shall seem to be mocking him, and bring a curse upon myself and not a blessing.' His mother said to him, 'Upon me be your curse, my son; only obey my word, and go, fetch them to me.' So he went and took them and brought them to his mother; and his mother prepared savoury food, such as his father loved. Then Rebekah took the best garments of Esau her older son, which were with her in the house, and put them on Jacob her younger son; and the skins of the kids she put upon his hands and upon the smooth part of his neck; and she gave the savoury food and the bread which she had prepared, into the hand of her son Jacob.
>
> So he went in to his father, and said, 'My father', and he said, 'Here I am; who are you, my son?' Jacob said to his father, 'I am Esau your first-born. I have done as you told me; now sit up and eat of my game, that you may bless me.' But Isaac said to his son, 'How is it that you have found it so quickly, my son?' He answered, 'Because Yahweh your God granted me success.' (Genesis 27:5–20)

Jacob's deception knows no bounds as he credits God, rather than his mother, with his rapidity in meeting his father's request. Perhaps he was convinced, as Jews now clearly believe, that God was on Rebecca's side.

This superiority became clear-cut in rabbinic law. Because of their responsibility in the home, Jewish women had no obligation to pray at fixed times; but on the other hand they did not share any of the rights given to men to lead the community. Because they were the 'weaker' and dependent sex, men thanked God every morning for not making them women. In Progressive synagogues, women are in fact today given equal rights: for over twenty-five years they have been ordained as rabbis, and for even longer they have been lay leaders of synagogues. Now in Orthodox synagogues, the struggle for sexual equality is growing in strength, and enlightened rabbis are seeking to find a way to meet the demands of a changing world.

The strange power given to Jewish women can be seen, in the portrayal of the Jewish mother as the dominant figure in the household. Tradition, which persists in fiction and in films, shows Jewish children who love their mothers but feel overwhelmed by their protectiveness, 'over-concern' and guilt at not meeting their expectations. Fathers, tired from the pressures of work, are depicted as more than happy to allow their wives to have the major say, or to be arbitrators, in planning their children's future or in determining the affairs of the household, maintaining only their right to a veto.

But with more Jewish women working, and many taking the lead in the feminist movement towards equal roles for men and women, this is all changing. Jewish men have indeed been trained over the ages to respect their wives. The Talmud directs a man to love his wife as much as himself and to honour her more than himself. The tradition that since the destruction of the Temple and the abolition of sacrificial worship the Jewish home has become the 'small sanctuary', in which the dining table is the altar, and the man and wife are the Priest and Priestess, has encouraged a sense of respect and mutual responsibility between Jewish husbands and wives.

Living in a hostile or ambivalent world, couples worked harder to make home a safe haven, a 'dwelling of peace'. Especially on Friday night, as the Sabbath begins, an aura of holiness pervades the household. As the woman lights the Sabbath candles, covering her eyes as she recites the blessing, husbands, wives and children sing their welcome to the Sabbath Angels, 'the messengers of the Most High, the Holy One Praised be He'. In the verses of this song they ask them to come in peace, to bless the house with peace and to depart in peace. Before the traditional blessings over wine and bread, the father recites the Priestly blessing over the children, and praises his wife as a 'woman of valour whose worth is greater than rubies' (Proverbs 31:10).

Some of these traditions may now only be maintained in observant households, but their influence, making the Jewish woman the pillar of the Jewish home, still survives. The matriarchal, house-proud, over-protective mother has become a caricature of the 'Jewish mother'. The Gentile impression that all Jewish husbands are dominated by their wives could be the result of Jewish men being conscientious about going home after work. A Jew asked by a colleague to join him at the pub in a friendly drink after work might surprise him by his regular refusal and the statement that he is expected at home. If pressed into a celebratory drink, he may feel that he has to ring home first. This may give the impression that Jewish husbands are subservient to their wives, and in fact they feel it only a matter of courtesy to keep their families informed. This 'sense of accountability' may be taken to extremes, and has been the subject of jokes by comedians such as Jackie Mason, who scoffs at the Jewish man 'who is a boss everywhere except in his own home, and who rings his wife when he begins to cross a road and when he gets to the other side'. Jewish audiences roll in the aisles at this caricature, so there must be some truth in it.

Some non-Jewish women about to marry Jews wax eloquent over the consideration shown by their boyfriends, and the example of co-operation and sharing they find in the home of their future in-laws. Is the Jewish matriarch a myth or a reality? There is obviously no stereotype, but I would hazard one generalization. In traditional Jewish homes, the man is only theoretically in charge. He is, to draw a comparison from the business world, the non-executive chairman, while his wife is the managing director. She is working at it full-time, so is allowed a lot of leeway; but she gets on with it, although he expects to be consulted on major policy decisions. She, on the other hand, will take a dim view if he makes any domestic decision without full discussion and agreement.

In non-traditional homes, especially where the wife is employed, there may be more sharing in the decision-making processes of caring for the home. But mutual respect should continue to be a hallmark of their relationship.

That women may be more expressive of their feelings and needs than men may be true in many Western households. The chortling appreciation of the following joke among Jews proves that at least it is prevalent in their homes: 'A Jewish boy returns from school and proudly tells his mother that he has been given a role in the school play. She asks him, "Is it an important part?" He replies, "I play the husband". "Never mind," she consoles him, "next time you may get a talking part!"'

On account of a bad wife, a man ages quickly.

Midrash

From the Talmud

Homa, the widow of Abaye, came before Raba to claim monies for her maintenance from her husband's estate. She said to him: 'Grant me an allowance for food.' He did so. She said: 'Grant me an allowance for wine.' He objected: 'I know that Abaye did not drink wine.' She exclaimed: 'By your life, he gave me to drink from drinking horns like this.' As she was showing it to him her arm was uncovered and its beauty shone like a fire in the Beth-Din. Raba rose up, went home and made love to his wife. 'Who was in the Beth-Din today?' she enquired. He answered: 'Homa, the wife of Abaye.' Thereupon his wife followed Homa, beating her with a strap until she drove her out of the town of Mahuza.

Every Jew who has no wife lives without a wall as it is written: 'A woman surrounds a man.' (*Jeremiah 31:23*)

Samuel said: 'Even *if* a man have many children, it is forbidden him to remain without a wife, as it is written: "It is not good for man to be alone."' (*Genesis 2:18*)

Rabbi Hiyya was constantly tormented by his wife. Yet, when he would find something pretty, he would purchase it and bring it to her. Rab, his nephew, asked him: 'Why do you bring her gifts when she is always troubling you?' He answered: 'I do it because we should be grateful to them for they raise our children and save us from sin.'

Three things enlarge the mind of a man: a beautiful dwelling, a beautiful wife and beautiful furnishings.

Three things bring a man to poverty, among them: a wife cursing her husband. Raba said: 'This is when she curses him in regard to cosmetics – when he has the money and doesn't allow her to buy them.'

A man must always be careful about the respect he shows to his wife, for a home is blessed only on account of his wife. 'And He treated Abram well on account of her.' (*Genesis 12:16*). For this reason, Rava said to the people of Mahoza: 'Defer to your wives that you may prosper.'

When a husband and wife are worthy, God's presence abides between them; when not worthy, fire consumes them.

What is a bad wife? Abbaye said: 'One who belittles him after sex.' Rava said: 'One who turns her back on him after sex.'

There are three beautiful things: the beauty of a place for its inhabitants, the beauty of a woman for her husband, and the beauty of an acquisition for its purchaser.

JEWISH INTERMARRIAGE ...

22 Jewish Intermarriage

'Mixed marriages never work'

The dynamics of Jewish life make out-marriage a very complicated matter for both the Jewish and the non-Jewish partners. Indeed, non-Jews usually find it harder to cope with the problems of their Jewish partners in this connection, than to reconcile themselves to their own situation, which is usually quite straight-forward.

This stems from the fact that Jews marrying out have the double stigma of rejecting a community and a religion, and often have to work out the long-term psychological impact of their action. What does their choice of partner say about them in relationship to their roots, their family and their community? The matter is not usually made easier by the reaction of their parents. The lack of a religious upbringing and the air of general tolerance for non-Jewish friends will have led the children to expect instant acceptance from parents when they introduce future non-Jewish spouses.

Even if they anticipate some disapproval of their choice in marriage, they cannot understand the intensity of opposition from parents for whom Judaism was a peripheral element in their lives. There are even those rare cases of Jewish parents informing their children that marrying out will spell the end of the family relationship. This may be a bluff, but particularly among the very Orthodox it does occasionally happen. Some parents even act as though their errant child had died and recite *Kaddish*, the memorial prayer for the dead.

It is more usual for parents to lay a few obstacles, but by the time the children have informed their parents of their intention, the decision has anyway been made and no family conferences, confrontations or meetings with rabbis will alter the situation. Often, however, the non-Jewish partner may convert for the sake of family unity, and win the sympathy of the family. During the educational process the Jew may indeed learn as much about Judaism as the non-Jew, and converts often gain a deep appreciation of the religion, and a feeling that they have struck new roots in an ancient people and have added a welcome dimension to their lives. A sincere convert to Judaism often helps create a more intensely Jewish household than two born Jews.

But if the non-Jewish partner does not feel able to convert, there are a number of possible scenarios. If the woman is Jewish but the man not, their children will automatically be Jewish, according to Orthodox law. So, provided the husband agrees, the household can be a Jewish one, although the husband may not himself be able to participate in some of the ceremonies. Often, in such cases, the Jewish relatives will provide the necessary ceremonies at their own homes on Sabbath and Festivals and invite their daughter and her family.

On the other hand, if the husband is Jewish and his wife not, their children will not be Jews, according to the Orthodox rules, unless they convert. One important difference for American Reform and British Liberal synagogues is that they recognize as Jewish the children of a couple only one of whom is Jewish, without stipulating that this must be the mother. If the children are raised in the Jewish faith, they will be considered Jewish. Once again, provided the non-Jewish parent is co-operative the household can be Jewish in religious identity and content, and the children may participate at services and in the life-cycle ceremonies such as child naming, Bar Mitzvah and marriage.

It occasionally happens that an identifying Jew will want to marry a believing Christian. Such couples often propose to bring up their children with an awareness of both religions, and allow them to make a choice at maturity. It must be said that this does not usually work, because religious education in church or synagogue requires a high level of commitment, and religion is an emotional experience in which 'choice' on the basis of 'logic' is probably impossible. Children also need to have a clear idea of their identity for social reasons. How they should relate to questions of identity is a matter which such parents should consider. Their children's emotional security may depend on it.

If the mother is a devout church-goer, therefore, her husband would expect their children to be raised in their mother's religion. Both partners should be aware that this would normally result in the Jew cutting himself off from the life of the Jewish community, and effectively bringing Judaism to a stop with him. He may feel a loyalty to the Jewish community, may express his association and support for it at certain times in his life, and may still be regarded as Jewish by his friends. But he is failing to perpetuate his role in it.

Christians should bear in mind that Jews are tied to their roots not only religiously but by folk memories and practices which make for strong common loyalties. For this reason irreligious Jews will usually be more motivated to preserve their ties to their Jewishness than irreligious Christians, for whom Christianity is primarily a religion. Non-Jews usually accept that their Jewish partners' 'religious' needs are greater than their own, and will go along with their wishes even if they do not comprehend their basis. Yet Jews who do marry outside the community, and argue that their hearts cannot be ruled by the community, may *also* not be able to find a coherent explanation for their persistent desire to remain Jewish and to transmit their culture to their children.

Jews from an Orthodox background who marry partners who do not convert are in an awkward position. They may find it difficult to remain part of the community, because they will be viewed by many Jews as bad children who have let the side down. Jewish life tends to revolve around couples, and the single (even if married) Jew will find limited acceptance in the social life of Jewish families. Progressive synagogues, however, *will* welcome non-Jewish spouses who join together with their partners in synagogue worship or functions. Progressive Judaism recognizes the realities of living in an open Western culture, and rather than condemning Jews for marrying out, chooses to encourage their desire to remain Jewish, especially when they wish to transmit it to their children.

Although the children of mixed marriages are regarded as fully Jewish provided they are raised as Jews, Progressive synagogues may vary in the level of participation they will offer the non-Jewish spouses, even in religious rites involving their own children such as baby blessings, Bar Mitzvahs or weddings. In most synagogues full participation is allowed.

It is part of accepted wisdom, in these times of soaring divorce rates, that people who are united by a common background will have a greater likelihood of making a successful marriage. But the large increase in divorce among Jews shows that this can be an over-simplification. While shared interests may cement relationships, differences may also keep marriages fresh and challenging. It is also true that many individuals who marry a person of a different religious background will have considered the risks and challenges with greater care than someone choosing a partner from within their own religious and social environment.

In this increasingly individualistic society, so much has come to depend on the successful interaction between personalities, and on the blending of characters and characteristics. In the end, almost anything is possible in relationships where proper understanding and goodwill exist. For this reason, Jews in mixed marriages who have confronted the psychological significance and consequences of their action, and have come to terms with it, should have no difficulty in integrating themselves and their families happily within the Jewish community, or at least certain parts of it, provided they and their partners so desire.

And Pharaoh called Joseph's name Zaph'enath-paneah; and he gave him in marriage As'enath, the daughter of Potiphera priest of On.

Bible, Genesis 41

And Moses was content to dwell with the man [Jethro, the priest of Midian], and he gave Moses his daughter Zipporah.

Bible, Exodus 2

Then Boaz said to the elders of the people, 'You are witnesses this day that .... I have bought Ruth the Moabitess, the widow of Mahlon, to be my wife.'

Bible, Ruth 4

Solomon made a marriage alliance with Pharaoh King of Egypt; he took Pharaoh's daughter, and brought her into the City of David.

Bible, 1 Kings 3

23 Jewish Weddings

'The world is a wedding'

The Jewish wedding ceremony, like other such ceremonies, has developed out of a conglomeration of ancient civil practices and rituals. While the Jewish content remains constant, certain aspects of the ceremony will vary from country to country according to national custom.

In antiquity, the Talmud records, a Jewish man could acquire a wife for himself in one of three ways: by contract, by monetary purchase and by sexual intercourse. All three methods required two legal witnesses. In regard to cohabitation, the witnesses were not required to be present during the act of consummation, but to hear the man declare his intention to wed in this manner before disappearing with his new wife into a room to do it.

The wedding ceremony incorporates the symbols of all three methods. The *Chupah* (canopy), under which the couple are united in marriage, symbolizes the room of cohabitation; the ring which the man places on his bride's finger represents the purchase price; and the *Ketubah*, or certificate, which is read out at the ceremony is the marriage contract.

These basic procedures are accompanied by other traditions picked up from the Diaspora cultures in which Jews lived. In ultra-Orthodox weddings, for example, the bride walks around the groom seven times. This, a survival of medieval practices, was designed to create a magic circle to guard the groom from wicked fairies. Translated into rabbinic terms it symbolizes the idea that a good woman protects a man against all misfortunes.

There are many other signs of adjustment to the non-Jewish environment. The Eastern European tradition is for the groom as well as the bride to be accompanied to the canopy by both parents. In Britain, however, the groom's parents and the bride's mother stand beneath the canopy waiting for the bride to be escorted by her father down the aisle.

The wedding service is introduced by the singing of psalms or hymns, and a prayer or address, after which the service begins by blessing God for wine – both the bride and groom drink from a cup – and for the institution of marriage. The groom then places a ring on the bride's right forefinger and says, usually in Hebrew and prompted by the officiant, 'Behold you are consecrated unto me by this ring according the Law of Moses and Israel'.

The *Ketubah* is then read by the officiant, after which seven blessings are recited. They are beautiful and worth quoting in full:

> Blessed are You, Lord our God, Sovereign of the Universe, Creator of the Fruit of the Vine.

Blessed are You, Lord our God, Sovereign of the Universe, He who created everything unto his glory.

Blessed are You, Lord our God, Sovereign of the Universe, Fashioner of Mankind.

Blessed are You, Lord our God, Sovereign of the Universe, He who fashioned mankind in his image, in the Form imagined of his Genius, Yea, He arranged for him endless procreation – Blessed are you, O Lord, Fashioner of Mankind.

May the Childless one rejoice and exult, Yea, let her revel – when her children are gathered into her midst, with gladness – Blessed are You, O Lord, who brings gladness unto Zion through her children.

O do You cause joy, yea rejoicing, unto these companions of love, like You did gladden your Model of creation in paradise of yore – Blessed are You, O Lord, who gladdens Groom and Bride.

Blessed are You, Lord our God, Sovereign of the Universe, He who created rejoicing and gladness, groom and bride, revelry, singing, merriment and good cheer, love and brotherliness, harmony and fellowship, O Lord our God! May there soon be heard in the towns of Judaea, even in the concourses of Jerusalem – sounds of rejoicing, Yea, sounds of gladness, sounds of groom and bride, sounds of nuptial jubilations from under marriage-canopies, even, of youngsters from their singing parties – Blessed are You, O Lord who gladdens the Groom with the Bride.

Following these blessings, the bride and groom once again drink from the cup of wine, and a glass is broken underfoot by the bridegroom.

The bridegroom nowadays breaks a small glass underfoot at the end of the wedding ceremony, a practice perhaps rooted in the desire to frighten away evil spirits by making a loud noise. Jewish sources, however, interpret it as a memorial of the destruction of the Temple in Jerusalem, which casts its shadow of sadness over the joy of every Jewish wedding. This would be consistent with the comment of a Talmudic rabbi who said, 'From the day the Temple was destroyed, the savour of intercourse was taken away from Israel and given over to sinners.' Whatever the value of these interpretations, it is hard to resist the feeling that the glass may symbolize the breaking of the hymen. When the glass is broken, the guests cry out: *Mazal Tov*, which is the equivalent of 'good luck' but literally means a 'good constellation'. The words seem consistent with the view that the glass is shattered to frighten away evil spirits.

In Progressive Jewish services, an exchange of vows between the bride and groom has been introduced because of the popularity of the Christian custom. Also, due to a belief in sexual equality and the mutuality of marriage, there may sometimes be an exchange of rings, with the bride repeating the formula spoken by the groom. She will do so at Progressive weddings, in Hebrew or English, even when there is no exchange of rings. The use of English in modern-Orthodox and Progressive wedding ceremonies will enable non-Jews to be more comfortable with the service – indeed, to understand what is happening.

A wedding, however, is more than the ceremony, and the receptions before and after also vary according to the sect of Jews or the country concerned. In Israel and the United States it is more common to have the ceremony and reception in a hotel or at home. In Great Britain the service is usually at a synagogue, because the synagogue's marriage secretary is required to give the wedding civil legitimacy.

Hasidim and other ultra-Orthodox groups hold pre-nuptial receptions in separate rooms for males and females, with much drinking and Eastern European folk dancing. Several minutes before the ceremony a group of young men will fetch the groom, often hoisting him on a chair, into the male area and then carry him with shouting and singing to the ceremony. After most Orthodox weddings, the bride and groom will be ushered into a room to be alone for a few minutes to symbolize their 'unification'. The ceremony over, there may be further drinking. In ultra-Orthodox families, men and women will sit in separate sections with a partition between them, but such arrangements tend to be the exception.

The meal will end with Grace and a further recitation of the seven wedding blessings; and now the dancing begins. In modern weddings the bride and groom are the first to step onto the dance floor, but in very Orthodox weddings the men will dance on their own accompanied by their own singing, or by a band, to entertain the new couple. When I participated in these wedding receptions, I felt their objective was to expend as much energy as possible, as a way of expressing their affection for the couple. The men might dance something that resembles the Israeli *Hora* in circles, while two or three of the more athletic individuals might go into the centre to dance at a more maddening pace. Two of them might start the Russian gazatchka, shooting out one leg after the other from a squatting position, without losing their balance. Ties are loosened and brows are beaded with perspiration. The women will meanwhile dance on their own. When the excitement really rises the groom will be hoisted on his chair into the centre of the circle. Perching precariously, he might achieve a wan smile as the men continue to dance for him, but soon the bride will be lifted up in her chair and brought to her husband in the circle. A handkerchief, usually white, will be handed to the groom who will give the other end to his bride, both holding it while their supporters dance with the chairs. This marriage dance is a remarkable sight, and I often wonder how these men, whose physical activity is limited by scholarly or commercial pursuits, muster up the strength for these performances. Perhaps they convert spiritual reserves into physical energy!

Modern wedding receptions are very different affairs, with discos or bands playing popular Western music intermingled with the traditional East European or Israeli dances prevalent at Orthodox weddings. But because of the excitement they add to the celebration, even sedate Westernized Jewish weddings may introduce the 'chair dance' and use a white handkerchief to join the bride and the groom or other dancers. The origin of the handkerchief, incidentally, lies in the need to avoid passing ritual impurity from one individual to another, but in the dance it has become a symbol of modesty and discretion.

Of course at all weddings there will be speeches. Modern weddings will follow the cultural format of the host country. In Britain, the bride's father will welcome the guests and say how much he loves his new son-in-law (but not as much as he loves his daughter), the best man will toast the groom by making fun of him, while the groom will respond by praising his new wife, to which she may then respond. In Great Britain there may also be official toasts to the Queen and the President of the State of Israel, after which 'God Save the Queen' and the Israeli National Anthem will be played.

As marriage marks the transition from single status to responsibility for and commitment to another life, it is the greatest occasion in the life of most couples. In particular, by joining two lives, two circles of families and friends will also become interlinked. Children will be born to create new families. In Jewish life both these elements are important – the bonding between Jews and the passing on of Judaism to future generations.

Jewish weddings, like all weddings however, bring out mixed feelings: nostalgia for lost youth or long-past wedding ceremonies, concern over the state of relationships, or anticipation of weddings to come, when they too will be raised high in chairs among dancing admirers, amid hopes that their happiness (unlike the chairs) will never come down to earth.

From the Talmud

It is forbidden for a man to betroth a woman until he sees her, lest he afterwards see in her something ugly which will make her repulsive to him. This would not be in accordance with the Torah, which reads: 'And you shall love your neighbour as yourself.' *(Leviticus 19:11)*

It is forbidden for a man to betroth his daughter while she is small, he must wait until she grows up and says: 'This is the man I want.'

Our masters taught: With what words do we dance and sing a bride's praises? The School of Shammai says: 'We praise her according to what she is.' The School of Hillel says: 'We praise her by calling her a beautiful and lovely bride.' The disciples of Shammai questioned those of Hillel: 'Suppose she is blind or lame? Shall we say that she is a beautiful and lovely bride? Does not the Torah command: "From a false matter stay far away"?' They replied: 'Suppose a man made a bad purchase in the market place? Do we praise the article before him or do we call it ugly? We say that we are to praise it!'

When Rabbi Dimi arrived in Babylonia, he said: 'This is the way they sing the praises of the bride in the West: "No eye paint, no rouge, no hair dressing, and still she is as beautiful as a doe."'

24 Jewish Funerals

'I wish you long life'

Jewish funerals are unfamiliar in many ways to people from other backgrounds. Flowers are not sent as a tribute to the bereaved, and mourners usually help bury the dead by throwing a spadeful or handful of earth over the coffin (but never flowers). Attending a funeral is one of the most important good deeds in Jewish life, since it is seen as a tribute to a family in grief. Accordingly, non-Jewish friends of the person who has died, or of the bereaved, are particularly welcome to attend.

At funerals, the body is never viewed. More surprisingly, it is traditional for the coffin to be made of simple wood and unornamented. At Orthodox funerals the men and women will be separated and prayers and psalms recited by the rabbi either on his own or responsively with the congregation. In Progressive synagogues, men and women will sit or stand together and the service will have sufficient English to enable most participants to comprehend the prayers. These might include psalms such as 'The Lord is my Shepherd', or 'I lift up my eyes to the hills', and prayers from the daily service or special prayers, the most notable beginning 'O God, full of Compassion', and asking God to give the dead eternal rest under his protecting wings. The most moving text is a reconciliation with death which includes the statement from that great study of suffering, the biblical book of Job: 'The Lord gives, the Lord takes, blessed be the name of the Lord.'

Orthodox Judaism forbids cremations, largely because of the belief in physical resurrection, although the non-Orthodox accept cremation as an alternative. The ashes might be buried under a small memorial stone or rose bush.

But the funeral is only the beginning of Jewish mourning. Bereaved Orthodox Jews will not return to work until after the seven days of mourning, known as a Shivah. These days exclude the Sabbath, on which mourning is not allowed, but otherwise the mourners will remain at home, sit on low stools or chairs, and accept condolences from family and friends. A memorial candle will be flickering to symbolize the soul of the dead. In Orthodox homes, mirrors will be covered. The origins of this custom are steeped in the primitive belief that the ghost of the deceased might wish to snatch away the souls of the living which are reflected in water or in mirrors. The modern interpretation is that they are covered in order to discourage vanity in the presence of human mortality.

In the evenings, communal prayers will be led at home by a rabbi, and then tributes may be paid to the dead. In those less traditional homes where prayers are limited to one evening, it would be normal for a large number of people to attend. The Shivah is as solemn an occasion as the funeral, but once the service is over and visitors have expressed their sympathy to the mourners, people might break up into small circles for drinks or tea and cakes, and the mood will usually be neither morose nor depressing. People who have not met for years find themselves brought together by a common relationship with the deceased or the mourners, and strike up animated discussions. The mourners do not appear to mind, partly because it has the effect of lessening their sense of isolation, and of reminding them that in spite of their tragedy life goes on.

According to Jewish law, there are three stages of mourning. The most intense period is the first week; slightly less so are the first thirty days; while the period of mourning comes to a complete end only after a year. Orthodox Jewish men will not shave during the first thirty days, or go to any form of entertainment during the year of mourning. Approximately a year after the death, it is normal to hold a service in which family and friends again congregate to consecrate the tombstone and say their last farewells, and to end their period of mourning.

In times of ancestor worship it was normal for people to tear their flesh, hair and clothes when a parent died, perhaps to assuage their guilt and placate the departing spirit. While the Bible forbade any self-mutilation, it became traditional for chief mourners to cut their garment as a symbol of grief. The traditional formula for comforting the bereaved when taking leave of them after a visit to the Shivah is: 'May the Lord comfort you among the mourners in Zion.' In English-speaking countries the conversational formula sounds almost ironic: 'I wish you long life.' Personally, I have always winced at this form of consolation. Perhaps it took hold because it expresses the Jewish view that, while the dead must be mourned, the bereaved should hold on to life for as long as possible. It is the Jewish way of saying: 'The King is dead, long live the King.'

It is better to go to the house of mourning than to go to the house of feasting; for that is the end of all men, and the living will lay it to his heart.

Bible, Ecclesiastes 7

Remember his doom, for it is also yours – his yesterday, yours today!

Apocrypha, Ben Sira, 38

Rabbi Simeon ben Eleazar said: 'Do not try to comfort your friend while the body of his deceased lies before him.'

Mishna

They used to carry food to the house of mourning, the rich in silver and gold baskets, the poor in wicker baskets. Then, in respect for the poor, all had to carry in wicker baskets.

Talmud

When Rabbi Hanina's daughter died and he did not weep for her, his wife reprimanded him: 'Was it a mere hen you carried out of your house?' He justified himself: 'Do you want me to suffer two evils – not only bereavement but also blindness from incessant weeping?'

Talmud

'Weep not for the dead, neither bemoan him' *(Jeremiah 23:10)*. What does this mean? Three days of weeping, seven for lamenting, and thirty days [for abstaining] from wearing pressed clothes and from cutting the hair. 'From then on,' says the Holy One, 'you are not expected to be more compassionate to him than I.'

Talmud

All go to the house of mourning and each weeps over his own sorrow.

Ibn Shuaib, Olat Shabbat

Rav said: 'Only after twelve months does one begin to forget the dead.'

Talmud

According to ancient Jewish custom, the ceremony of cutting our garments when our nearest and dearest on earth is lying dead before us, is to be performed *standing up*. This teaches: meet all sorrow standing upright. The future may be dark, veiled from the eye of mortals – but not the manner in which we are to meet the future. To rail at life, to reel against a destiny that has cast our lines in unpleasant places, is of little avail. We cannot lay down terms to life. Life must be accepted on its own terms. But hard as life's terms are, life (it has been finely said) never dictates unrighteousness, unholiness, dishonour.

J. H. Hertz, British Chief Rabbi

Weep for the mourners,
Not for the souls that have departed
For they are at rest and we suffer grief.

Talmud

JEWS & IMMORTALITY —
MAY YOU LIVE TO 120 . . .

25 Jews and Immortality

'May you live to 120'

Most people view death with apprehension. Not only the process itself, but what happens after death, 'is that which makes cowards of us all'. The traditional Jewish belief in immortality, however, seems to stem less from the fear of death than from the desire for ultimate justice in the 'affairs of men'. The world to come is where there will be amends for the prosperity of the wicked and the suffering of the just. The biblical view was of a gloomy nether world, *Sheol*, where no distinction was made between good and bad souls. The Bible, for instance, records King Saul raising the protesting seer Samuel from the grave to receive a prophecy on the future of his Kingdom.

The Talmudic period possessed a far more complex concept of a God who rewarded the righteous by illuminating them with His presence and punished sinners by withholding it. But God's judgement, at which he rewards the righteous and punishes the wicked, takes place not after death but annually on the Jewish New Year. We are also told that the good may suffer in this life for their sins and enjoy their full reward in the next life, while the wicked may benefit in this life for their good deeds but inherit the painful consequences of their evil after death.

There is little description in the Bible of what life after death is like, but there is no pleasurable anticipation of death as a release or as solace. The Psalmist praying for salvation from enemies reminds God that the 'dead do not praise You, nor do those who go down to the place of silence'. The Torah forbade witchcraft, magic and spiritualism, and Rabbinic literature records no raising of spirits, although the spirits of great men, particularly Elijah, may occasionally appear voluntarily to guide the living. Jews indeed pray for the dead to enjoy eternal rest, which suggests that they believe the spirit survives death.

The vast Jewish literature contains many descriptions of the World to Come, many often inconsistent with each other. Generally, the Jewish image of immortality is of the good basking in divine bliss while the wicked suffer discomfort, and the Rabbinic Masters posited faith in the afterlife as an essential element of the Jewish religion, arguing that those who deny the principle of the World to Come will not enjoy it! The logic of this resembles 'Pascal's Wager', in which he wrote that it is advisable to believe in God, because if there was no God you lost nothing, and if He did exist you were on the winning side. The suggestion that the World to Come is reserved for those who believe in it, was echoed by the great twelfth-century Jewish philosopher Maimonides, who hinted that only people of intellect – such as philosophers whose thoughts bring them into spiritual spheres – would enjoy continuity after death.

But this élitist view of immortality is not shared by mainstream Jewish tradition, which states categorically that well-behaved non-Jews as well as Jews have a place in an afterlife. One image of post-mortal bliss is of the righteous sharing in the feast of the great Leviathan fish; while another has the righteous studying Torah with God. One might occasionally hear it said, on the death of a learned Jew, that he has joined 'the Academy on High'.

Jewish traditional faith is one matter, but the reality is another. What do Jews actually believe? In fact they are as confused as any others in the face of the unknown. Most are agnostics who take a wait-and-see attitude. Many are moved, by the prospect of the death of loved ones, to believe that this is not the end of life. The pain of separation is so great that consolation is sought in the hope that there will eventually be a reunion of the dead, and that death is but a new beginning. For some this is not enough, and there are Jewish spiritualists who claim to make contact with the dead, though this is against Jewish law; and others who believe that, when a body dies, the spirit moves into another living creature, which seems a credible option and finds a prominent place in Jewish mysticism.

The anxiety, repressed and revealed, in individuals over death is too deeply personal to be resolved by ideas taught by religions or speculations of different philosophies. People will look for some meaning in death to sustain faith in the significance of their own lives. The Jewish affirmation of a worldly life and its opportunities is highlighted by the rabbinic admonition 'to repent the day before you die'. As one never knows the day of one's death, one is instructed to live each day with the fullest goodness and joy.

Then his servants said to him, 'What is this thing that you have done? You fasted and wept for the child while it was alive; but when the child died, you arose and ate food.' He said, 'While the child was still alive, I fasted and wept; for I said, "Who knows whether Yahweh will be gracious to me, that the child may live?" But now he is dead; why should I fast? Can I bring him back again? I shall go to him, but he will not return to me.' Then David comforted his wife, Bathshe'ba, and went in to her, and lay with her; and she bore a son, and he called his name Solomon.

Bible, 2 Samuel 12

For there is hope for a tree,
  if it be cut down, that it will sprout again,
  and that its shoots will not cease.
Though its root grow old in the earth,
  and its stump die in the ground,
yet the scent of water it will bud
  and put forth branches like a young plant.
But man dies, and is laid low;
  man breathes his last, and where is he?
As waters fail from a lake,
  and a river wastes away and dries up,
So man lies down and rises not again;
  till the heavens are no more he will not awake,
  or be roused out of his sleep.

Bible, Job 14

Because man goes to his eternal home, and the mourners go about the street; before the silver cord is snapped, or the golden bowl is broken, or the pitcher is broken at the fountain, or the wheel broken at the cistern, and the dust returns to the earth as it was, and the spirit returns to God who gave it. Vanity of vanities, says the Preacher; all is vanity.

Bible, Ecclesiastes 12

He will swallow up death for ever, and the Lord God will wipe away tears from all faces, and the reproach of his people he will take away from all the earth; for Yahweh has spoken.

Bible, Isaiah 25

This world is like a vestibule before the world to come. Prepare yourself in the vestibule so that you may enter into the palace. Better is one hour of repentance and good deeds in this world than the whole life in the world to come; and better is one hour of blissfulness of spirit in the world to come, than the whole life of this world.

Mishna

Two ships were once seen to be sailing near land. One of them was going forth from the harbour, and the other was coming into the harbour. Every one was cheering the outgoing ship, and every one was giving it a hearty send-off. But the incoming ship was scarcely noticed.

A wise man was looking at the two ships, and he said: 'Rejoice not over the ship that is setting out to sea, for you know not what destiny awaits it, what storms it may encounter, what dangers it may have to undergo. Rejoice rather over the ship that has reached port safely and brought back all its passengers in peace.'

It is the way of the world, that when a human being is born, all rejoice; but when he dies, all sorrow. Rather ought the opposite to be the case. No one can tell what troubles await the child on its journey into manhood. But when man has lived and dies in peace, all should rejoice, seeing that he has completed his journey, and is departing this world with the imperishable crown of a good name.

Talmud (as retold in the Book of Jewish Thoughts)

There are those who gain eternity in a lifetime, and others who gain it in one brief hour.

Talmud

The day of death is when two worlds meet with a kiss: this world going out, the future world coming in.

Talmud

I often feel that death is not the enemy of life, but its friend, for it is the knowledge that our years are limited which makes them so precious.

Peace of Mind, Joshua L. Liebman

DIETARY HABITS —
FUSSY ABOUT FOOD...

26 Jewish Dietary Habits

'Jews are very fussy about food'

Jews tend to pride themselves on being logical people, but when it comes to what they will or will not eat and where they will eat it, all logic breaks down. Furthermore, individuals will not seek to defend their idiosyncratic observance of the dietary laws by anything more than the statement that the degree of their observance is right for them. Thus, if non-Jews are confused as to the Jewish view of what is permitted and prohibited, they are not in any worse a position than Jews. For when Jews invite each other to meals, either to their homes or to a restaurant for the first time, they too must ask their guests' dietary habits, and discover their attitude to eating food that is not *Kosher* – a word that literally means 'fit'.

Besides those who observe either everything or nothing, there are Jews who will keep a Kosher home, in which no forbidden foods are eaten and in which separate dishes and cutlery are kept for milk and meat produce, yet will eat anything at all in restaurants or other people's homes, excepting, perhaps, pork. And even pork might be ignored if it is chopped into small pieces and made to disappear in the camouflage of a Chinese egg roll.

The strictest observers will not even eat in restaurants supervised by Orthodox rabbis, because these will be regarded as not to be trusted to be as meticulous about dietary rules as they are in their homes. In my Orthodox parental home there were constant debates as to how far one had to go to keep the rules properly. All I can hope to do here is to outline to non-Jews the mentality of Jews towards the rules concerning food, so that they will not feel completely at a loss when they encounter the large variety of Jewish eating practices.

How did it all begin? The Torah – the written law given to Moses – tells Jews what they may or may not eat, and the categories are clearly defined. Mammals which chew the cud and have a split hoof may be eaten, while the others may not. This means permitting sheep, goats and cows, but forbidding some wild animals such as rabbits, and certain domesticated animals such as horses, dogs and cats. The pig, for instance, though it has a cleft hoof, does not chew its cud, so is also forbidden. Shellfish and crawling sea animals are similarly forbidden, as are fish without scales and fins. The reasons for these taboos are uncertain, but according to tradition they are to be obeyed without seeking any explanation.

What is permitted is called *Kosher*, and what is forbidden is called *Trayfah*, which literally means 'torn'. *Trayfah* became the collective word for all forbidden dietary practices, because to eat a limb torn from a live animal was considered the height of barbarism. According to the Torah, this was forbidden even to non-Jews.

Yet even animals that one may not eat must still be preserved. When Noah gathered the animals into his ark, he was under divine instruction to save one pair of 'impure' animals and seven pairs of 'pure' animals. A description of the animals, or an explanation of the meaning of 'pure', is not given. As Noah lived before God's covenant with Abraham, it must be assumed that even non-Jews had taboos when it came to foods.

Jews have sought to rationalize the dietary prohibitions on the basis of cleanliness, but I think this is far-fetched. The avoidance of pig because it was identified with muck (and was later found to be a common transmitter of tape-worm) assumes greater medical knowledge than is likely at the period in which the laws were given. Stomach ailments could have come from any animal food, and the different causal connections between one species or another would not have been detectable by ancient medicine. What is more likely is that the abhorrence of so many Jews for pork originated because boars and pigs were part of the Hellenistic sacrificial cult. In the days of the Seleucid rule of Judaea (175–135 BCE) Jews were required to participate in these pagan practices and many died as martyrs when they refused.

In addition, Kosher animals have to be slaughtered by humane methods, and the meat cannot be eaten with the blood still in it, because blood was considered to be the life of the animal. While some people may have felt that eating the 'life-force' of animals gave them added strength, the Israelites were discouraged from taking this view. It became traditional in preparing meat to salt it, so as to draw out the blood, before cooking it.

The Torah includes several laws designed to have a civilizing impact on Jews. One was to shoo away the mother bird before taking eggs from her nest, so as not to cause her additional anguish. And another, which led to unbelievable complications, was the command against cooking a kid in its mother's milk. Some say that this was a pagan practice against which Jewish lawgivers rebelled, but whether or not this is so, it showed sensitivity on their part. For Jewish legislators it was part of the sadness of natural life that humans killed fellow creatures for food. To desist from cooking an offspring in the food which would have nourished it was a projection of civilized human feelings for hapless victims.

But this prohibition was given more than once in the Torah, and since the Rabbinic Masters assumed that no holy word or phrase is superfluous, they gave a different dimension to the commandment each time it appeared in the Torah. Thus the rule was expanded to mean not only in its mother's milk, but in any milk. Also, that neither milk nor *any* dairy products should be eaten together, and a required period of time be allowed to elapse between the eating of meat and of milk products. Anxiety over the way meat or milk might be absorbed in the utensils led to separate dishes and cutlery. Piety, that some will feel approaches fanaticism, leads certain Orthodox Jews to have separate dishwashers for dairy and meat dishes. But most Orthodox families, or those who keep a Kosher kitchen, will have separate dish cloths for the two sets of cutlery, dishes and cooking utensils.

Non-Jews may also be interested to know why Orthodox Jews will not eat filet mignon. The biblical reason is rooted in the description of how Jacob wrestled with a 'Man of God' the night before he was to meet Esau, the warrior brother from whom he stole the birthright and their father's blessing. Jacob was victorious, and he was blessed and given a new name, Israel, to symbolize the blessing. But he suffered an irreversible limp, because his thigh ligament had been torn. Thus, according to Genesis, 'the children of Israel eat not of the tendon which is upon the hollow of the thigh, unto this day, because he [the Man of God] touched the tendon of the hollow of Jacob's thigh [Genesis 32:32].' It would be possible to remove the tendon to enable Orthodox Jews to eat filet mignon, but this is a laborious business and non-Jewish beef-eaters benefit, as the thighs of kosher-killed cows are sold to the non-Jewish market.

Kosher wine also requires explanation. According to the Talmud, Jews are not permitted to drink pagan wine because it was used for libations in idolatrous rites. Only wine grown and put into casks and pitchers by Jews may be drunk. Yet in spite of the fact that the Talmud also ruled that Christians are not pagans – since they are not 'worshippers of the stars and constellations' – Orthodox Jews to this day will drink only wine produced and bottled by Jews. They are punctilious to the extent that the bottle can be decorked only by a Jew.

Yeyn Nesach, 'forbidden wine', appears to be one of the more absurd features of Orthodox Judaism and is ignored by many. But when I asked my father why the rule was still kept even though wine was never used for pagan libations, he gave me an honest answer: 'Son, it is to keep us apart from the Gentiles.'

For most Jews, this helps explains why Jews keep the dietary laws: not so much because it puts a divide between Jews and non-Jews, but because it has become the most pragmatic method for maintaining Jewish identity. Jews will still invite their non-Jewish friends to their family events and will have them share their meals, but they will keep the dietary laws because it is the most basic reminder that they are Jewish.

Precisely because a sense of identity is so personal a matter, Jews observe food practices often not on any rational basis but for their emotional value. As a Progressive rabbi, I used to make fun of friends who, I argued, had *Kosher* homes but *Trayfah* bodies, in that outside the home they ate anything. I reminded them that Jesus, whom Jews reject as a messiah, had said that 'a man is not defiled by what goes into the mouth but by what comes out of it'. 'You', I said, 'act as though the body can be defiled so long as the house is not.' Yet I have reconciled myself to the fact that, although the majority of Jews do feel an obligation to remain Jewish, they do not know why. Loyalty to their ancestors has made for many a 'Kosher home' and 'my son must marry a Jewish girl' – their two major criteria for guaranteeing Jewish survival.

All this explains why some Jews will eat everything – not because they have no attachment to Judaism, but because they hope to maintain Jewish identity on different religious grounds. I knew a man in Texas who was proud of his ancestors who had founded the Reform synagogue in his home town. He proudly stated, 'I am a fifth-generation pork eater', to indicate that he had retained his Jewishness without being Kosher. Most Jews, however, believe that once you ignore the dietary laws in their entirety, you are leaving not only Judaism but Jewishness.

To round off the picture, let me identify the main varieties of dietary practice among Jews in ascending order:

1 Jews who ignore the Kosher rules entirely at home and outside.
2 Jews who eat anything (and anywhere) except pork and perhaps seafood.
3 Jews who have Kosher kitchens but eat anything outside their homes.
4 Jews who have Kosher kitchens and eat anything outside their homes except pork and perhaps seafood.
5 Jews who have Kosher kitchens and eat Kosher fish or vegetarian meals outside their home.
6 Jews who will have Kosher kitchens and only eat in other Kosher homes or Kosher restaurants.

Progressive Jews do not make the dietary laws their highest priority. The more radical consider it purely a matter of personal conscience; the middle of the road will encourage some form of *Kashrut* (the noun for Kosher) as a means of identification. All Progressive synagogues will respect the sensitivities of the Orthodox by either serving only Kosher meat or fish meals at their synagogue functions.

Because Kashrut is considered so vital a part of Jewish life among Orthodoxy, its supervision has become a business. People are engaged by various rabbinical authorities to supervise and monitor Kosher restaurants and manufactured food. Food made in Israel and the Diaspora appears in specialized Jewish food stores, and in some ordinary supermarkets, with labels or signs on the packages indicating that they have been approved by these authorities. Some of these authorities may inform their followers that the food agreed by others cannot be trusted because the controls are not sufficiently meticulous, which leads to community squabbles, and claims that the motives are commercial rather than religious as there is a price to be added to the cost of the foods. Sadly, for the Orthodox, *Kashrut* in Diaspora communities does lead to a far costlier food bill, which discourages some, especially in periods of recession, from being as observant as they otherwise might be.

Non-Jews need be no more concerned than Jews when they invite Jews to a meal or accept an invitation from them. In inviting Jews, one need only ask whether there are any foods they cannot eat. Usually, if they are observant in any way, they will volunteer their needs. If they are strictly Kosher, they will apologize for not being able to accept the invitation. This should not trouble non-Jews, as such people would probably not accept invitations to meals even in Jewish homes unless they were friendly enough with the people to know that they shared the same dietary standards.

If non-Jews are invited to a Jewish home for a meal, they can accept in the knowledge that nothing special will be expected of them, and that there will be no ceremonial with which they would feel uncomfortable. An Orthodox household would begin and end the meal with a blessing, but one would not be expected to participate. Generally speaking, non-Jews invited to any Jewish home or occasion can expect to be put at their ease. Anything they will need to know will be explained before or during the event. But if non-Jews are going to an

Orthodox home and do not want to go empty handed, they should bear in mind that flowers would be more appropriate than chocolates (which might contain something non-Kosher) or wine.

Lastly, it is possible that you expected this chapter to include a description of Jewish food. But in fact there really is no such category. What has been regarded as Jewish food originates in fact from the kitchens of Eastern Europe and Germany, or from the Mediterranean or Oriental countries in which Jews lived for centuries. As Jews have been raised to enjoy life, and as the drinking of wine is a normal way of celebrating religious events, eating rather than drinking will be the essence of a Jewish meal. Jews love good food whatever its national origins, though certain cultures such as the Japanese should appreciate that some Jews, because of their religious upbringing, may find it difficult to eat raw food. Their refusal should not be considered offensive.

Among the *Essays of Elia*, by Charles Lamb, there is one titled 'Imperfect Sympathies', in which he explains that he cannot really get on with Jews because they do not eat what he eats. One appreciates this feeling, because eating together is the essence of a significant life-event, be it a wedding or a funeral wake. Shared hospitality marks a bonding between individuals and is a sign of trust. But since he wrote this essay times have changed, and except for that small section of the ultra-Orthodox who live in seclusion, Jews welcome the opportunity of sharing meals with non-Jews, and do not allow dietary practices to limit the pleasures of good food combined with good company.

And God blessed Noah and his sons, and said to them, 'Be fruitful and multiply, and fill the earth. Every moving things that lives shall be food for you; and as I gave you the green plants, I give you everything. Only you shall not eat flesh with its life, that is, its blood.'

Bible, Genesis 9

You shall not eat anything that dies of itself; you may give it to the alien who is within your towns, that he may eat it, or you may sell it to a foreigner; for you are a people holy to Yahweh your God. You shall not boil a kid in its mother's milk.

Bible, Deuteronomy 14

A Rabbi did tailoring in the home of a heathen in Rome. One meal time meat of a forbidden animal was served to him, and the heathen said, 'Eat.' He replied, 'I cannot eat.' The heathen: 'Eat, for if you do not, I will slay you.' 'If you wish to slay me, do so, but I cannot eat forbidden meat.' The heathen: 'How did you know that if you had eaten it, I would have slain you? For a Jew should act like a Jew, even as a heathen should act like a heathen.'

Talmud

The dietary laws train us to master our appetites…and not to consider…eating and drinking the end of man's existence.

Guide for the Perplexed, Maimonides

Some say that all the animals that are unclean in this world will be declared clean by the Holy One in time to come.

Midrash

JEWISH SABBATH —
WORLD TO COME. . . .

27 The Jewish Sabbath

'The taste of heavenly bliss'

Friday night at home is the most important hallmark of Jewish life. Parents will not accept social invitations, and teenagers living at home will hesitate before asking to be excused from the Sabbath evening meal. This respect for Friday night has little to do with the level of Sabbath observances. While the rituals may have fallen away, the nostalgia has remained and the majority of Jewish families feel that the end of the working week should be celebrated *en famille*.

This home institution derives from the commandment to observe the Sabbath – perhaps the greatest Jewish contribution to the moral and religious life of the world. Two moral principles form the basis for the Sabbath: First, Jews should imitate God; they must rest because the Lord 'rested on the seventh day, wherefore the Lord blessed the Sabbath day and hallowed it' (the Exodus version of the Ten Commandments), and Jews should seek to be like God. Secondly, Jews should rest on the Sabbath and allow all their servants and even animals to rest because 'you were a servant in the land of Egypt … therefore Yahweh, your God, commanded you to keep the Sabbath day' (the Deuteronomy version of the Ten Commandments). The instruction that all Jews, their servants and any alien residents must rest, implied the equality of all humans in their rights to freedom from labour on at least one day out of seven, because all were made in the image of God.

Liberation from servitude and labour, and living like God are the essential message of the Sabbath. Worldly cares are to be set aside as one enjoys the freedom from work and the pressures of life. For Jews the major purpose of the Sabbath is pleasure. According to the Talmud, as mentioned earlier, three things are intimations of the delights of the World to Come: Sabbath, sunlight and sex. While the vagaries of the climate cannot guarantee Sabbath sunshine, the Rabbinic Masters praise those who make love on the Sabbath, thus combining two foretastes of heavenly bliss.

Since according to biblical tradition the twenty-four-hour day starts in the evening, Sabbath begins at dusk on Friday and concludes with nightfall on Saturday. Christianity moved the observance from the seventh day to the first day of the week.

The Sabbath is ushered in by the woman of the house kindling at least two candles, which are interpreted to signify the command to *remember* the reasons for the Sabbath (Exodus 20:8) and the command to *keep* the Sabbath (Deuteronomy 5:12). In observant Orthodox families, the men will attend synagogue for the Sabbath prayers. On their return a festive meal will await them, to be introduced by the blessing of children, the recitation of Kiddush (the prayer which declares the Sabbath as 'holy' or special). Hands are washed, accompanied by a special blessing which is recited before every meal, not only on the Sabbath. A blessing over bread is then recited over two twisted loaves, representing the double portion of Manna which was collected in the wilderness on the sixth day, to provide for the Sabbath as well.

The meal will vary from country to country and from family to family, based on cultural backgrounds. In the United States, the four-course meal for Friday night usually consists of chicken soup, *gefilte* fish (a fish cake made up of white fish and carp), chicken and compote, a combination of stewed fruit. In Great Britain, cold fried fish accompanied by various salads and pickled cucumbers as the main course has become traditional fare, perhaps because it freed the women from the drudgery of serving up a cooked meal.

Between the courses, the custom of singing prayers and poems praising God and the Sabbath still prevails among the more religious and knowledgeable families. At the conclusion of the meal, a series of blessings is recited which praise God for food, ask his blessing for the households of Israel, and pray for the coming of the Messiah.

What I have described is prescribed practice but does not always reflect what happens. In most Jewish families for whom Friday night retains its importance, there will be the lighting of the candles, a blessing over wine and bread, and no more. In some families there will be a tradition for its immediate members to come together, perhaps with a few guests, for a festive meal without any of the ritual trappings.

For traditional Jews, other than attending synagogue for prayers on the eve, morning and afternoon of the Sabbath and the rituals connected with the meals, the observance of the Sabbath is a matter of prohibitions rather than positive instructions. The biblical commandment to desist from work was not left to the individual to interpret. The Bible tells graphically how a man collecting wood on the Sabbath was put on trial before Moses. After two witnesses gave evidence of his crime, he was found guilty and executed. In biblical days there was no difference between religious and civil law, and avoidance of penalties for Sabbath violation required detailed definition.

While there is no record of capital punishment for Sabbath violators in the post-biblical period, and there is every reason to believe that peer pressure was sufficient to keep people in tow, the Rabbinic Masters defined work as comprising all types of labour involved in the building of the Tabernacle in the Wilderness as prescribed by Moses and the High Priest Aaron. Thirty-nine major categories were discovered and each of these had many derivatives.

The consequences of those ancient laws turned out to be more restrictive than I am sure they were intended to be. As an example, in biblical days writing was done by engraving on stones or slates, which was recognized as work. Today, writing would still be considered by the Orthodox as labour, although it requires comparatively little physical effort to move a pen across paper. Of course, modern writing could be considered as labour if it were a matter of a person's normal work, such as preparing contracts or recording research. But for traditional Jewish law, no distinction is made; writing is writing and therefore forbidden.

I give this as an example because it is this prohibition that became the basis of a turning-point in my own life as a Jew. Being raised in a very Orthodox family, once the Sabbath began lights were not switched on or off because of the ancient prohibition of making a fire, and all one could do as a means of recreation was to talk or read by lights strategically placed for comfort. Wall lights in the kitchen, bathroom, toilet and hallway, as well as a reading lamp in the living-room, would remain alight until nightfall on Saturday. In addition, the light bulb in the refrigerator would be removed before the Sabbath so that the light would not switch on and off with the opening and closing of the door. Without radio and the ability to use public transport to reach my friends (because the vehicles were operated on the basis of electrical sparks, and the drivers and conductors were working), the only way to avoid boredom bordering on despair was to become an avid reader. My brother, who had broken ranks with family and community by becoming a Reform rabbi (and how my family coped with this betrayal is another story), had forced me to face the reality of the plurality of religious truths. But I had not broken with family tradition until one fateful Sabbath afternoon.

I was fifteen and reading a play by the Greek dramatist, Euripides, as I swung lazily on the swing sofa on our front porch. I came across a line which I wanted to mark for future reference. Aware that it was the Sabbath, I went to my bedroom, found a pencil and secretly underlined the sentence. Nothing happened. I decided to challenge the Orthodox Jewish God and quickly switched on and off the bedroom light. No lightning struck me and I decided that my God did not mind if I wanted to underline a profound thought. Years later I still have the same Everyman's Library Classic which had travelled with me across the Atlantic, and I find that what I had underlined in the play, *Electra*, and for which I had 'broken' the Sabbath, was a religious sentiment which is still the basis of my personal belief: that faith in God without the conviction that good must ultimately be victorious over evil is a faith without meaning. The 'Sabbath breaking' words were those of Electra herself:

> I am assured; or never must we more
> Believe that there are Gods, if impious wrongs
> Triumphant over justice bear the sway.

In good Orthodox Jewish homes, parents and children will converse, visit and receive visits from local friends. Some will go on walks and commune with nature in parks and woods. The more studious will study Torah. Many will read as I did. Fathers might disappear for a few hours on the Sabbath afternoon for the *Shabbas shloof*, Yiddish for the 'Sabbath nap'. And the day may pass pleasantly enough without any radio, television or shopping – as buying, selling or even handling money, let alone carrying objects out of one's home or garden, are forbidden.

The strain of such prohibitions can be understood in a commercial age, where for the working Jew so many jobs depended on working from 9:30 to 5:30, even when the Sabbath began earlier than 5:30 on Friday, or indeed on working on Saturday. Many refugees from closed Jewish communities found that they had little choice but to work during Sabbath hours, or were moved by ambition to ignore those restrictions in order to move up the ladder of success.

Even for those who had the opportunity to observe the Sabbath, the restrictions seemed too burdensome and irrational. During long summer days one could do nothing physical (even sports such as tennis and football were by ancient definition interpreted as work), or even be an onlooker in areas of entertainment. Most Jews do not have the moral resources to restrict themselves in this way, especially as they see no virtue in it, for the reason that the definition of work has been modified.

Progressive Judaism has accepted that as the times change, so must the observance of the Sabbath. A founder of the Liberal Jewish movement in Great Britain established the religious right of Jews to garden on the Sabbath if this was their hobby and made them feel closer to themselves and to God. Technological advances were accepted; driving and the use of electricity were permitted, as was listening to radios or viewing television. Jewish leaders emphasized the spirit rather than the form of the Sabbath. Sabbath observance was not linked to actual nightfall; it began at a civilized time on a Friday evening and ended twenty-four hours later, which enabled them to have their Sabbath meal at a reasonable hour rather than at 10:00 on Friday evening, as would be the case in summer if they were Orthodox and living in London. They could also go to the theatre or cinema on Saturday night.

The reality of the Jewish Sabbath is that less than 10 per cent observe it at all, except for the family get-together on Friday evening. It is a pity that one of the greatest of Jewish institutions, in terms of its humanitarian and spiritual basis, should have become – through the accretion of restrictions over the centuries – a burden rather than the source for human delight.

I have quoted the rabbinic thought that the pleasures of the Sabbath are a foretaste of the peace in the World to Come. There is another rabbinic quotation that if all the Jewish people were to keep one Sabbath properly, the Messiah would come, since the Sabbath is the equivalent to all the other divine commandments. The validity of this pronouncement has never been tested. But one could surmise that, were all humans able to celebrate one day in the week as a day of total peace and contentment, free of mundane worries and hassle, full of joy, and of the freedom to enjoy convivial company, good food and drink, recreation, sport and self-discovery, this would mean that the Messianic Era had indeed arrived!

What a shame that the Sabbath has fallen short of keeping its promise, not only for Jews but for Christians as well. Religion, over the centuries, except in very special families, has had almost every ounce of enjoyment squeezed out of it, by giving it a harsh solemnity circumscribing meaningless prohibitions. This is what often happens when a divine concept gets into the hands of holy men and pious do-gooders who value the authority of past traditions over the command 'to serve the Lord with gladness'.

28 The Jewish Festivals

'Holy Days or holidays?'

How can one explain the role of holy days and festivals in the lives of Jews – be they religious or not – to someone who has not had direct experience of them? Consider the pleasures and conflicts around the place of Christmas in Western life. While religious people argue about the commercialization of Christmas, two-thirds of the business world are merely anxious whether Christmas profits will be high enough to satisfy their bank managers. For two months, children antici-pate presents, parents worry about what to buy them, where to find the money, and how to enjoy the Christmas break.

Jesus chased the money-changers out of the Temple. Little did he know that two thousand years later the celebration of his birth would be one of the greatest money-spinners ever devised. Perhaps the role of Christmas in the totality of human experience would console him, for it shows how religious and business activities are integral to life, and interweave like the warp and woof of a single garment. Indeed, it would be interesting to research how much is spent on religion-related enterprises, such as votive candles, Bibles, rosary beads, the build-ing of churches, the support of clergy, and food and drink for religious celebra-tions. Also, it would be informative to know how many working days are lost due to holy days.

The fact that holy days have become 'holidays' is not only an indication of the secularization of life, but of the religious basis and origins of the recreational and festive components of modern life. Similarly, Jewish life revolves around Sab-baths and Festivals and milestones in the life-cycle such as birth, coming of age, marriage and death, regardless of the extent to which they inspire devotional practices.

The Christian reader should not be surprised to find that there are numerous similarities between the festivals of Judaism and Christianity, since they share the same origins. The Jewish year is rooted in the cycle of the natural seasons and their impact on ordinary life. But, as in all festivals, there is a vast difference between the theory and reality of how they are observed.

Let us begin with the theory. The basic events are the three harvest festivals in autumn, spring and summer. They are known as Tabernacles (Sukkot), Passover (Pesach) and Pentecost (Shavuot) respectively, and are referred to as the 'pilgrim festivals' because Israelites used to make pilgrimage at these times to the Tem-ple in Jerusalem, where they would witness the priests offering sacrifices and thanking God for the bountiful harvest.

In later Judaism each of the harvests was assigned an historical significance: Tabernacles to commemorate the wandering of the Israelites during their forty years in the wilderness; Passover, their liberation from slavery in Egypt; Pentecost, the giving of the Law at Mount Sinai. The first two festivals were originally celebrated for seven days, the first and last days being especially holy on which no work was permitted; the third lasted for only one day. Because the Jews used a lunar calendar, the dates of the festivals were determined by the sighting of the new moon; and when Jews were scattered outside of Judaea, there was a system for conveying the dates of the festival from the Court in Jerusalem. But since there was concern in the Diaspora that communications could be faulty and that the holy days would not be observed properly, a day was added to each festival, so that the first two and last two days were declared Holy. Ever since, despite the invention of calendars which leave no doubt as to the occurrence of the festivals, Orthodox Jews outside Israel still do not work for four days at Tabernacles and Passover and for two days at Pentecost. This helps explain the frustration of employers and teachers of Orthodox Jews, who find they will not be at work or school for ten days for these festivals, and three more for the New Year and Day of Atonement.

On Tabernacles, traditional Jews will build a temporary *Sukkah*, the Hebrew word for 'shed', in which they will eat their meals during the festival. Perhaps this arose from the temporary shelters of field labourers away from their homes during the harvest, or from the need for temporary accommodation in Jerusalem because of the wave of pilgrims that flooded the city.

The specifications for a *Sukkah* include a roof of leaves, supported on slats or branches which have to be laid well apart so that one can see the stars at night. There is something poetic about the transiency of the shed being defined in terms of the eternity of the stars. And it is not coincidental that the autumn festival is melancholic. One of the special biblical readings is the book of Ecclesiastes, which begins with the words, 'Vanity of vanities, all is vanity... There is nothing new under the sun.'

Tabernacles is a nature festival par excellence, full of fertility symbolism. On the first day the rabbi and male members of the community will pronounce a blessing over a palm leaf (to which are tied sprigs of myrtle and willow) and a citron fruit. Adulatory psalms are sung in the synagogue while the phallic-like palm branch and citron are held in both hands and waved to the four points of the compass, as well as to the heavens and the earth, to acknowledge God's sway over the entire universe. Numerous moral interpretations are given to the citron, palm branch, myrtle and willows, but Jewish city dwellers are so remote from their agricultural origins that the fertility aspects are hardly mentioned.

Unlike Tabernacles, the historical interpretation of Passover as the birth of the Jewish nation quite overshadows its nature-festival origins. Spring festivals are celebrated by many peoples to mark the rebirth of nature after winter's death, and are rich in symbols such as eggs, new-born lambs and magical dances. In the same way at Passover a lamb was eaten as a sacrifice before the exodus from slavery; Christ became the Paschal Lamb; and at Easter, the death and rebirth of the Son of God are celebrated by all believing Christians. The analogies are numerous and fascinating but their full exploration goes beyond the purpose of this chapter.

The major symbol of Passover is unleavened bread (which became the wafers of the Christian communion), and the prohibition against eating any leavened food. The highlight of the celebration is the family gathering on Passover eve, called the *Seder*, to re-enact the experiences of their Israelite ancestors on the night of their departure from Egypt. The ingredients of the last Israelite meal in Egypt are explained: they ate unleavened bread, *Matzah*, because they had to leave in such a rush they could not wait for the dough to rise; a shank bone represents the ancient Paschal lamb; bitter herbs, such as horseradish, remind modern Jews of the bitterness of slavery; *haroseth*, a sweet mixture in which the bitter herbs are dipped, now symbolizes the earth used by the Israelites for building Egyptian royal cities.

The youngest child asks about the meaning of the night's celebration, and is told by the leader, in a ceremonial narrative over 2000 years old called the *Haggadah*, 'This is because of what the Lord did for me when I was a slave in Egypt.' The spiritual genius of the *Seder* is to link every generation to the primary experience which formed the family of Abraham into a people.

The next festival is Pentecost, which occurs fifty days after Passover and celebrates the revelation at Sinai. There is no special symbolism for this festival, but a salient feature is the reading of the biblical story of Ruth, perhaps one of the best short stories ever written. The scene is the summer harvest in Judaea. Naomi is a widow bereft of her two sons killed by a plague in Moab, the country to which her husband and she had migrated because of a drought in Bethlehem. She now returns with her Moabite daughter-in-law, Ruth, who loves her deeply. Ruth finds herself among the poor folk in Judaea, following the harvesters to pick up the sheaves and grain that they have missed, and a romance unfolds between her and the field's owner. She later marries him, bearing him a son who will be the grandfather of King David, the Sweet Singer of Israel.

In the autumn there are the High Holy Days – the New Year (*Rosh Hashana*) and the Day of Atonement (*Yom Kippur*), which concentrate on the individual's relationship to God. On New Year, all human beings are judged and sentenced by God for their behaviour during the past year. On that day, Jews begin to acknowledge and ask forgiveness for their sins. In the home, apples are eaten with honey as families pray for a good and sweet New Year.

The Day of Atonement falls just ten days later, and closes the period of repentance opened at New Year. While divine judgement was passed on *Rosh Hashana*, it is traditionally subject to appeal until the conclusion of *Yom Kippur*. The ten days are called Days of Penitence, or the Awesome Days.

Yom Kippur, which begins, like all Jewish commemorative days, in the evening and lasts through to the following nightfall, is a day of total abstinence – no food, drink, sex, washing or shaving. It is a day devoted to prayer, repentance and to resolving to improve one's life. Traditionally the eve and the whole day, from morning until the sighting of three stars, will be spent in the synagogue, awaiting God's forgiveness and for a reprieve of the evil decree passed in heaven which could ruin one's life or cut it short in the coming year, perhaps through disease, famine or war.

Immediately following *Rosh Hashana* and *Yom Kippur* in the autumn comes the Feast of Tabernacles. Scholars assume that Tabernacles was the major festival of the year, and that the solemn days before it were break-away festivals to give individuals the opportunity to look after their personal needs, rather those of an agricultural community or an historic people. Another spin-off of this grand harvest festival was the holiday known as 'The Rejoicing in the Torah', which falls on the day after the end of Tabernacles. This was introduced to celebrate the reading of the final chapter of the book of Deuteronomy, the fifth book of Moses, in the annual cycle of reading the Torah. It is celebrated by parading the scrolls of the Torah in synagogue: enthusiasts even dance with the scrolls in their arms. On the morning of this festival, the concluding paragraphs from Deuteronomy describing the death of Moses are read from one handwritten parchment scroll, followed by the reading from Genesis of the story of creation from a second scroll. Two members of each synagogue are honoured by being called to read, or say the blessings over, the two readings. They are known as the Bridegroom of the Torah and the Bridegroom of Genesis, symbolizing the belief that Jews are wedded to the Torah, their Sacred Book. And indeed, the joy in this celebration evokes a wedding. Sweets are distributed to children along with paper flags, sometimes with apples stuck to their wooden sticks.

Two other festivals require mentioning, although they are not prescribed in the Torah. One of them, *Purim*, whose historical context is in the biblical book of Esther, celebrates the victory of the Jews in Persia against the villain Haman who planned their destruction. A Jew, Mordecai, and his cousin Esther, who became the Persian queen, were able to foil the plot, and to mark their salvation, Jews were commanded to exchange gifts and to be merry. Today, on the eve and morning of *Purim*, which means 'Lots' – as Haman used this method to determine the day on which to mount his attack on his Jewish victims – they read the book of Esther and deafen the synagogue with rattles or noise makers every time the name of Haman is mentioned.

A second festival, which is not mentioned in the Bible, is referred to in the Apocrypha in Maccabees: it is the festival of *Chanukkah*, which commemorates the successful rebellion, led by the priestly family of the Hasmoneans, against their Hellenist ruler in 165 BCE. The uprising reached its climax in the reconquest of the Jerusalem Temple and its cleansing of pagan worship. The event is celebrated around the winter solstice, and the ceremony is based on the legend that a cruse of sanctified oil, which should have kept the eternal light kindled for only one day, miraculously lasted for eight.

Beginning with the kindling of one wick or candle on the first evening and increasing this daily, Jews celebrate *Chanukkah* for eight days. It is also called the Festival of Lights; and since Jewish dates are determined by the lunar calendar, it rarely coincides with Christmas. Although this festival is post-biblical and relatively minor in comparison with the High Holy days and the Three Pilgrim Festivals, its proximity to Christmas has increased its importance in those countries where Christianity is the dominant culture. The seductive quality of the exchange of presents, Christmas trees and decorations has led Jews to make *Chanukkah* an imitation of Christmas, as a major opportunity for exchanging gifts and jollification. The celebration of *Chanukkah*, like *Purim*, has no restrictions regarding work or school attendance.

The coincidence of Christmas and *Chanukkah*, and the way both are celebrated with lights at a time of year when the days are very short and the nights long, makes one feel that both hark back to an age when people were terrified that the earth would ultimately descend into total darkness. Perhaps they thought that through magical means, such as kindling lights, they could influence the natural forces and bring light back to the world. Christmas is still called 'Yuletide' because at this season a wheel of tapers was rolled down mountains in primitive Europe. The timing of major religious events was originally tied to nature festivals, which had a universal following, in order to guarantee their observance. It made little material difference to the worshipper when Jesus was actually born or died, or when the Israelites really left Egypt or defeated their Hellenist overlords. What mattered was that the spiritual messages they bore should be celebrated, and if harnessing them to primitive customs was the best way for achieving this, so be it. To those who believe in the importance of belief over literal chronology, and who value truth over blind faith, the convenient dating of religious festivals will appear an additional element of interest. Such aspects may have little obvious impact on the lives of the average Jew, but the moral and ethical aspects of the festivals should not be neglected.

Religious festivals seek to reveal the nature of God's relationship to humanity, and especially to those who worship Him. For Jews, the Passover is a celebration of freedom and the use of human freedom in the service of God. Pharaoh was commanded to free the Israelites, 'so that they may serve Me'. This concept of freedom implies that every Israelite is equal as well as free. His only master and king is God. The Exodus from Egypt is given as one of the two reasons for the commandment to devote one day a week – the Sabbath – to utter freedom, when employers and employees are equal, neither working nor being a slave to their labours or material ambitions.

The main ethical concept in Tabernacles is the virtue of humility. Life is transient; men are flesh and blood, frail and subject to death. Only by linking oneself to God's purpose can one achieve a life of lasting worth – immortality. Tabernacles was meant to teach Jews to view life in the perspective of eternity.

Pentecost – the time of the Giving of the Law – teaches that without the moral law there would be chaos in human society, just as there would be in the cosmos without natural law. Human freedom requires the law as its guarantor.

The High Holy Days – the New Year and the Day of Atonement – bear the overall ethical message that all humans have the obligation to develop their own lives without harming others. Because of the human weaknesses of greed and lust, they are in danger of harming each other and themselves, but because they are 'little lower than the angels', they have the strength to repent and to improve their lives. In this way they achieve forgiveness from God and a new beginning to life. It is a simple message, but it is the basis of Jewish and of all religious truth.

In describing the Jewish holy days I have omitted some commemorative fast days, the modern celebration of Israeli Independence and the commemoration of the Holocaust. Outside Israel these are for the most part ordinary workdays and would not make any impact on non-Jews.

Although I felt it would be useful to outline the ordained festivals and how they are practised, Judaism – like Christianity or Islam in a secular age – is observed more in the breach, 90 per cent of Jews ignoring most holidays or giving them the minimum of observance. For example, on *Yom Kippur*, the holiest day of the Jewish year, every religiously identifiable Jew will attend synagogue (although at least 10 per cent of people who maintain their Jewish identity will not even do that), but the majority will leave after the morning service, perhaps to return for the memorial service in the late afternoon. Many will not fast, arguing that that would be taking religion too far, or because it would give them a headache.

Strictly observant Jews will take a day off from work or close their businesses on biblically ordained festivals. But the others might miss out on a festival because it does not appear in their diaries and they have no observant Jewish friends to draw it to their attention. Orthodox Jews will obviously have trouble in obtaining employment if they feel required to stay away on so many Sabbaths and holy days, as well as periods of bereavement, especially if they have to leave work hours before sunset on short winter days in order to be home on time. The Sabbath Observance Employment Bureau was established in Britain to place such individuals, usually with Jewish employers. Also, Jews with recognized professional skills will be able to determine their own schedule, as it is the quality of their work and their achievements which are valued rather than the number of days they clock in.

Jews living in a secular society may also observe Holy Days as social events, for family gatherings. Jews who never attend synagogue except to celebrate a Bar Mitzvah or wedding will gladly accept invitations to the Passover Seder or a *Rosh Hashanah* family lunch. Jews who do not fast on *Yom Kippur* will still join their families for a break-the-fast party at its conclusion.

While religious people might disdain the merely social acknowledgement of the festivals, we should remember that in earlier times, when there was no division between religious and secular life, the chief function of holy days, feasts and festivals in all cultures was to create and reinforce bonds between families and the community, as both thanked the gods for favours and sought to urge nature to smile on them. Jews still celebrate their festivals to a lesser or greater degree, and, to the extent that they have assimilated to non-Jewish culture, may even celebrate the social aspects of the Christian holy days that have become public holidays. A few Jewish families in the Christian Diaspora have a Christmas lunch, turkey and all. Some may even have a discreet Christmas tree to please their children, or exchange gifts on Christmas day. But this does not mean they have given up their Jewish roots; only that the branches of their neighbour's tree are hanging over their garden.

The continued identification of Jews with their culture will depend on the way religious observances have an impact on their lives. Those with a large quantity of observances are perhaps more likely to pass on their traditions and faith to future generations. Those with fewer observances will doubtless find that their culture is like a tree: the death of the branches and the lack of leaves or fruit is the surest indication that the trunk and the roots have also died.

29 Jews and Jesus

'If Jesus was a Jew, why won't Jews
believe in him?'

'Why don't you Jews believe in Jesus?' is a question which has been asked of me many times. My first reaction as a child to this enquiry was shock. How could I believe in someone who over the centuries had become the bane of my people's existence? Christian-based anti-Semitism did not leave me untouched. Many civilized readers may not know that the most common anti-Semitic remarks hurled at Jews is that they are 'Christ Killers'.

As children we could dismiss this accusation as nonsense, because we certainly had nothing to do with his death, and even if some of our ancestors had had a hand in it, they were of a kind that every nation has; and of course we all knew that without the crucifix there would have been no Christianity, so perhaps felt that we should be thanked rather than beaten up. When I became a rabbi, a beloved and now departed colleague of mine, Sholom Singer, raised a chuckle when he related the advice he gave to a mother who complained that her son was called a Christ Killer by his schoolmates. 'Tell him to say, "We meant well".'

Still, the verbal abuse and physical punch-ups did not make Jews very sympathetic to Jesus. Those Jews who were spared anti-Semitic outbursts were aware of its history. While Christian children took delight in the heroism of the Crusaders, Jewish children learned that during the Crusades thousands of their ancestors had been killed throughout Europe by knights on their way to the Holy Land, with the cry, 'Kill a Jew and save your soul.'

Considered dispassionately, the fact that Jews have suffered mercilessly at the hands of Christians is past history, and ideas and individuals should be judged on the basis of truth and present behaviour. But most Jews are not so forgiving, and for them the crucifix has become as much the symbol of their persecution as for Christians it is the sign of their salvation. For this reason, leaders of the Jewish community are particularly resentful of the Evangelical mission directed towards its members. They are appalled by this insensitivity. They maintain, 'We Jews have suffered so much at Christian hands to maintain our Jewish faith, and our persecutors' descendants now want us to betray the faith for which our ancestors died, and to accept Jesus as our saviour.'

In spite of this natural reaction, over the centuries many Jews have converted to Christianity. Even today there are many who do, most notably the 'Jews for Jesus' movement. Among many of the others who retain their Jewish loyalty there must also be the buried feeling, 'Wouldn't it have been better if we could have believed in Jesus; after all, he was one of our own.'

The worship that Jesus inspired in so many millions of people is surely a point in his favour. Also, during Christmas in Christian countries it would be nice to be a believer, not only because of the presents, but because the 'whole world' is aglow with lights and full of talk of love and good will to all men. The Christian carols are so beautiful, and many Jewish children, had they been able to believe, would have joined their classmates in their warm camaraderie rather than suffer the sense of exclusion.

Yes, it would be better to be on the winning side; but religiously and intellectually it is just not possible! Jews, even discounting their persecution in the name of Jesus, cannot believe in him as their Messiah. They could not *en masse* accept Jesus, because the advent of the Messiah, 'anointed King', was believed to bring the restoration of Jewish independence under a scion of the House of David, and he would rid the Judaean hills of the tyranny of Rome. This is something that Jesus had not done, and the Roman executioners mocked him and his disciples for his failure by putting the words 'King of the Jews' on the cross. Jews still believe that a Messianic Age will inaugurate the Kingdom of God on earth.

In addition, much as many Jews would be delighted to accept Jesus in order to be at one with their neighbours, the concept of a suffering Messiah is alien to the mainstream of Judaism and would require a conversion of the type which Paul encountered on the road to Damascus.

Beyond these difficulties, classic Christianity demands more than the belief that Jesus was simply the Messiah. He is part of the Trinity of God, and one cannot remain Jewish and believe in a God the Father, who sent his son, begotten of a virgin, to redeem the world through his suffering. This change from the perception of Jesus as the slain Messiah to Christ, the Son of God, has made faith in him by Jews quite impossible. Jews may be atheistic and still retain their Jewish identity, but to believe in the Trinity means rejecting the foundation stone of Jewish history – the faith in one invisible God. It is for this reason that the secular Israeli Supreme Court recently rejected the application of Father Daniel, a Jew who had converted to Christianity, to be admitted to Israel as an Israeli citizen under the Law of Return.

Jews can, of course, appreciate Jesus without worshipping him as the Son of God or accepting him as their saviour. No open-minded Jew would want to deny the charisma of Jesus, the teacher and preacher. He shared in the oratorical gifts of the prophets and the homiletic genius of the great rabbinic masters. But what made him unique and different from both the prophets and the rabbis was that for his followers he spoke 'not like the Pharisees but as one with authority'. Mainstream Judaism always believed in the continuity of authority. The prophets spoke in the name of God. The Rabbinic Masters spoke in the name of received tradition. What made Jesus so powerful a religious figure for his disciples was the very factor which precluded him from an established place in Jewish institutional life.

This scepticism did not prevent Jews from savouring and studying the poetry of the parables, which is easy to compare with the recorded wisdom of the ancient rabbis. No one will deny the appealing mystery of the many oracular utterances of Jesus. Jews, like Christians, can beneficially spend hours seeking the secret meaning of statements such as 'to him who has, shall be given more, and from he who has not, it shall be taken away'. What will also appeal to the liberal tendencies of thinking Jews is the prophetic ring to the verse, 'a man is not defiled by what goes into his mouth but what comes of it'.

The force of these arguments may persuade Christians not to expect Jews to worship Jesus. Many may still feel it churlish of them not to give him some place of respect in their hall of heroes. There are some Jews who would feel happier if their tradition could acknowledge Jesus as a prophet or great rabbi. But this too is not possible since the Rabbinic Masters, when establishing which books were to be included in the Bible, had determined the end of the Prophetic Era, and this predated the rabbinic period in which Jesus lived by several centuries. Also, the judicial privileges and responsibilities which the title of rabbi implied were handed down by a laying on of hands by a Rabbinic Master on his deserving disciple. Jesus did not fall into this category. All that Jews could honestly do was to make of Jesus an Honorary Prophet or Rabbi.

But even were it possible to find a place for Jesus in the Jewish tradition, as have the Bahai and Islam, it would not be desirable for the mass of Christians. The essence of Christianity is that Jesus offers a new revelation and promise of eternal salvation, and any attempt by Jews to find a place for him within their existing structure would risk offending believing Christians, and would certainly confuse Jews whose identification with their community is based on historical bonds in which neither Jesus nor Christianity played a positive role.

On the other hand, the success of the Ecumenical movement of Christians and Jews has led to greater understanding between the two faiths. Councils and societies of Christians and Jews have been organized throughout the Western world. Meetings and journals reflecting the views of scholars and clergymen explore differences and similarities between the two religions. As a result, Christians are examining the Jewish roots of their faith and removing those vestiges in their teachings and prayers which have nurtured the cancerous growth of anti-Semitism.

While this is happening on the Christian side, Jews should seek to overcome their prejudice against Jesus and Christianity based on generations of persecution in his name. They should read what he has to say and seek a clearer understanding of his personality and message; Jews must attempt to grasp why the faith that was created around the life and death of Jesus continues to shape the world in which they live.

For their part, Christians, and particularly Evangelists, should recognize that acquiring an appreciation of Jesus is not an easy task for Jews, and the difficulty is in large measure due to the nature of Christianity itself, for in making its Saviour into a God, it became almost impossible for Jews to relate to him even as a man.

THE JEWISH MESSIAH...

30 The Jewish Messiah

'When will the Jewish Messiah come?'

'Messiah' is the transliteration of the Hebrew word meaning 'anointed'. Jewish prayers for an 'Anointed One' are rooted in the ancient longing of the defeated Israelites for the restoration of national sovereignty under a descendant of King David. The Anointed One would rebuild the Temple in Jerusalem and sacrifices would be offered again to Yahweh, God of the Jews.

The coming of an 'Anointed son of David' would be so miraculous that it would be akin to a second liberation from Egyptian slavery. Jews who celebrate the Passover – the feast of redemption – in the countries of their dispersion imagine the new Exodus to be followed by a period of independence and benign rule, when Jews would once again be filled with pride and sanctity.

Even today when Jews celebrate that Egyptian Exodus on the eve of Passover, the story is told of four Rabbinic Masters who on one Passover eve under Roman oppression in about 135 CE, spent the whole night expounding the biblical texts regarding the Exodus, until their disciples came to call them for morning prayers. Since the Passover is always celebrated with families and friends, and not with colleagues, it is surmised that the Masters were using the feast as a cover for plotting against Imperial Rome. One of them, the great Akiba, was later to be martyred for his part in a great rebellion whose leader, Bar Cochba, Akiba believed to be the Anointed One, destined to defeat the Romans. But this revolution was quashed, as were the others before.

When Romans ended Jewish self-rule, faith in a messiah was the only source of hope, and it is not surprising that Jews flocked to the charismatic Jesus, or that when he failed to fulfil their messianic hopes, the Romans mocked them by emblazoning over his cross: 'King of the Jews'.

Yet Jesus was neither the first nor the last of the 'messiahs' who, although they started with large followings, did not meet Jewish expectations. Bar Cochba followed, but even his failure did not remove the need for a messiah. Christians were unmoved by the failure of their messiah to save the world from oppression and war, because they believed him to be Son of God and their personal redeemer. Also, since the Christian Church wielded great temporal as well as religious power, the need for a messiah in the Jewish mould was less immediate. Jews, however, continued to look to a messiah to bring them redemption. For this reason, the need for an Anointed One was especially felt during periods of despair. When a need becomes desperate, the human mind may create its own reality. Like the mirage of water to the desert wanderer dying of thirst, Jews created messiahs to quench their thirst for salvation, and generated the belief that the messiah had already come.

The most extreme example of this phenomenon was the appearance of a false messiah (who warrants an entry in the *Encyclopedia Britannica*) called Sabbatai Zebi, who was born in Turkey in 1626. An ecstatic mystic, he enjoyed an enormous following; in 1648 he declared himself the messiah, and achieved almost total support. By 1666, the year predicted by some Christians to be the beginning of the millennium, Sabbatai was hailed by Jews throughout the world as 'King of the Jews'. Whole communities in Europe and the Turkish Empire packed their bags in anticipation of their triumphal return to Zion. But this messianic hope collapsed when he was arrested by the Turkish Sultan and persuaded to convert to Islam.

Another famous charlatan was Jakob Frank from Galicia, who declared himself the messiah in 1751 and also attracted a large following. Many believed that he was the reincarnation of Sabbatai Zebi because he announced that there was a higher 'Torah' which released God's élite from obeying the words of the worldly Torah. This was a pretext for his followers to engage in sexual orgies, but he still won the protection of Roman Catholic authorities who favoured his sect as anti-Talmudic and thus ripe for conversion to Christianity. Their prediction proved correct, and he and his disciples did finally convert to Christianity.

Jewish beliefs about the messiah have developed throughout history and have become confused in folk culture with the End of Days and the faith in bodily resurrection. What began as a political desire for the return of a Davidic head of a Jewish State soon became a vision of a supernatural messiah-king who would lead all Jews, living and dead, to a Jerusalem rebuilt and restored.

But this is a fantasy which most Jews have not been able to sustain. When Jews express their longing for a messiah, they are mostly now expressing their hope for a time when Jews will enjoy independence and security, and when the whole world will conform to God's moral laws. This has become the theology of Progressive Judaism, although there are Orthodox Jews who see the establishment of the State of Israel as the beginning of the messianic days.

In recent years, however, a messianic movement has again begun to revolve around the person of Rabbi Schneerson, the head of the mostly American Lubavitch movement. In 1991 some 50,000 of his disciples predicted that the identity of the messiah would be revealed on the Jewish New Year. When asked whether it would be their own revered rabbi, they responded that he had all the qualities required of a messiah. The fact that he had advised his followers living in Israel not to leave during the Gulf War because Iraqi scuds would never harm them was cited as an example of his prophetic powers. Yet the Jewish New Year passed and there was no revelation of any messiah.

The pessimism, or realism, of Jews when faced with the question of a Jewish messiah is revealed in an engaging story:

A rich American Jewish manufacturer before the Second World War decided to pay a pilgrimage to the Polish village where he had been born but which he had left as an infant. On arrival at the train station he was given directions and began to walk the few miles to his village. At a crossroads he saw a man sitting on a stool, and approached him to ask the way. The man pointed to a cluster of houses nestling below a hill about a mile away, and it soon became apparent that he too was Jewish and that he was a native of the rich Jew's birthplace. They exchanged pleasantries. When asked why he happened to be sitting on a stool at the crossroad, he replied that it was his job to wait for the messiah. When he came, he would run ahead and inform the villagers. 'And how much are you paid to do this job?' A minuscule amount, was the reply. 'I will pay you a hundred times that amount if you agree to work for me.' 'Ah,' came the immediate response, 'but could you offer me such job security?'

Realistic or not, the image of a messiah is still powerful in Jewish life. On Passover Eve, many Jewish families sing of the advent of Elijah the Prophet, the messiah's precursor. The song concludes, 'Even though he tarry, yet I believe with a complete faith in the coming of the messiah.' Those who are close to Jews will realize that this is a religious poetic image. Intellectually pressed, Jews would admit that they could not accept, in a free and democratic age, the possibility of one person, human or supernatural, appearing to impose his benign will on the Jewish people. The time for kings – even 'messiah-kings' – is over. Human fulfilment will be attained by earlier prophetic visions, according to which God will be the only king, and no man will rule over another. The elected leaders would be those who could be trusted to judge honestly between one human and another so that each could pursue their own salvation without interference.

This hope is deeply embedded in Jewish lore and tradition, and the personal messiah has become its symbol. I would give the final word to Samuel, who led one of the talmudic academies in Babylonia at the beginning of the third century. He stated that the only difference between the times in which he lived and the Messianic Age would be the end of subjugation and the right to enjoy freedom. While he limited his observation to the Jewish people, in the interdependent world in which we live the full liberty of each and every individual and nation to fulfil their human and divine potential still remains a truly Messianic vision, not only for Jews but for members of all religious faiths.

Every Israelite, the Jewish Mystics teach, has the spark of the Messiah in him; and because of this, he is fitted to become a co-worker in the holy task of establishing the reign of righteousness on earth. 'No duty is more sacred,' said Rabbi Nachman of Bratzlav, 'than for man to cherish that spark of the Messiah in his soul, and save it from extinction.'

A Book of Jewish Thoughts, J. H. Hertz

THE CHOSEN PEOPLE . . .

31 Jews – The Chosen People?

'Why do Jews think they are chosen?'

Since early childhood, I remember the prayer said before reading the Sacred Scroll, 'Blessed are you, Lord, who has chosen us from among the nations to give us his Torah.' As a child of immigrant parents from Jerusalem living in a declining neighbourhood of Philadelphia, I felt anything but chosen. Nor did my parents, who were Orthodox practising Jews, ever lead me to believe that we had been chosen. We certainly were different. Our lives were organized around Jewish learning and observance, and all my parents' relations and friends shared the same value system. It was assumed that none of us would ever achieve the American dream of fame and fortune, primarily because it was not our dream.

What helped to raise my morale in these poor circumstances was that I was Jewish and believed I could trace my ancestry back to Abraham. I was still living the way God had commanded the first Jews. I never felt that I was better because I was Jewish, but I did feel that, for whatever reason, I was special to God.

The meaning of chosenness changed for me over the years. When I studied and experienced the persecution of the Jews, I felt that we had perhaps been chosen to suffer, or that it was because we suffered so much that we were chosen. These two feelings coalesced into the conviction that it made no sense to suffer so much unless there was a reason – a purpose which is the meaning of chosenness.

I began this discussion by giving my own reaction to the question of chosenness, because it is the only place to start thinking about a subject which is not about theory, but about emotions, which are by their very nature personal. I can only answer the question from my own perspective. I cannot answer for Judaism or for any other Jew, nor can anyone answer for me.

There are pockets of ultra-Orthodox Jews who feel superior to any other people; they are like Seventh-day Adventists or Jehovah's Witnesses, who believe that they have an exclusive truth. The majority of Jews brought up in Israel or in Western communities recoil at the very idea of chosenness. It goes against the democratic spirit, the desire for universality, and it tastes too much of racism. If Hitler made the concept of Aryanism detestable, he also made any exclusivist interpretation of Jewish chosenness questionable.

Yet Jews are the People of the Book, and the Bible makes it clear that God did indeed choose the ancestors of modern Jews and give their lives a purpose. Those Jews who still want a Jewish dimension in their lives will have to relate to the meaning of chosenness and find an interpretation which will be morally acceptable and emotionally satisfying. This is not as difficult as it appears. The original biblical verses describing Abraham's chosenness are helpful and worth quoting in full.

Now Yahweh said to Abram, 'Get you out from your country, and from your Kinsmen, and from your father's house to the land which I will direct you. And I will make of you a great nation and I will bless you and make your name great and you will be a source of blessings. And I will bless them that bless you and him that curses you, will I curse and through you shall all the families of the earth be blessed.' (Genesis 12:1–3)

As most people are not believers, it is best to ignore the claim that it was a divine command which motivated Abraham. It is better to look at his journey in a human psychological context. Abraham abhors the culture in which he was raised, and believes that the only way to change his life is to start anew in a new and unknown land.

In the age of Abraham the sense of divinity was all-pervasive. In a pre-scientific age such as the one in which he lived, every tree and brook was inhabited by a god, and every inspiration and driving impulse appeared to be the power of a god flying on wings. In such a world it would have been incredible for him to decide to turn his back on family and land without believing it to be the result of a divine command. To discard his past and to build an uncertain future required the conviction that he was in the company of a protecting as well as a directing God. Is this not a meaning of chosenness ?

The risks that Abraham took in going to a strange and hostile country were enormous. The rewards would consequently have to be more than transient wealth and power. His ambition was a vision of descendants as numerous as the stars of the heaven and the sands of the seashore, who would be loyal to his own god and give his name eternal life. This, it seems to me, is, no more but also no less, the meaning of 'chosenness' for the Seed of Abraham.

And because among his descendants there were sufficient heroes who believed that God had spoken to Abraham, they carried this relationship forward into the history of their people. Every momentous event, tragedy or victory, every moral inspiration was perceived as a further revelation of that ancient encounter with God. So God and the Jews kept meeting each other. Every religious genius who met Him – prophets or kings – believed they were discovering God just as their ancestors had, and that the demands God made of them were not for their personal benefit but for the sake of His people.

This is the essence of Jewish chosenness, the collective faith of a people in the God of its ancestors. In this, as in all relationships, there were mutual obligations, and this was the Covenant between the two. The Jews would obey, and God would be their protector.

The understanding of chosenness changed over the ages. Individuals and generations of Jews had different concepts of its meaning, depending on their personal inclinations and social circumstances. Deutero-Isaiah saw the rejected prophet as God's suffering servant through whose afflictions others are healed. Jewish readers of the Suffering Servant passages may perceive them as a description of the role of the Jew in history, just as Christians will read in it the description of the Christ who died for their sins.

As one can see, therefore, the image of God as well as of chosenness can change.

God ceases to be the protector of Israel's physical well-being, and allows his people to become the unpopular bearer of his truth. The God who redeemed Israel from Egyptian bondage appears different from the God who did not prevent His Temple from being destroyed by Nebuchadnezzar, or his people from being exiled to Babylonia. Equally, the Israelites who sang a poem of Praise to God after their salvation after the splitting of the Red Sea did not feel the despondency of their conquered descendants who wept by the rivers of Babylon as they were driven into exile.

Two things, however, are consistent. Firstly, that having a special relationship to God did *not* make the Jews better people. It only increased their responsibilities. Secondly, they did not consider it mandatory to conquer the world in God's name. Only once in its history did a Jewish king forcibly convert a vassal kingdom (Idumaea) to Judaism. The prophets were satisfied that each people should walk in the name of their own God, even though the Jews had a clear vision of their own Jewish God as King of Kings, leading the way, and of his teachers giving instruction from his Holy Mountain in Jerusalem. All peoples who lived by civilized standards would enjoy God's grace. The prophet Jonah was sent to the non-Israelite city of Nineveh to appeal to them to turn from their evil ways. It is this prophetic message which is read on the Jewish Day of Atonement, the holiest day in its calendar.

Chosenness is the sense of feeling special, and people will interpret this concept according to their own psychological needs. It would not be remarkable, therefore, if a persecuted people were to bolster its morale by deciding that chosenness meant that they were in fact better than their persecutors. This would be a natural defence mechanism, and I am sure that there were many times in their history when Jews took comfort in the prophetic passage which asserts that, because God loves Israel, He punishes her. This kind of cold comfort should not be an excuse for the accusation that Jews consider themselves to be a superior race. The opposite is revealed by the races encompassed by the Jewish people – black Jews from Ethiopia, almost black Jews from Yemen, as well as blond blue-eyed Jews from Europe, are among the many racial types living in the State of Israel.

Of course there are some Jews who interpret chosenness in this arrogant manner, but I am sure that they are no more numerous than British, French, American or Japanese people who feel a sense of superiority which they may excuse as national pride. Some might feel that it is arrogant for a people to believe that it had a special role to play in history or that God had designated a special land for it. But this is not a reasonable charge. Most nations and individuals who spur themselves on to great achievements do so with a sense of purpose and a belief in the call to excel. Modesty in this regard is the justification for the non-achiever. The quality which makes a belief in chosenness or specialness tolerable is the realization that so much of human creativity is due to God-given talents as well as determination and hard work.

As to the Promised Land, every migrating people who have conquered the land which was to become their final home have felt that their gods supported their conquest. What makes Israel different is that the belief in that promise was recorded, while the histories of other peoples were either never written or lost.

What I have found interesting in my many discussions of Jewish chosenness is that most Jews are appalled by the idea, while many non-Jews have adopted and accept it at face value. Christians will at the very least believe that Jews were at one time the Chosen People, and that their chosenness was passed on to the Community of Christ.

Most sensible people, I think, would be prepared to understand the emotions which led the Liberal Jewish theologian, Leo Baeck, to put the whole matter in the following way: 'Every people can be chosen for a history ... but more history has been assigned to this people [Israel] than to any other people.' The romance of sharing in the fate of so ancient a people has made various other groups claim descent from the Ten Lost Tribes of Israel. Indeed, there is a similar romance for some about belonging to the Tribes that have *not* been lost. The large numbers of converts to Judaism over the centuries do indicate some inexplicable attraction which goes perhaps even beyond religious faith.

The fact that Jews have arguably survived longer, contributed more, suffered more and remembered more than most other peoples, should be understood and not held against them. And if 'chosenness' inspires some of them to seek to reach greater moral heights, they should be praised rather than condemned. In this attempt, as in the efforts of all good people, all humans are the beneficiaries.

Now therefore, if you will obey my voice and keep my covenant, you shall be my own possession among all peoples; for all the earth is mine, and you shall be to me a kingdom of priests and a holy nation.

Bible, Exodus 19

I am Yahweh, I have called you in righteousness,
I have taken you by the hand and kept you;
I have given you as a covenant to the people,
a light to the nations.

Bible, Isaiah 42

You only have I known of all the families of the earth; therefore will I visit upon you all your iniquities.

Bible, Amos 3

Are ye not as the children of the Ethiopians unto Me, O children of Israel? saith the Lord.

Bible, Amos 9

How odd of God to choose the Jews
It's not so odd the Jews chose God.

Anonymous

32 Jewish Ethics

'If I am only for myself, what am I?'

Many people assume that what is good and what is wicked are incontestably agreed, and that in essence the moral code of one religion does not differ from that of any other. In the West, the person in the street tends to consider the Ten Commandments, or those of them that they remember, to be the basic norms of behaviour whether one is Jewish, Christian, Muslim, Hindu or Sikh. It will also be assumed that, despite the binding nature of the Ten Commandments, there are no sanctions against those who do not obey them, with the exception of murder and theft. For instance, the seventh commandment, against adultery, has been broken by royalty, prime ministers and presidents – as well as rabbis and priests – with impunity; while the tenth commandment, against covetousness, would today be dismissed from the outset as totally unrealistic in the light of current attitudes towards the desire to 'better' one's neighbour.

Generally, ethics is considered to reflect the world of 'what should be' and not the 'real' world. We in the Western world may tend to raise our children to be good, teach them to respect each other and to share their toys, and that their goodness will be rewarded. Yet ironically, when some of the more sensitive among them become young adults and continue to believe in a fairer distribution of wealth, and the need to fight world tyranny, we consider them 'idealists' and look forward to the passing of a phase we like to regard as 'immature'.

For the most part, Jews are no different from others in this respect. There are, of course, decent individuals who lead their lives according to a consistent moral code. But what is there to be said about the specific character of Jewish ethics? The practice, with few exceptions, is indistinguishable from that of non-Jews, all of whom can be seen to obey or disobey the law of the land and suffer the consequences of transgression to a similar degree. Significantly, however, the theory of Jewish ethics does make a difference to Jewish life, as it is a foundation to Jewish attitudes to life, even though it is buried deep in the unconscious, and remains invisible even to those whose lives are influenced by it.

'Old Testament' morality, to use a Christian concept, is the basis of modern Jewish ethics and values. It posits a God who rewards the good and punishes the wicked. The biblical ancestors of the Jews believed in this God and took the promise of prosperity to the righteous and the threat of drought, disease and defeat of the wicked very seriously. Accordingly, the book of Proverbs expresses no more than the common faith of the day when it says, 'The lips of the righteous feed many, but fools die for lack of sense. The blessing of Yahweh makes rich, and he adds no sorrow to it... What the wicked dreads will come upon him, but the desire of the righteous will be granted' (Proverbs 10:21–2, 24). Jews living in biblical days clearly believed that the righteous were clever, and the wicked foolish – the reverse of our own more heartless times, when the kind man is seen as naive and the ruthless as clever.

Rewards and punishments were believed to be dispensed in this life and not saved up for some future existence. The agreement between Yahweh and the descendants of Abraham to protect them was dependent on their obedience to His law. If they strayed from it, they would be punished. The laws were all-embracing, but they did have one general aim, expressed most succinctly by Jacob Licht in an article on biblical ethics in the *Encyclopedia Judaica*: 'The Bible requires nothing other than the proper behaviour which is necessary for the existence of society.' In ancient days, the Tribes of Israel believed that it was God who brought destruction on wicked communities. Even today, most people believe that the seeds of self-destruction are to be found in every evil society, and that no tyranny can last for ever. This philosophy results in a sense of collective responsibility, in which one sees peer pressure exerted on individuals to deal honestly with their fellow citizens and to care for the poor and dependent of society.

Compassion for the disadvantaged was never viewed as a merely idealistic option: it was, and is, essential if society is to function effectively. A large dissatisfied element in any community would weaken it in the face of calamity such as famine or war. Charity used to be, and remains, a pragmatic way of preventing civil unrest, and the verses in Deuteronomy, Chapter 15: 7–11 make this objective of lending money, free of interest, abundantly clear. It advises the well-to-do not to fear the cancellation of all debts on the Sabbatical year to the extent that they refuse to make loans when the Sabbatical is approaching.

> If there is among you a poor man, one of your brothers in any of your towns within your land which Yahweh your God gives you, you shall not harden your heart or shut your hand against your poor brother, but you shall open your hand to him and lend him sufficient for his need, whatever it may be. Take heed lest there be a base thought in your heart, and you say, 'The seventh year, the year of release is near,' and your eye be hostile to your poor brother, and you give him nothing, and he cry to Yahweh against you, and it be sin in you. You shall give to him freely, and your heart shall not be grudging when you give to him; because for this Yahweh your God will bless you in all your work and in all that you undertake. For the poor will never cease out of the land; therefore I command you, You shall open wide your hand to your brother, to the needy and to the poor, in the land.

The text accepts that the 'poor will never cease out of the land', and recognizes how necessary it is to give relief to those without means. Significantly, when the rabbinic master Hillel discovered that the rich would not lend to the poor as the Sabbatical year approached, he took the extreme step of annulling the release of debt on the Sabbatical year.

It is also true that many Christians, even Jews, are unaware that the command to love your neighbour as yourself appears in the Hebrew Bible, Leviticus, Chapter 19:18. Has anyone realized that when Jesus said, 'You have heard that it was said, love your neighbour and hate your enemy, but I say to you love your enemies' (Matthew 5:43–4) he was misquoting Leviticus. Nowhere does the Bible or Jewish Law say, 'Hate your enemy'; on the contrary the biblical command is clearly to love one's enemy, as one can see from the verses preceding the command:

> You shall not hate your brother in your heart, but you shall reason with your neighbour, lest you bear sin because of him. You shall not take vengeance or bear any grudge against the sons of your own people, but you shall love your neighbour as yourself: I am Yahweh.

It is apparent that the 'neighbour' that the Israelites were to reason with, lest they 'bear sin because of him', as well as the 'brother' they were not to hate and the 'sons of your own people' against whom they were 'not to take vengeance or bear a grudge' was their personal enemy. How else can you describe someone whom you hate and against whom you plot vengeance? It is this enemy neighbour whom the Israelite is instructed to love as himself.

The command to love your enemy (and this command has been, rightly I think, interpreted to mean 'that which belongs to your enemy') is not a generalization to be ignored. Some implications of this order are given in Exodus 23:4–5:

> If you meet your enemy's ox or his ass going astray, you shall bring it back to him. If you see the ass of one who hates you lying under its burden, you shall refrain from leaving him with it, you shall help him to lift it up.

This was both an ethical and pragmatic command. Hatred and vengeance weaken communities as they tear families apart. St Luke recognized as much when he said, 'A house divided; it will not stand.' Abraham Lincoln quoted him in modern times in arguing to preserve the American Union: 'A house divided against itself cannot stand,' he said. 'A chain', as either of these might have said, 'is as strong as its weakest link.'

Collective responsibility and rewards and punishments are the foundation of biblical morality. But as I have mentioned elsewhere, the 'collective' was limited to the society in which one lived, and did not apply to foreigners. What may be unique about the law of the Israelites is that they were also commanded to 'love the stranger as yourself' (Leviticus 19:33). Citizens and strangers living in Israel were to be treated equally:

> You shall not oppress a hired servant who is poor and needy, whether he is one of your brothers or one of the sojourners who are in your land within your towns. (Deuteronomy 24:14)

What strikes the modern mind, however, is the unfairness of the way in which righteous individuals suffer merely for being part of an evil community. This sense of injustice led to a remarkable confrontation between Abraham and God, when it was announced that the twin cities of sin were to be destroyed:

Then Abraham drew near, and said, 'Will you indeed destroy the righteous with the wicked? Suppose there are fifty righteous within the city; will you then destroy the place and not spare it for the fifty righteous who are in it? Far be it from you to do such a thing, to slay the righteous with the wicked, so that the righteous fare as the wicked! Far be that from you! Shall not the Judge of all the earth do right?' And Yahweh said, 'If I find at Sodom fifty righteous in the city, I will spare the whole place for their sake.' Abraham answered, 'Behold, I have taken upon myself to speak to Yahweh, I who am but dust and ashes. Suppose five of the fifty righteous are lacking? Will you destroy the whole city for lack of five?' And he said, 'I will not destroy it if I find forty-five there.' Again he spoke to him, and said, 'Suppose forty are found there.' He answered, 'For the sake of forty I will not destroy it.' Then he said, 'Oh let not Yahweh be angry, and I will speak. Suppose thirty are found there.' He answered, 'I will not do it, if I find thirty there.' He said, 'Behold I have taken upon myself to speak to Yahweh. Suppose twenty are found there.' He answered, 'For the sake of twenty I will not destroy it.' Then he said, 'Oh let not Yahweh be angry, and I will speak again but this once. Suppose ten are found there.' He answered, 'For the sake of ten I will not destroy it.' And Yahweh went his way, when he had finished speaking to Abraham, and Abraham returned to his place. (Genesis 18:23–33)

Whether or not Abraham really did discuss the matter in exactly this way with God is irrelevant to the fact that the people of Israel perceived the moral problem, and included it in the Jewish Bible.

The moral dilemma of the 'righteous [individual] faring as the wicked' is constantly with us even today. It is assumed that Abraham was teaching God a moral lesson, but he was not. The question is whether God should spare the many wicked, who will doubtless continue to violate society and the world, so that the innocent may live. Put differently, how many good people does a community require if it is not to destroy itself?

Biblical morality is open to criticism for its exclusion of non-resident foreigners, but this would apply to all ancient peoples. It would be a naive expectation on our part to demand a different attitude of nations or individuals who were living in totally closed societies. And indeed we still applaud governments that act in the self-interest of their nations, while condemning our government for sending soldiers to 'wars which are not our business'. The death of one British soldier in Bosnia received far more attention in Britain than the death of hundreds of Bosnians, for the simple reason that for the British, he was 'one of our boys'. Only when the world's communities become interdependent, and act on the premise that *all* life is equal, can we hope to see the application of morality on an international scale.

Yet even in this the Hebrew prophets gave a lead. Amos criticized not only the sins of his own people, but those of the neighbouring peoples of Damascus, Philistia, Edom, Amon and Moab. A universal God, according to him, will punish all, not only the nations of Judah and Israel, and Amos rebukes his own people, 'Are you not like the Ethiopians to me O people of Israel, says Yahweh' (9:7).

What relevance does such ancient Hebrew morality have to Jewish life today? Probably very little in the day-to-day life of Jews distinguishes them from the rest of the world. They seem to have been influenced by the utilitarian ethics of their biblical forebears, which happens to coincide with the prevailing ethics in the secular West, based on the recognition that, although all humans will seek to fulfil their worldly needs, some will not be as able as others in doing so. A healthy society will accept responsibility for looking after these individuals.

Other vestiges of old Jewish morality are less widely accepted by others, however. Many Jews believe that if they give charity, their businesses will prosper. This seems to hark back to the time of the Bible, and in a way it does. For Jews who listen to the Bible being read in their synagogues or read it in their homes, looking after the poor is not an obligation or a voluntary act, but a natural duty and a privilege of wealth.

There is tension between individual and collective responsibility among Jews, and the extent to which the latter is favoured continues to challenge, unite *and* divide Jewish life. For example, Jews are discouraged from inter-marriage with Gentiles because it further reduces a small and scattered people. Many Jewish individuals, however, will maintain that their personal fulfilment and happiness have priority over the desire for the largely abstract idea of the survival of the Jewish people. The Jewish parents of such a child are caught in the tug-of-war between two loyalties, their child's happiness as he or she perceives it, and the desire to transmit their Jewish identity, as their ancestors passed it to them. Imagine the guilt and outrage when a former British Chief Rabbi declared that Jews who marry out collaborate with Hitler in destroying the Jewish people.

To a large extent, however, modern Jewish ethical morality remains collectively based. To this very day, personal confessions on the Day of Atonement are made in the plural: all individuals joining together in repeating, 'For the sins we have sinned, forgive us and give us atonement'. Individual Jews do not expect to be spared the sufferings inflicted on their people, even if they believe they have been more righteous than their fellow Jews. Jews appear to recognize that if someone bores a hole in a ship, be it an outsider or one of their own, when the ship sinks, all are likely to suffer drowning. This ethic of collective responsibility is a model that should be assumed by all. Only when the search for human salvation becomes a joint rather than a purely individual effort will the chances of human survival improve.

Humans are social animals, each with their own unique fingerprint and right to fulfilment, but in isolation their humanity cannot be fully realized. This was recognized by one of the greatest of Jewish moral geniuses, Hillel – at whose feet some say that Jesus sat. Did Jesus perhaps hear him teach these words?

> If I am not for myself, who will be,
> If I am only for myself, what am I
> and if not now, when?

WHO IS IN CHARGE ?...

33 Jewish Pluralism

'Who is in charge of the Jewish Faith?'

The need for responsible authority is natural to humans. 'Who is in charge here?' is one of the first questions asked by an outsider. From early childhood, we need our parents or guardians to prevent us from touching a flame or falling down stairs. We grow up accustomed to being told what to do. Even our first independent steps are taken at the urging of others. As working adults we will spend much of our time either ordering others about or being ordered by them, and even in situations of shared responsibility, there may be one partner whose view is accepted because it is more authoritatively expressed.

What is true for the individual and the family is true also for society. Democracy is government by consent of the governed. But the electorate only temporarily votes away its authority over certain areas of life, and retains right of redress for grievances through ombudsmen, and still sterner responses at the next election.

Power remains a very personal matter: we know that certain individuals accept authority and others resent it. Some long to be leaders while others are content to be followers. Some want to be told what to do, and some resent it.

Judaism rests on authority. It began with a command to Abraham: 'Get out from your land and go to the land which I will show you.' Loyalty to this commanding God is passed on to Abraham's son, Isaac, and He later appeared to his son Jacob, identifying Himself as the God of his fathers, and promising to look after him. Jacob responded by promising a tenth of all he earns. The treaty or 'covenant' which God first made with Abraham, is still sealed in the individual's flesh, by male circumcision. The covenant with the entire community of Israel was made at Mount Sinai when God gave Moses the Ten Commandments, and other laws which regulate in greater detail how each individual is to relate to others and to God.

A tradition was passed down about how authority was passed from generation to generation and period to period. According to the Talmud, 'Moses received the Torah at Sinai and handed it down to Joshua; Joshua to the elders; the elders to the prophets; and the prophets handed it down to the men of the Great Assembly.' From the Great Assembly came the Rabbinic Masters who transmitted their authority, through ordination, to their disciples.

It seems that when religions are first established there remains little sense that they had once not existed. The truth revealed by God's prophets is eternal, static and unchanging. There is no allowance for the possibility that the times in which they lived and wrote could limit the truth of the revelation for other times. For example, the seer Samuel commanded King Saul to wipe out the tribe of

Amalek and all their possessions. When Saul spared Agag, king of the Amalekites, an enraged Samuel hacked Agag to death, and told Saul that he had transgressed the word of God and would lose his kingdom to a better man than he. For generations, pious Jews have read this tale and believed that this actually happened and that Samuel had acted according to the will of God. But I, and many Jews like me, believe that, great and virtuous though Samuel was, his moral vision was limited by the times in which he lived. Had he lived today, he would have acted differently.

There is progress in the life of humanity, in moral conduct as well as in the natural sciences. The Rabbinic Masters asserted this in their interpretation of the verse, 'Noah was righteous, perfect in his generation', in which they argued that this verse from Genesis actually meant in *his* generation, and that he would not have appeared so in the generation of his descendant, Abraham, who had progressed still further. Judaism seems to have the channels for changing and for meeting new circumstances. There is within the Jewish nation, as in all societies, a tension between tradition and change – conflicts between the Rabbinic Masters and the priestly class, between Pharisees and Sadducees, between the Rabbinic Academies of Hillel and Shammai – and out of these conflicts, Judaism developed.

Once the Jewish nation lost its sovereignty and autonomy, its population was dispersed all over the world, and became strangers even in their own land. All they possessed were their holy books, their laws and their customs. It was on this common tradition that their survival was based. The lack of physical security made them clutch their spiritual heritage with even greater tenacity. In this context, change had to be viewed as threatening and divisive.

The fact that the past is pictured as glorious (as indeed it had been at certain periods), and that the present was bleak in comparison, led Jews to have an even greater reverence for tradition. Over the centuries, nothing was subtracted from it. But under the subtle influence of the cultures in which Jews lived, much was added, and in time those additions also took on sanctity. The past had an authority which was never questioned.

Shock waves, however, went through European Jewry in the eighteenth century. The Age of Enlightenment began to break down the ghetto walls. Jews were obtaining civil rights. Jewish converts to Christianity could reach the highest levels of society and influence. It is difficult to imagine the feelings that an enquiring Jew experienced when comparing the insularity of Jewish life with the universalism of Christian art and science. True 'civilization' of a higher level seemed to be beckoning to the adventurous and creative spirits in the Jewish ghettos. For these Jews, breaking down the cultural barriers must have seemed like promising sight to the blind.

A large number of Jews seized the opportunities, assimilated, and even converted to Christianity. But the majority remained in their spiritual shells. In between these two extremes were the beginnings of groups who wanted to bridge the two worlds – loyal to their tradition and determined to maintain it, but with adjustments to bring it in line with reason and science. These changes were designed to make them feel comfortable with their Jewish and Western identities.

The justification for change was the new scientific approach to the critical study of the Bible: critical studies revealed that the Jewish Torah – the Five Books of Moses – was not written at one time or by one inspired man. And once the divine authorship of the Bible was questioned, traditional Jewish law was also put under the moral microscope, and was in certain instances found lacking. The Talmud, the authoritative interpretation of the Written Law, in particular was viewed as the work of men and, therefore, subject to alteration.

The rejection of the doctrine that Jewish law is altogether divine established the battle lines between the traditionalists and other religious sections in Jewry which are still in existence today. Traditionalists begin with the belief that religious truth was at its zenith when it was first revealed to Moses, and has been diluted over time. Alternative forms of Judaism, born in the period of European intellectual enlightenment of the eighteenth and nineteenth centuries, held that progress in human affairs implied that progress was also made in the understanding of God and religious faith.

The terms used to describe these opposing schools of thought are, on the one hand, Orthodox, a Greek term meaning of 'right opinion', and, on the other hand, Progressive, which highlights the belief that God's revelation of his will is not static but progressive. Between these two poles are varying degrees of belief that vary according to particular religious philosophies. The centrist position is called Conservative, its main thrust being to conserve as much tradition as possible, even though the foundation stone of divine authority had been weakened. Within the Progressive wing there are also differences of emphasis, similarly reflected by suitable adjectives. 'Reform' Judaism in Britain puts its emphasis on the renovation of faith within the framework of a reinterpretation of Jewish law. British 'Liberal' Judaism gives more weight to the freedom of the human conscience. In the United States, however, 'Reform' Judaism reflects both tendencies, and can lean either to a more conservative or a more radical approach.

The rabbinic leadership of the Orthodox is very hostile towards both Conservative and Progressive Judaism, attacking them for destroying the foundations and essence of Judaism. While moderate Orthodox rabbis may be personally polite to Reform and Liberal rabbis, they will deny that these people are teaching Judaism. For them, any Judaism but their own is merely a convenient accommodation to modern life which must lead to assimilation. But there are secular Jews who belong to Orthodox synagogues who believe little and practise less, while still feeling that only Orthodoxy is authentic Judaism. Many non-Jews will sympathize with the Orthodox view, for surely, if Jewish survival over millennia is due to the refusal to compromise with other faiths and cultures, any movement away from this pattern could be dangerous to Jewish survival.

Progressive Jews are accused of wanting to have their cake and eat it. But what alternative do they have? If they believe in the human capacity for progress and the necessity to build on the moral as well as scientific knowledge of their ancestors, what can they do but reinterpret Judaism in the context of modern thought?

In fact, Orthodoxy is also the product of a Judaism that developed over the centuries, but because it happened for the most part gradually, it was not felt to challenge the sanctity of ancient law. Progressive Jews maintain that the tradition of an Oral law, by its very nature, compels change and allows for compromise, as there will be differences of opinion on what was the true tradition. The very phrase 'Talmudic logic' developed as the result of disputes on every detail of the Law.

Whether or not the Rabbinic Masters actually believed that they were transmitting oral traditions which God had taught to Moses, we will never know. There is one charming legend which would suggest that some of them knew they were engaged in creating new precedents while merely pretending to adhere to tradition. According to this tale, the prenatal soul of Moses saw God decorating the letters of the Torah which He would one day give to Moses, and he asked God why He was doing it. When God responded that one day the great Rabbi Akiba would expound laws based on each ornament, Moses asked to be sent ahead in time. He then found himself in the eighth row (the ancient rabbis were sticklers for detail even in regard to legends) of Akiba's Academy, where he could hear Akiba arguing cases, but was able to understand nothing of the discussion. When, however, a disciple asked Akiba the origin of a certain ruling, the Master responded, 'It is the law that Moses received at Sinai'. At this, Moses was most impressed and gratified, and returned to heaven. Once there, he asked God, 'With such a man as Akiba, why do you not give the law through him rather than me?' God replied that He will do what He has to do. The lesson the Sages were teaching, however, is that Moses was right for his generation and Akiba for his.

A few decades later, war and expulsions endangered the survival of the Oral tradition, and it was recorded. As a result, the Oral Law, now in the form of Talmudic debate, anecdote and commentary, has become almost as sacred and unchanging as the Mosaic Law. Jewish Law at this point lost its ability to adjust to the times.

Progressive Jewish leaders of the early decades spent much of their time and effort removing what they believed to be accretions to Jewish life, like moss gathered on stones. They sought to return to the 'purer' forms of Judaism, and to what they considered the essence of Judaism, namely the ethical teachings of the prophets, rather than the minutiae of ritual observance. The leaders of this new movement felt that the Enlightenment was the opportunity to refine the human spirit and not to cramp it with outward forms.

They also believed that what they were witnessing in the life of modern Europe was the beginning of a new age of human brotherhood, freedom and equality. They looked forward to a Messianic Age, when the differences between people would be overshadowed by a universal unity of purpose. They believed that rituals and observances that bind individuals of a shared faith or community to each other, also separate them from other groups. The Jewish dietary laws were considered particularly unfortunate in this respect, as they prevented free social contact between Jews and non-Jews. Progressive Judaism declared *Kashruth* to be a matter of personal conscience, unlike Orthodoxy which continues to regard it as one of the essential marks of Jewish life.

But, however persuasive leaders of alternative forms of Judaism will be, they are aware that the Orthodox, as a matter of principle, cannot accept that logic can replace faith, or that human reason can challenge divine revelation. The conflict between Jewish Liberals and the Orthodox appears irreconcilable. Liberals assert the autonomy of the individual within a God-given structure; the Orthodox assert divine authority which allows each person certain freedoms. The Liberals believe that freedom and choice are the most effective channels for coming closer to God and for realizing his Kingdom on earth, while the Orthodox feel that this will be achieved through faith and obedience.

The polemical battle between the two movements leads to a loss of clarity on both sides, as often happens when emotions run high. Liberals may condemn as 'medieval' the unquestioning faith of the Orthodox, without understanding that this is the very heart of their religion; and Orthodox Jews may mock the lack of authority within Progressive Judaism, without appreciating that this is essential to the meaning of Liberalism.

Such an analysis of the situation may indicate that the Orthodox tend to be individuals with a greater yearning for security and structure, while Liberals lean towards spontaneity and flexibility. If so, it is the tendencies of the Liberal personality that the Orthodox find so threatening, since for the Orthodox, any change in religious faith or observance is dangerous. One change will lead to another. It is 'the thin end of the wedge', 'down the slippery slope', or 'an escalator out of Judaism'. The Liberals in turn accuse the Orthodox of pushing modern Jews into secularism or religious hypocrisy.

A central element in the debate – and this is what makes it so vitriolic – is the concern for Jewish survival. It is common, even among the irreligious, to regard the rituals, traditions and customs which bind Jews to each other as essential even if they are not motivated by sincere belief. It matters little whether you believe or not, so long as you live as a Jew!

Non-Orthodox Jews confess that their relaxed attitude to the formalities of Judaism does present a problem of Jewish survival. If one's life is not totally saturated by Jewish observance, one must fall back on intellectual ties which may be insufficiently powerful to resist the seductions of secular life. But Jews with a Liberal temperament feel that they have no alternative. They cannot feign faith in absolute authority, nor make the survival of Jewry a greater priority than their own integrity.

The dilemma for the Progressive is in certain respects far greater than that of the Orthodox. The decision to open your life to religious choices means continual choice, each religious act requiring a decision which is emotionally and intellectually demanding. Nor can one ever be sure that the choice made is correct. The Orthodox surrender the freedom of choice, which means that decisions come easier; and if the consequences are not beneficial, they have the solace of knowing that they acted in obedience to time-hallowed tradition.

The differences in attitude between the two wings of Judaism lead to an unequal debate. While the Progressives, because of their flexibility, have no difficulty in accepting that the Orthodox may live according to their belief, the Orthodox are unable to be tolerant of a faith which for them is not Judaism. As a

Progressive Jew with an Orthodox upbringing, I can understand the extent to which they are locked into their intolerance.

The practical consequences of the intolerance are another matter, however. Many Orthodox communities will not allow a Progressive rabbi to participate in a panel discussion, far less in a joint service. By this exclusion, they stamp the Progressive or Liberal as not authentically Jewish, and demonstrate to all doubting Orthodox Jews that to accept another way of Judaism is to court the rejection of their own community. The children of Progressive Jewish converts are rejected by Jewish day schools because they are regarded as not 'really' Jewish, and it is argued that allowing relationships with 'real' Jews to develop would lead to tragedy if they discovered that a marriage between them is impossible.

So a division has appeared. There is an increase in mixed marriages in which children are raised as Jews, as well as a growing number of Progressive converts not recognized by the Orthodox. The Jewish community is divided to the point where Jews from one section cannot marry Jews from another section. A resolution of the 'Who is a Jew' issue is essential if the community is not to be irrevocably divided. In spite of the efforts of many, including myself, a reconciliation on this issue appears unlikely to be reached. The inability of the community to agree that anyone who wishes to live as a Jew is Jewish, only decades after the murder of six million Jews by Nazis and their sympathizers, is no less than tragic.

Fanaticism in Jewish religious life is beginning to have an impact on non-Jewish attitudes, to the increasing embarrassment of secular, Progressive and moderately Orthodox Jews. Some ultra-Orthodox Jews have recently, for example, asked permission of the civil planners of a north-west London suburb to erect poles several yards high connected by thin wires to 'fence off' the area in which they and their neighbours live. This legal fiction, called an 'eruv', converts the public domain into a private domain, and enables Orthodox Jews to carry small items and push baby prams and wheelchairs within the area enclosed, rather than confining them to their homes and gardens.

The ultra-Orthodox maintain that as the poles would hardly be noticeable, and would make it possible for disabled individuals to go to synagogue, the authorities should oblige. And it is creditable that in our tolerant and pluralistic Western society, the extreme Orthodox should feel sufficiently secure and confident to make this application for special treatment. Some non-Orthodox Jews, however, for whom such ways of evading the laws of Sabbath appear ludicrous and intrusive, will not wish to break ranks with fellow Jews, but at the same time want to distance themselves intellectually from what they consider 'hocus-pocus'. Nor do they wish to accept responsibility for those albeit insignificant poles surrounding the area in which they may live; or to have to explain to non-Jews what to them seems inexplicable. Jews who express the conviction that the request itself is an unwelcome imposition on the hospitality of the majority non-Jewish society in which they live will be accused by Orthodoxy of betrayal and of the crime of assimilation.

The increase of polarization within the Jewish community is not unique; it is happening among other religious sections. Moderate Muslims are also embarrassed by the sentence of death on Salman Rushdie or concerned that a

self-appointed Muslim Parliament seeks to impose a state within a state by insti-
tuting self-taxation on their community to fund social welfare. These moderate
Muslims, like Jews, do not want to decry their co-religionists, but are also unable
to support their efforts.

The Sabbath 'eruv' may be as trivial an issue as the poles and wire of which it
consists, but it reflects the complexity of pluralism within Jewish life. Non-
Orthodox Jews like myself might find it easier to support the 'quaint', albeit
sincere conviction of the Orthodox, were they to acknowledge publicly that their
beliefs and practices reflect their own interpretation of Judaism as one among
several, and not, as they currently insist, the only true form of Jewish faith. The
attempt of Jews to persuade their more Orthodox colleagues to accept pluralism
must succeed if Jews are to live at peace not only with themselves but with the
society in which they make their homes.

God is not a fundamentalist

The sages had a dispute with Rabbi Eliezer whether a certain oven was susceptible to ritual defile-
ment. On that day, he brought forward every conceivable argument to prove that it was not, but they
were not persuaded.

Finally, he said to them, 'If the Law agrees with me, let this carob tree prove it.' Immediately, the
tree was flung a hundred cubits away where it took root. They said to him, 'A carob tree proves
nothing.' He then said, 'If the Law agrees with me, let this stream prove it.' The stream began to flow
backwards. 'A stream proves nothing,' was their response. Then he said, 'If the Law agrees with me,
let the walls of the Academy prove it.' The walls of the Academy began to lean over. Rabbi Joshua
cried out to them, 'What business is it of yours when the Sages dispute the Law?' Rabbi Eliezer
spoke once more, 'If the Law agrees with me, let Heaven prove it.' A divine voice was heard, 'Why
do you argue with Rabbi Eliezer when the Law agrees with him in every case.' Rabbi Joshua protested, 'It [the Law] is not in Heaven [Deuteronomy] and we take no notice of divine voices because
long ago at Mount Sinai, you wrote in the Torah, "One follows the majority" [Exodus 23].'

Rabbi Nathan met the prophet Elijah and asked him, 'What did the Holy One do at that moment?' Elijah answered, 'He laughed joyously and said, "My children have defeated me, my children have defeated me."'

Talmud

JEWISH SPIRITUALITY —
ARE THERE MYSTICS? ...

34 Jewish Spirituality

'Are there Jewish mystics?'

According to the Talmud, four rabbis entered the 'mystical realm' (the actual term used is *pardes*, which means 'orchard', but has given us the word 'Paradise'). These were Ben Azzai, Ben Zoma, Elisha ben Abuya and Rabbi Akiva. Ben Azzai delved deeply into the mysteries and died; Ben Zoma delved deeply and became 'touched' in the head; Elisha ben Abuya became an infidel; and only Rabbi Akiva survived without harm.

This tale was recorded not only to praise Akiva, but also to discourage even the cleverest and saintliest of Jewish scholars from dabbling in the occult; and the reason given is that it is fraught with unforeseen dangers. As we have explored in other chapters, Judaism has never encouraged the 'spiritual' life to the exclusion of the material, for both were viewed as elements of the whole. As a religion, however, with a history of three thousand years, subject to all human experiences and cultural influences, Judaism would be incomplete if it did not provide some of its members with the means for experiencing mystical thought and practice.

The *Kabbalah*, meaning 'that which was received', took form in the twelfth century and was the source of Jewish mysticism, the exploration of the mysteries of creation and the non-rational. Since that period Jews have been able to delve into the esoteric and occult, study magical formulae and seek identification with the mind of the Universe. But, as the tale cited above indicates, all but the most learned and emotionally secure were discouraged from the study of mysticism, and very few Jews, therefore, have engaged in such pursuits. Today there are those who study the *Kabbalah* for its scholarly interests, and some Jewish psychotherapists also explore Jewish mysticism for keys to the understanding of the human mind.

Of all contemporary Jewish sects, the Hasidic movement has been most influenced by mysticism. It was founded in the mid-eighteenth century by Israel ben Eliezer, who was called *Baal Shem Tov*, the 'Master of the Good Name', because he was believed to perform miracles through his knowledge of God's name. Hasidism was the attempt of the *Baal Shem Tov* and other Hasidic leaders to make the worship of God an intense and ecstatic experience for Jews who, due to poverty and ignorance, could not find fulfilment through Jewish learning and wisdom. Spiritual concentration during prayer and ritual observances, and the joyous worship of God under the tutelage of the *Rebbe*, the Hasidic Master, were the hallmarks of the movement.

Over the last two centuries, the power of many Hasidic groups has focused around their *Rebbes* (who often fiercely competed with each other) and continued to grow until the Holocaust swallowed them up. Some still remain, the most popular and numerous being the 'Lubavitch' movement (the name of its original centre in Eastern Europe) under its dynastic head, Rabbi Schneerson. Theirs is a missionizing movement towards the Jewish community, and pictures can often be seen of them dancing or demonstrating their love of God and Judaism. Often dressed in clothes reminiscent of seventeenth-century Poland, with beards and long earlocks, they appear spiritual and other-worldly.

Ironically the movement, whose original popularity was due to spontaneous worship and intuitive observance of rituals, today boasts of the most rigid adherents of Jewish law and practice. There is no item of ritual too small to escape attention. Loyalty to custom and to their own leaders has become so great that there can be riots between opposing sects of Hasidim over the clothes they ought to wear. Intermarriage between members of different sects is often forbidden. But the spirituality of Hasidic Jews is sensed most when one witnesses them either at worship or studying the Talmud. There is on these occasions an intensity about them which makes the observer feel that they are in a state of rapture. I, as a rabbinical student, had the experience of meeting the Lubavitcher Rebbe at a midnight interview at his headquarters in Crown Heights, New York. There was a glow about him. Whether this was the result of his scholarship or saintliness, or the worship he inspired in his followers, is difficult to assess. His words did not make as great an impact on me as did the glazed looks in the eyes of his disciples who crowded around me, and the others who had been privileged with this audience, to ask what precious pearls of wisdom the Rebbe had dropped.

The fierceness of Hasidic loyalty often turns into fanaticism, but this does detract from their spirituality. When 'Satmar' Hasidim in Jerusalem throw stones on the Sabbath at cars who cross into their territory, or Jewish women are accosted in Hasidic neighbourhoods for the immodesty of their short-sleeved dresses, the spirituality of their faith is not very apparent.

Jewish spirituality can be found in other circles than the Hasidic. One senses it at those brief moments when Jews divorce themselves from their everyday humdrum existence and join themselves to the world of the 'holy'. This can be felt when a woman covers her eyes after she has lit the Sabbath candles, or by scholars lost in thought while they consider a biblical verse. Spirituality is most manifest among Jews when they are, and give the appearance of being, in deep concentration, to the exclusion of all else, on something which they consider holy, be it prayers or study or any form of communion with the 'other world'.

As in all peoples and religions, there are Jews who have spiritual faces which suggest an inner contentment of deep wisdom or piety. I have sometimes discovered that the reality of the personalities behind these faces is a disappointment. And on occasion, I have been impressed by the deep spirituality of individual Jews whose exterior demeanour would indicate the opposite. I am sure that we have all had similar experiences.

I feel it important for Gentiles not to confuse Jewish religiosity with spirituality. Just as religious Jews can lack spirituality, so can irreligious Jews be very spiritual. Pious Jews who are bigoted and intolerant cannot be spiritual, because they lack the love which is the essence of spirituality. Irreligious Jews such as Albert Einstein or Yehudi Menuhin impress me as very spiritual beings.

Organized religions, like all organizations, are attempts to achieve influence through power. Among their leaders will be those whose drive for power will thwart the spiritual flow, which depends for its existence on giving and letting go rather than grasping and being possessive. A moderately religious Muslim scholar may be more spiritual than a mullah who incarcerates young girls for listening to popular music. Fanatically religious people can never be spiritual, for while spirituality resides in humility before God, the fanatic is always arrogant. The fact that fanatics feel driven to claim that they act on behalf of God or his prophet does not diminish the quality of their arrogance, for they do so merely in order to claim that only they know God's will.

We often see television pictures of fanatically pious Jews in their outmodish clothing, and the tendency is to identify these as spiritual Jews and to classify all others as irreligious or secular. This impression is the fault of ignorance, coupled with the power of imagery. The spirituality of Jews can be enhanced by faith and observances, but the core of it will be the purely human qualities of goodness and generosity of spirit.

It needs to be added that Judaism does not believe that people 'are' or 'are not' spiritual. There is no equivalent of the Christian concept of grace which is a gift of God given to certain individuals and denied to others, nor is it the gift of healing which 'spiritualists' believe is given to a select few. For Jews, the spiritual dimension is always available, and individuals can open themselves up to it at any time in their lives. A tale from the Midrash symbolically echoes this truth. A Roman executioner in the second century CE was responsible for burning Jewish rebels at the stake. To prolong the agony, he was instructed to keep a sponge of water next to the heart of a Rabbinic Master who had disobeyed the emperor. The victim begged for deliverance, and the executioner was so moved by the suffering that he removed the sponge and threw himself into the fire. A voice from heaven was heard which declared that both the rabbi and the executioner had achieved eternal life. The survivors then reflected on the irony that some, like the rabbi, must work their whole lives for salvation, while others may achieve it in an instant. As in death, so in life. From the Jewish point of view, spirituality is a dimension of life open to all; achieved by some during the whole of their lives and by others at only isolated moments. As the psalmist says, 'When you seek the Lord He shall be found'.

'Where is the dwelling of God?' This was the question with which the Rabbi of Kotzk surprised a number of learned men who happened to be visiting him. They laughed at him: 'What a thing to ask! Is not the whole world full of his glory!' Then he answered his own question: 'God dwells wherever man lets him in.'

Tales of the Hasidim, ed. *Martin Buber*

WORLD WITHOUT JEWS—
WOULD IT BE BETTER?

35 A World without Jews?

'Would it be better?'

When I informed friends that one of the questions I would be asking in this book was, 'Would the world be a better place without Jews?' there were deep in-drawings of breath and shakes of the head. For Jews, this question touches some raw nerves, and this is hardly surprising so soon after Hitler's attempt to find a 'final solution' for the 'Jewish problem'. Even Gentile friends have expressed amazement that I was prepared to be so blunt, let alone to seek an answer to what seems less a question than a gibe.

Admittedly, a comprehensive approach would require one first to ask 'better for whom', and 'from whose point of view'? None the less governments or social groupings have on more than one occasion related to the Jews on the premise that the world would indeed be better off without them. The Holocaust perpetrated by the Nazis was not the only example. The Crusaders on their way to the Holy Land may have seen personal benefit in randomly pillaging and killing Jews, but the cry, 'Kill a Jew and save your soul', suggests a theological basis for ridding the world of Jews.

The Christian evangelical movement, although for purer motives, also acts on the basis that a world without Jews would be a better one. True, they seek the conversion of the whole world, which they think would be better if there were no non-Christians in it at all. Although I would not wish sincere evangelists ever to be compared to those who sought physically to annihilate the Jews, their greater enthusiasm for converting them indicates a special interest in their removal from the scene.

The urge to eliminate any group reflects the belief that it constitutes a threat to universal well-being. Demagogues will, for their own purposes, exaggerate dangers in order to whip up popular support, but they will select their targets to agree with popular perceptions.

In modern life, however, voices are raised against any assertion that a certain group can threaten another by its mere presence. One can attribute wars between nations to irreconcilable hatreds, but governments continue to stimulate crude emotions for their own reasons. The German and British soldiers who played football in no-man's land during a Christmas truce were expressing their mistrust of officially sponsored hatred, and George Orwell movingly described how he intended to shoot an enemy soldier during the Spanish Civil War, but was thwarted by the sight of him lowering his trousers to defecate.

Such instances of individual responsibility and personal fulfilment are the hallmark of Western civilization, and subvert the idea that any group, by its very character, poses a general threat. The current tendency towards greater unity in

Western Europe breaks down century-old enmities, but is conceivable only because the common individual desire for prosperity and well-being is now seen to over-ride the national differences which divide people. While ethnic wars in the Balkans seem to contradict this tendency, in fact they do not. Old national hatreds, once repressed by an absolute tyranny, flared up once independence was restored. Old unsettled scores, combined with conflicting economic interests, revived certain national enmities; but individual interests will eventually win out over historic hatreds.

Today, it is increasingly difficult to argue that the Jews, or any people for that matter, could pose a serious danger to mankind. Only rabid anti-Semites, indoctrinated in racist schools to believe in a world Jewish conspiracy, would maintain that the world should rid itself of Jews. Yet there are others, equally misguided, for whom Jews still seem a nuisance. In the popular imagination they 'seem to be everywhere', 'causing trouble' and 'creating division'. The prejudice against Jews has earned compound interest over the centuries, so that even the nicest people, including Jews, find it difficult to escape. The prominence of Jews in the imagination, and the popular interest in them, continue to form a self-generating fountain for distrust and suspicion.

It is scarcely credible that until very recently the world was being warned that a nuclear war could be ignited in the Middle East unless the stubborn and belligerent Israelis made peace. It is now known that this was being argued at precisely the time that the atomic and chemical arsenal of Saddam Hussein's Iraq was being developed. Not only was this fact totally ignored, but Israel endured diplomatic attack by every nation for destroying the Iraqi nuclear reactor in 1982! Luckily for the Jews, the world is now suffering the aftermath of the dissolution of the Soviet Empire, so the Jewish State is no longer in the limelight.

Jews often seek to 'spot the Jew' in every arena of life, perhaps to feel more secure in themselves, and many non-Jews are also quick to join in, especially if there is a scandal involved. Is it possible that the statement, 'the Jews are every-where', may have the subconscious undertone that the world would be better if 'they were nowhere'.

I am aware that my remarks will have no pragmatic impact; even if I concluded that on balance the Jews are non-beneficial, no civilized person would say, 'Ah, case proved, let's get rid of them'. Nor, indeed, if my conclusion were highly positive, would prejudice against them cease. I am attempting only to understand feelings and to clarify thoughts. As this book is about understanding the Jews and non-Jewish attitudes towards them, any investigation into the Jewish contribution to the world is justified.

Any fair-minded person would be dismayed by the disappearance of an entire people from the map of the earth, be they Hottentots, Bosnians, Gypsies, American Indians or Jews. Even attempts to save whales, elephants, seals and penguins from extinction gain ardent supporters. Consider our interest when we are told that a species of bird or bear has only a few remaining members. The world, we feel, would be poorer without them. And what is true of the lower animal world is just as true of the higher animal world. Every tribe, people or nation adds its colour and texture to the tapestry of human life.

Philosophically speaking, one might imagine someone wishing to extinguish a species or a nation or people if it could be proven beyond doubt that its members, all and severally, are a danger to the wellbeing of mankind. But no rational person would maintain that each and every Jew is that. On the contrary, apart from the dignity which comes from their being part of the human race, individual Jews have made and continue to make large contributions to society. History provides ample evidence for Jewish genius in every field of human endeavour. A world without Jews would be one without the Bible, Christianity and Islam. Who knows how long it would have taken for psychoanalysis or the theory of relativity to have been discovered had it not been for Freud and Einstein? The 1992 Nobel Prize winners for chemistry, physics and medicine were Jews. It would be a matter of apologetics to list the Jews prominent in the sciences and the arts and professions. Let it suffice to say that the world would be less advanced had Jews not been part of its history.

But I would be embarrassed to justify Jewish existence merely by what Judaism and Jews have done for the world. Human existence needs no justification – but it is interesting to consider whether something in their religious faith can account for the contributions they have made to human history. My instincts tell me that when the distant ancestors of the Jews decided that their God must not be personified or visualized, and that He has no rivals, they set out on a lonely course which would have a direct bearing on what they did and thought. Their concept of God made them, in the words of the Bible, 'a people apart'; and they have indeed remained outsiders in every age and wherever they have lived, cast as the great 'nay sayers' of history. Jewish tradition reports that Abraham began his rebellion by breaking the idols in which his father dealt. And ever since then Jews have excelled in iconoclasm, in defying myths and breaking new ground, often pushing forward the frontiers of science even in opposition to their own heritage. Baruch Spinoza said God was in everything; Sigmund Freud said the previously unthinkable about the human sub-conscious and passions, and opened a new world of self-understanding. Both these trail-blazers rejected Judaism as myth, just as their ancestors had rejected idolatry.

Like Spinoza and Freud, many Jews who contribute to human progress do not count themselves as Jewish in any traditional sense. Some secular individuals, while affirming their identity as Jews, do not relate their creativity or leadership to their Jewish heritage. It is possible to assert that religiously observant Jews make a relatively small direct contribution to the improvement of the world, even if, by preserving the tradition and accepting the discomforts of being outsiders, they produce future generations who will be innovators and risk takers like their predecessors.

This leads us to a response to my opening question: the world, I believe, would *not* be a better place without Jews. This is to ignore, however, the feelings of the Jews themselves, who have suffered persecution and destruction for centuries precisely because they were Jews. For them it would undoubtedly have been better had they not been so identified. But people, regardless of the consequences, do not commonly turn their backs on their history and community. Justifiable pride in the contribution that Jews have made, and continue to make, to society is one further reason for them to defend themselves against anti-Semitism and to resist assimilation. The non-Jewish world has every reason to wish them success.

JEWISH HUMOUR...

AND ITS TRAGIC SIDE...

36 Jewish Humour and its Tragic Side

'Funny, you don't look Jewish'

This is a chapter which was almost never written; I simply could not see how the subject fitted into my desire to explain Jewish life to non-Jews. But looking through the completed proofs, I asked myself, 'How could there be a book on Jewish life without a chapter on Jewish humour?', and set myself to explaining how Jewish humour can give Gentiles an insight into Jewish mentality.

The ability to laugh at oneself is the most acceptable definition of 'a sense of humour' and is in direct contrast to the desire to laugh at others. An analysis of how Jews poke fun at themselves is a key to the appreciation of how they perceive themselves. It also explains why non-Jews are not permitted to tell the same jokes as those which Jews tell about themselves. It is a fact that, while it may be all right for a husband to make fun of his family, it would be the height of rudeness for another to do so. But the fact that certain Jews do not like these jokes, even when told by their co-religionists, is an indication of a desire to distance themselves from a perception of Jews which makes them feel uncomfortable. On the other hand, non-Jews will know that they have been totally accepted among Jews once they are told a Jewish joke by their Jewish friends.

The number of Jewish jokes is endless, so I have rummaged through my memory for stories which reflect the perception of certain Jewish attributes or aspects of Jewish life. My purpose is only to give a sample, in order to sensitize my readers to appreciate what it is that makes a particular story funny for Jews. Sometimes the jokes will border on the anti-Semitic, because they deliberately caricature the truth, and for this reason it is advisable for non-Jews to be wary of sharing a Jewish joke even with close Jewish friends. One has to keep in mind that there are certain Jewish jokes which even Jews feel go beyond the bounds of good taste.

The right of Jews to expect charity from the wealthy.
A rich Jew was in the habit of meeting a weekly request for support from a Schnorrer (poor Jewish supplicant). Like clockwork, the man would arrive on Friday morning and receive his donation. But the rich man was surprised when one week passed and there was no visit. When, the following Friday, a strange man appears, to make a claim on the man's charitable purse, he objects that he does not know who he is. The stranger says he is the closest kin of the man whom he had been supporting for years, but the man had died and that was why he was there to collect his weekly allowance. When the rich man said that he owed him nothing, the schnorrer looked at him in disbelief. 'Am I his heir or are you? '

Jewish women are house-proud.
An impotent elderly Jewish man sees a sexual consultant who gives him the latest plans for an apparatus which causes an erection. It is very expensive and he decides to consult his wife. 'Darling,' he says to her, 'we can make love again; look at these plans and this is the estimate. What do you think?' 'Fantastic,' is her response, 'but first let's do the kitchen'.

Jewish men are hen-pecked.
Question: Why do Jewish men usually die ten years before their wives?
Answer: Because they want to.

Persecuting Jews is endless.
A pogrom takes place in a Jewish Russian village. The Cossacks come into a family home, line up the men against the wall and make them witness the ravishing of all the women. After the 16-year-old is raped, the mother of 35 years and the grandmother of 55 are ravished. They begin to strip the great grandmother and the men plead with them. 'Have you not done enough, leave the poor old lady alone!' She interrupts their plea, 'Sh… a pogrom is a pogrom!'

You can always rely upon a Jewish mother.
A young Jewish mother rings her own in desperation. 'Hello, Mum,' she blurts out, 'I am desperate, the baby has the flu, my help hasn't come, the washing machine is flooding, and I have to pick up Danny from school in an hour. Will you come over?' When she pauses to take breath, the woman on the end of the line says, 'I'm sorry but you have the wrong number, I am not your mother.' There is a moment's silence. 'Does that mean you're not coming?'

You can never satisfy a Jewish mother.
A mother presents her son with two ties for his birthday. The next time she sees him, he is wearing one of the ties. The mother asks, 'So what's wrong with the other tie I bought you?'

Jewish family pride.
A proud woman is parading her grandchildren. She meets a friend who courteously praises them. Bubbling over with pride, she says, 'That's nothing, wait until you see their photographs!'

Jewish identity.
An old woman sits down in a train next to a man reading a paper and engages him in conversation. Eventually, she tells him that she is Jewish and asks him whether he is also Jewish. 'No madam, I am not.' She persists, 'You sure you're not Jewish?' He politely says he is sure that he is not Jewish. She cannot accept his denial. 'Maybe you have a Jewish grandmother or father' is one of many investigative questions. Finally, in the man's desire to rid himself of the tortuous inquisition and to return to his newspaper, he says, 'OK, OK, I am Jewish'. 'Funny,' she replies, 'you don't look Jewish'.

The Jewish love for moaning.
An old woman on a train without any food service cannot stop moaning, 'Oi, am I thirsty.' She does this without interruption for fifteen minutes. 'Oi, am I thirsty; oi, am I thirsty.' A man sharing the carriage cannot suffer her complaints any more and there is no other seat. At a stop he sees a confectionery stand. He jumps out, buys a drink and makes it back to the train just in time. He gives her the drink for which she expresses her undying gratitude. He relaxes and looks forward to a more restful journey until he hears her mumble, 'Oi, was I thirsty; oi, was I thirsty!'

Jews should play it safe and not make waves.
Two Jews are in front of the execution squad. The guard offers them a last wish. One of the two asks for a cigarette. The other rebukes him, 'Don't make trouble!'

Jewish refusal to give up.
A Protestant, Catholic and Jew are told that their illnesses are terminal and they do not have long to live. The Protestant asks to see his lawyer, the Catholic asks for a priest, the Jew asks for a 'second opinion'.

Jewish respect for authority.
A man has a stroke. The doctor is called in, feels the pulse of the man and declares him dead. The man sits up and objects, 'I'm alive.' His wife rebukes him, 'Be quiet, the Doctor knows best!'

Jewish priorities.
Jack Benny, the well-known American radio and TV comedian, tells of a robber who held him up with a gun. 'Your money or your life.' Jack Benny did not reach for his wallet. 'Well?' said the agitated robber. Benny said, 'Give me a chance, I'm thinking.'

Tradition over faith.
A son returns from university and confesses to his father that he is no longer a believing Jew. He begins by telling him that he no longer observes the Sabbath. No response. He tells him that he eats unkosher foods. Still no response. After further admissions without a response, he says, 'Dad, I no longer believe in God.' His father looks at him impatiently, 'Fine, fine, but if we keep talking we will miss the afternoon prayers in synagogue.'

Matchmaking.
The matchmaker brings his client to meet the proposed match. He is shocked. He whispers to him, 'You didn't tell me that she was short, had a hunch back and a squint in her eyes.' The *Shadhan* replies, 'Why are you whispering? She's deaf.'

Keeping up with the Cohens.
The Goldberg family decide that their son's Bar Mitzvah celebration is going to be the most unusual. Following the service, a jet plane is hired to take the party into deepest Africa for a safari. They arrive at night. The next morning they are helped by the natives and guides to put on their gear. They mount the mules and the long caravan proceeds towards its destination. An hour after the journey begins, they see water. They are instructed to stop. After a delay of thirty minutes, the party becomes fidgety. After an hour, people in the rear send up for information on the reason for the delay. It takes ten minutes for the answer to arrive. Why are they waiting? They have to wait for the Bloom Bar Mitzvah party to cross the river ahead of them!

Jews avoid giving answers.
A Gentile asks a Jew, 'Why does a Jew always answer a question by asking a question?' The Jew replies, 'Why do you ask?'

Feminine vanity.
Three women, a Christian, Muslim and Jew, come before St Peter at the Pearly Gates. Angela says, 'I always attended church and did charitable works.' St Peter says, 'Good, second door on the left.' Fatima comes next and says, 'I was very modest, looked after my household, prayed and fasted during Ramadan.' 'Good,' says St Peter, 'second door on your left.' Sarah appears before him and says, 'I have been a good Jewish mother, made a good Jewish home, looked after my husband and children.' St Peter nods with approval and says, 'Good, first door on the left.' She is surprised. 'Why am I different from the others?' St Peter says, 'I thought you would want to have your hair done first!'

Jewish rebellion.
A certain illiterate tailor was missed at synagogue on the Day of Atonement, the holiest day of the year when Jews ask for forgiveness. The next morning, the townspeople asked him how he could be absent on such a day. He explained, 'I didn't have to go. I said to God, listen, I confess that on occasion I have provided a cloth of lesser quality than I have charged for, I have been short-tempered with my wife, slapped my son when he didn't deserve it, held back from giving charity to a needy person. But compare that to what you have done. Rebecca who lives down the road was left a widow with three young children, Samuel's son was drafted into the Russian army and has not been heard of for seven years, and I don't have to tell you all the other things you let happen. When you compare what I've done with what you've done, I think if I forgive you, you should forgive me. As God is reasonable, He agreed, and I stayed at home, for why should I waste His time?'

These samples of Jewish humour could be expanded to incorporate other areas of Jewish life, but there are any number of anthologies of Jewish humour, which Jews are always buying because they love laughing at themselves. It is this ability which has doubtless made their hard lives more endurable. Humour is still the best way to lighten one's life.

The comparatively large number of Jewish humourists and Jewish-influenced TV comedies and films is due to this enjoyment of a good laugh at one's own expense. Woody Allen is the quintessence of Jewish humour, baring his soul and dissecting it before an audience of millions. Danny Kaye, George Burns, Barbara Streisand and many others from a Jewish background give joy to the world by seeing the funny side of life, and they have been inspired by and not limited by their Jewish experience. Jewish humourists, like Jackie Mason the New York comedian, make their living by exposing Jewish life to ridicule: the hen-pecked Jewish husband who is a boss everywhere except in his own home, the Jewish wife whose house is a museum where no one can sit down, the Jewish family on holiday for whom touring means visiting all the restaurants, and so on, keep Jewish audiences rolling in their seats with laughter. The popularity of this humour with non-Jews is proof that they too are beginning to appreciate the pathos and joys of being Jewish. This can only be a good thing.

But the tragic side of Jewish humour cannot be overlooked. For the capacity to laugh at oneself is not inborn. It comes from the realization that some people really think you absurd, out of place, a joke. The Jew of history, helpless before the loathing of those who thought him an outsider, had no option but to turn the howling laughter of his enemy inwards.

Jewish jokes are risqué because they teeter on the edge of self-hatred, the consequence of centuries of humiliation. And Jews, for all their contributions to the world, and the intense international respect that some have earned, are indeed like those endangered species I mentioned in the previous chapter. They are a tiny minority, but they bear a great culture.

It is this that has been my intention to outline in this book. None the less, this is not a full catalogue of Jewish life; it is only a brief guide written by an 'insider' seeking to see it from the 'outside' in order to interpret Jews and their culture for the outsider. But such a guide is sorely needed, for where there is ignorance, hostility stalks.

Perhaps it is the humour which sees Jews through the worst as well as the best, and which has enabled me, a Jew, to write this book in the midst of a labyrinthine, largely unhumorous world.

Glossary

Aliyah – (i) Immigration to the State of Israel. (ii) The honour of being called up to the reading of the Torah in synagogue.

Ashkenazim – Jews whose origins were in Germany or in West, Central or Eastern Europe, as contrasted with Sefardim.

Bar Mitzvah – Religious ceremony in synagogue and social celebration marking a boy reaching the age of thirteen and his initiation into the religious Jewish community. Literal meaning is 'Son of Commandment'.

Baruch HaShem – 'Praised be the Name [of God]'. An expression used by Jews following a declaration that one is healthy or prosperous, etc.

Bat Chayil – Orthodox synagogues, in their attempt to redress the lack of status given to Jewish girls, will have a synagogue ceremony for girls at about the age of thirteen. Unlike Bar Mitzvah, it will not usually be on the Jewish Sabbath and may well be for a group of girls. Literal meaning is 'Daughter of Valour'.

Bat Mitzvah – 'Daughter of Commandment'. Orthodox synagogues do not have a ceremony to mark a girl's initiation into the religious community at the age of twelve. Non-Orthodox synagogues often do, but Jewish families do not feel it as obligatory as Bar Mitzvah.

Bentsh – The Yiddish word for the prayers after meals.

Beth Din – Ecclesiastical court of law, presided over by a Dayan (judge) and two other rabbis.

Bris(t) – Circumcision. The word means 'covenant', because the circumcision was the physical sign of the relationship between God and the descendants of Abraham.

B'rocho – A blessing. Jews have special blessings to mark almost every occasion, although only the very observant will take every opportunity for saying them. The Hebrew origin of the word is 'water well', harking back to the pastoral time when water was considered the greatest blessing.

Broygess – Argument which has broken out between two Jews of the same family, or two close associates, leading to a rupture in their relationship.

B'shert (emphasis on the second syllable) – Yiddish word for 'fate' used when a Jew expresses his reconciliation to the inevitable.

Challoh – The twisted bread eaten on the Sabbath and Festivals.

Chumash – Yiddish for 'Pentateuch', the Five Books of Moses, the Torah.

Chutzpah – The Yiddish word for bravado and cheekiness. The popularity of this word has made it part of English slang. The example given of Chutzpah is the man accused of patricide asking mercy from the court on the basis that he is an orphan.

Diaspora – Areas of Jewish settlement outside Israel, from the word 'dispersion'.

Erez Yisrael – Land of Israel. Palestine.

Eruv – A loophole to enable Orthodox Jews to 'get around' the law (see p. 166).

Ganif – Yiddish for thief, used sometimes in an affectionate way for a person who is not trustworthy.

Gut Yonteff –'Have a good festive day.' Yiddish greeting used on Jewish Festivals (see Yonteff).

Haftorah – The second reading from the prophetic books of the Bible on Sabbath or Festival mornings.

Hasid or Hossid – A follower of a Hasidic sect.

Hasidim – Plural of Hasid.

Hasidism– Religious movement, founded in the first half of the eighteenth century, emphasizing joy and ecstasy in the service of God.

Hazzan – Cantor, one who leads Synagogue worship by musically intoning the prayers.

Kabbalat Torah – Often called Confirmation, when the graduation class of a non-Orthodox religion school affirm their Jewish loyalty at a synagogue service. The literal meaning of the Hebrew is 'Acceptance of the Torah'.

Kaddish – The prayer recited usually in memory of the dead but also during other parts of religious services. It is a paeon of praise of God. *See* Kadosh.

Kadosh – Translated as 'Holy', a word which also needs explanation. The original Hebrew word appears to mean 'special' or set aside for a special purpose. Thus, when something is hallowed or sanctified, it is to be declared 'special'.

Kapul – A small cap used by Jewish males to cover the head as a symbol of piety and respect for God. The Kapul is normally worn during religious services and on ceremonial occasions. Pious Orthodox Jews will wear a Kapul or hat at all times. Other names for the head covering are 'Yarmelka' and ' Kippah'.

Kenainahorah – Literally 'no evil eye', said after praising someone, in order to avert the evil eye.

Kiddush – Blessing over wine and prayer of sanctification on the eve of Sabbaths and Festivals before the meal. *See* Kadosh.

Kiddushin – The act of a marriage, when a man declares a woman to be his wife by placing a ring on her finger. He has by this act set her aside to be his wife, excluding her from all other men.

Kosher – The word originally used to describe permitted foods. The Hebrew root means 'fit' or 'correct'. Due to the growing popularity of Yiddish words in ordinary conversation, the word has come to mean anything which is right and proper.

L'haim – Meaning 'to life', the toast before taking wine or spirits. The Jewish equivalent to 'Cheers'.

L'voyah – Jewish funeral.

Mahzor – The books of prayer used during Jewish Festivals.

Mamzer – 'Bastard' according to Jewish law, the offspring of an incestuous or adulterous relationship. The child of an unmarried woman is not a bastard according to Jewish law.

Matzah – The flat unleavened bread which must be eaten during the Festival of Passover.

Mazal – Luck, literally 'constellation of stars'.

Mazal Tov – Greeting expressing wishes for good luck, extended after marriage, a birth, etc.

Mechuleh – A business bankrupt, literally someone whose business has 'ended'.

Mechutonim – Relations through marriage, normally the father and mother-in-law.

Mezuzah – Parchment handwritten with selected verses from the Torah, put into a container and affixed to gates and doors of Jewish homes and institutions. Also worn around the neck as decorative jewellery.

Midrash – Collections of moral interpretations of Scripture and stories about Jewish heroes.

Mikveh – Ritual bath used normally only by the ultra-Orthodox and prior to conversion to Judaism.

Mishnah – 'repetition', first codification of the Oral Law in six sections by Judah ha-Nasi at the begining of the third century.

Mishugeh – Yiddish for 'crazy', used to express any act or person which or who appear weird.

Mitzvah– Biblical or rabbinic commandment, also charitable deeds and honours given to individuals in synagogue.

Motzi – Blessing over bread at the beginning of a meal.

Naches – Yiddish word for the enjoyment derived from pride in the good qualities or achievements of loved ones.

Pogrom – An organized or spontaneous riot against a Jewish community involving rape, pillage and murder.

Rebbe – Yiddish form for rabbi or teacher, applied particularly to Hasidic leaders.

Schlemazzel or Schlemiel – An unlucky individual, a 'loser'. The origin of the word is disputed, but it appears to come from the Yiddish, meaning 'individual without luck, or person with bad luck'. The two descriptions are synonymous, but the two can be humorously distinguished in this way: the schlemazzel is the waiter who pours soup over the schlemiel!

Seder – Home evening service for the commemoration of Passover.

Sefardim – Jews who trace their origins to Spain and other countries once or still under Islamic rule.

Shabbat, Shabbos – Jewish sabbath.

Shabbat Shalom – 'Sabbath peace', greeting used on the Sabbath.

Shalom – Peace, derived from the Hebrew word 'Shalem', which means complete.

Shalom Alaychem – Jewish greeting meaning 'Peace unto you'. The response would be the words in reverse: 'Alaychem Shalom', meaning 'to you also peace'.

Shiva – Seven-day period of mourning, when the bereaved remain at home to receive consolation.

Shul – Yiddish for 'synagogue', from the German word meaning school. A primary use for the synagogue was for the teaching of children.

Siddur – The daily and Sabbath prayer book.

Simha – Joyous occasion. 'Nur auf simhas', meaning 'we should meet only on joyous occasions', is an expression of hope by Jews saying goodbye after a sad event.

Tallit or Tallis – Four-cornered garment with fringes (Tzitzit) worn during morning prayers by men.

Talmud – 'Teaching', compendium of debates and discussions revolving around the Mishna, which was the first codification of the Oral Law. Composed over several centuries by scholars in many different centres of learning, and completed by the sixth century CE.

TaNaCH – The Hebrew for the three sections of the Jewish Bible, derived from the first letters of their Hebrew titles: *Torah* ('Pentateuch'); *Nevee-im* ('Prophets'), *Ketuvim* ('Writings').

Tfillin – Two small square receptacles containing selections from the Torah handwritten on parchment, affixed to the forehead and left arm with leather straps by adult Jewish males during morning prayers on weekdays.

Torah – (i) The Scroll containing the first five books of the Bible: Genesis, Exodus, Leviticus, Numbers, Deuteronomy. (ii) Description of the Jewish Law as written in the Torah and interpreted in the Talmud and later rabbis.

Trayfa – The Hebrew word to describe any forbidden food.

Tzadik – Hebrew for 'righteous man', a term used often to describe the rabbinic leader of a Hasidic sect.

Yahrzeit – Yiddish for the anniversary of a death, commemorated by the burning of a 24-hour candle in the home of the bereaved.

Yonteff – Description of Jewish Festival. Yiddish corruption of the Hebrew *Yom Tov*, meaning 'a good day'.